Three Pastors and a Rabbi: Heavenly, Experimental, Dental Prosthetics for a Dyslexic Dwarf

By Marsha Lampert MBA MS

Miracle Dance Publications
Tucson, Arizona, USA

Copyright© Marsha Lampert
January 2020
ISBN:
978-0-578-61738-1

Cover art courtesy of Drew Super Photography

Dedicated to and inspired by and in honor of

Dr. Michael Schamis DDS

inventor of experimental dental prosthetics

Three Pastors and a Rabbi: Heavenly, Experimental, Dental Prosthetics for a Dyslexic Dwarf

Legal Disclaimer

This book contains many chapters on many different medical and dental topics; however, **no warranty whatsoever** is made that any of the information is correct tested or verified. There is absolutely no assurance that any statement contained or cited in a book touching on medical or dental matter is true, correct, precise, or up to date. This book is written by me a nonprofessional. Even if a statement made about medicine/dentistry is accurate, it may not apply to you or your symptoms.

The medical/dental information provided in this book is, at best, of a general nature and cannot substitute for the advice of a medical/dental professions (for instance, q qualified doctor/physician, dentist pharmacist/ and so on. I am not a doctor.

None of the individual contributors, not anyone else connected to this book can take any responsibility for the results or consequences of any attempt to use or adopt any of the information presented in this book.

Table of Contents

Contents

Dr Levinson's Testimonial

Marsha Lampert is a dyslexic/ADHD and phobic dwarf that truly stands tall. She has not only responded favorably to my medical treatment—but has attained intellectual and functional heights that have defied most others with lesser disabilities. Importantly, she has exemplified my
clinically derived belief that her complex cauldron of dyslexia-related and other symptoms are far simpler to understand than her gifted, talented and unstoppable endowments enabling her—really driving her—to thrive and excel. And thus, to soar far beyond and above her many differently named and poorly understood diagnostic deficits.

Marcia demonstrates the many paradoxes that I've repeatedly encountered among gifted others with similar impairments: a profound ability to grasp and pursue complex mental concepts and/or master initially hidden musical and related gifts— despite insufferable odds. Utilizing Merlin-like magic and hyperactive energy, she is somehow altruistically driven to repeatedly convert lemons into lemonade. As a clinical researcher, I have learned infinitely more about Marcia and her disorders by listening to suffering patients than their dedicated healers and experts. However, both sources are essential for positive outcomes and eventual solutions—often catalyzing one another. And by her uncanny ability to rapidly absorb and advance the scientific literature—often finding essentials hidden within complex and massive—even confusing— content streams, Marcia also became an "expert. "

So, I encourage all those with dyslexia, ADHD, Phobias, especially dental ones, and even those exhibiting some autistic traits as well as dedicated healers and loved ones to read Marcia's God-inspired words, insights, and book.

—Harold N. Levinson, M.D.

Ode to My Beloved Father

Since the original first publication of this book in 2019, My beloved "Daddy" died 5/7/2024 at age 90. Although we didn't always see "eye to eye" about the Experimental dental treatment, He understood that I was "destined" to become an " Experimental dental pioneer" which necessitated being in NY. He knew that I was "headstrong determined committed and devoted" to this Experimental Dental mission and didn't try to persuade me to "give up the dream."

He was a tough and hard-working person all his life until Alzheimer's stole him from me 5/7/2024.

Despite my grief I know Dad was always dedicated to writing including Musical jingles, & I knew he would want to see me put aside my grief to get the necessary work completed so that this extraordinary book could get reprinted/restocked. I know he is likely going to celebrate in Heaven when this book finally gets reprinted/restocked. Since my earliest Elementary school age
He taught me about writing and getting "published". It lit a "burning fire under my dwarf feet" to use books to share my unique knowledge.

Thank You Dad !

Your "Marshmallows" eldest daughter Marsha

Footnote:
https://www.google.com/books/edition/A_Scientific_Watergate_Dysle
xia/omINud2cvwoC?hl=en&gbpv=1&dq=scientific+watergate+levins
on+dying+%22father%22+harold+hospital&pg=PA384&printsec=fro
ntcover   Page: 384

Inspired by the old movie Field of Dreams.

An ode to Dr "Mickey" Schamis DDS

Mickey, go the distance and ease her pain.
And you went the distance and eased her pain.

Mickey, people will read the book. People will come Mickey. They'll come to your office for new dental hope they never dreamed would be possible. They'll walk up the steps, not sure if this is really what they ought to consider doing. They'll arrive at your office with youthful enthusiasm, longing to save their precious teeth.

Of course, I won't mind if you want me to take a look at your mouth. It's only a nominal consultation fee. They'll pay you without thinking twice for its finances they have and teeth they are terrified to lose.

And they'll walk into your dental operatory and happily sit "in the chair" eager as young kids waiting for a special treat. And as they observe you, it will be as if they found a little bit of dental heaven here on earth. For many, the tearfulness will be so profound that they'll be wiping the droplets streaming down their faces.

People will come Mickey. People will read Mickey.
The one crucial self-asset through the years has been pearly white teeth.

Many Dentists have come and gone, their past failures obliterated, redesigned, and improved upon and re-designed again.

But pearly white teeth have always been a self-priority, a part of human self-image eternally timeless over so many many years.

Your dental office & these dental prosthetics, it's a heavenly miracle and reminds us of loving old-fashioned dentists of yesteryear lovingly handcrafting artisan quality dental restorations.

People will read the book Mickey. They will most definitely read the book & come to you. You went the distance & so did your dwarf patient me. You lovingly built these prosthetics, and I definitely came to you. And you eased my pain.

Marsha

A mouth full of miracles

Book shares local dentist's life-changing procedure

Posted December 5, 2019

Dr. Michael Schamis gave Marsha Lampert a new set of teeth. Her mouth was constantly in pain until he replaced her teeth with prosthetics.

COURTESY MARSHA LAMPERT

<u>The Importance of Irlen Color tint Spectral Filter Eyeglasses in treating my DENTAL PTSD/ PANIC/PHOBIA/TERROR</u>

Thank You Dr Harold Levinson for referring me for IRLEN color glasses.

Special Dedication to Drs Jeri Lavigne & Carol Kessler, my IRLEN diagnosticians and to Dr George Boyle OD, my Vision People Optometrist & "Irlen ally" & Optician Carolyn at Vision People.

I PROPOSE THAT: Every dentally traumatized, panicked, terrified, phobic be tested for IRLEN Syndrome aka IRLEN SSS Scotopic Sensitivity Syndrome.

The cerebellar vestibular inner ear harmonizing medication help "filter " internally while the Irlen Color Tint Spectral eyeglasses help "filter" externally as per Dr Harold Levinson.

I and I'm sure other dyslexic and similar special needs patients needed something that persuades them to consider my extraordinary, experimental, dental treatment and the helpful, non-dental add-on therapies.
As the combining of it all can yield the most effective, mind, body healing and improve their overall functioning and coping skills.

The experimental dental treatment can yield a huge, rapid improvement such as decreased pain/bleeding. And can thus decrease anxiety, panic, and despair.

I wanted to reach as wide a reader base as possible. My multifaceted, experimental, holistic program is what Dr Levinson would call groundbreaking and I especially wanted to target what he calls "concerned healers." My research that I present in my book is vital and should help my fellow patients and their providers obtain miraculous results and remarkable improvements.

I kind of also feel that the best way to learn from me is to really listen to what I say and write in my book and related communications. It is really a bizarre and complex dental, medical syndrome that needs holistic, mind, body, healing approaches combined for synchronicity and effectiveness. It can literally be life, spirit, and soul saving.

Now everyone can know the root causes of my medical dental nightmare. It is also what Dr Levinson would characterize as a panoramic approach that greatly expanded the myopic and narrow-minded approach that is ineffective and even harmful and traumatic.

I gave indisputable, detailed, proof that is persuasive and realistic as well as being a huge step forward in treating me and other similar patients. It's filled with so many incredible discoveries that I made now presented in a cogent fashion for the world to learn from. It really envelops, explains, proves, and illustrates the totality of the medical, dental model I designed. It reveals hidden links and buried connections, and truly explains the bizarre network that this medical, dental disorder takes.

It's what Dr L would also call an explanatory solution that overcomes the devastating prognosis that had been around up to and including now. Such as ill-fitting dentures.

I hope it represents a beautiful contribution to my 1984-present mission to help my fellow patients and their providers to truly heal me and others.

Introduction-Preface

Who would think that a person would have to flee indefinitely from the so-called Sunshine State of Florida literally under stealth of night with little more than the clothes on their back in order to save their teeth and to treat their dyslexia? And ...Who would think that a person would choose polar fleece over palm trees? Who would think that Eskimo style winter coats would be nicer than colorful, tropical swimsuits? Who would choose insulated boots instead of beachy sandals? Who would think their new "beach" would be blue colored, beach style, bubble bath in an old tub? All to save TEETH and treat dyslexia? Sounds weird? Right? Well, that person is ME. In Florida I was repeatedly told to get my teeth extracted and replaced with dentures. Told I was hopeless, and nothing could be done to save my teeth. In Florida I was repeatedly told nobody in Florida would be willing to prescribe the dyslexia medication I need either.

The Florida Governor's office told me to go back up north from where I came from - I kid you not. The Florida dental/medical community told me to move back to Long Island as Florida isn't a progressive state and doesn't get involved in weird treatments for weird diseases. After crying and panicking I made the split-second, hardest decision in a lifetime – abandon the tropical life and embrace back the Eskimo winter life. Toss out the brightly designed bathing suits and the flip flops and welcome polar fleece and insulated boots. Goodbye palm trees and aqua pools, hello snow piles and metal shovels.

Who would think that Florida wouldn't even have a dental phobia, dental treatment center whereas NYC would have a world-renowned, dental phobia dental office to help treat me?

If I didn't want to be a toothless, dyslexic gal my future was to make a life U-turn and abandon the tropics and head back to Long Island NY and the Big Apple.

Even Florida's fried Twinkie's/Oreo's didn't tempt me to stay. Even their medical and dental schools and organizations and even POLITICIANS all insisted my only hope for my teeth and my dyslexia were to move back to the Apple and abandon the summery, tropical, citrus life. So, I did that, and it was the best decision I ever made. I received state of the art experimental dental prosthetics and plenty of my much-needed dyslexia medication.

My elderly parents begged me to move back south but there's no way I can be in a place that thinks being horribly toothless and badly dyslexic is ok! I'd rather wear 50 layers of polar fleece than have that. I laugh when people tell me they want to move to Florida. They look at me with glazed eyeballs when I tell them the answer to sick teeth is not dentures but rather teeth saving prosthetics. They look at me with stunned speechless stares when I tell them my dyslexia is fabulously controlled here with medication.

And to hear from even the politicians there and the governor's office there as well - that I should move back because Florida is not a progressive state and doesn't have the treatments that NY has- its mind bending. They told me dentures are the only option there for my sick teeth. I told them to go burn their confederate flag and bury their confederate currency. They even suggested I go on Social Security disability for my dyslexia. RIGHT. I suggest that the federal government take over Florida and bring it to NY standards.

The next time you gripe about your high taxes and corrupt politicians - that's a whole lot better than being sadly, toothless, and hopelessly dyslexic. I've already begun putting away my summery gear and yanking out my Eskimo, polar style, winter apparel.

I can't wait till my book comes out next year to tell the world my teeth saving and dyslexia spearing, treatment miracles here including the experimental dental prosthetics. Nobody should have to be Toothless in Florida when they can have the "white pearly big apple smile." Say goodbye to pink sand beaches and leafy, green palm trees. Say hello to hoodies, boots and Eskimo like winter coats. It's better than being a hopelessly dyslexic, toothless lady.

This "Nightmare journey is still ongoing as my rare medical based dental disease is incurable & chronic. The dental battle now continues every 2 weeks. So far So good. Thank God for MERCY MEDICAL ANGELS for the airfare for my winged air flight to NY 4/1/2016. Thank You MMA for being the powerful volition to spirit me like a bird to the "promised dental land up North. I would have died toothless in agony had I stayed in Florida. Unfortunately, there was NO treatment anywhere in Florida for my rare & severe condition. The botched oral surgery in Florida had failed & I was out of options there. Nobody in Florida was/is familiar with my rare & severe condition. A cerebellar, hypopituitary, dwarfism, Alopecia Ectodermal, periodontal / endodontic dental ravage

Inflammatory Auto-immune disease that had already left me bald from its alopecia defect. Bald is "yucky" enough, but bald & toothless is an unbearable nightmare. Meanwhile, this disease was destroying my teeth, my jawbone and my gums. I refused to even consider Dentures (see my short chapter on this). My mouth/face were badly swollen/inflamed/infected and painful, and a simple brushing/flossing would trigger severe bleeds with blood spraying everywhere like a homicide scene. The cerebellar, trigeminal neuralgia, hot searing, burning pain was worsening. My gums were bleeding internally into my chin, neck and jaw causing huge, inflammatory swelling that was disfiguring me. My teeth were loose sliding & shifting. Mere brushing & flossing were triggering massive painful and terrifying increasingly, worsening bleeds of bright red, blood spraying all over, creating homicide like "scenery" that was truly horrifying & terrifying. Rosacea, reddish, ruddy facial skin was looking pretty bad.

Even eating and drinking could trigger severe pain. And my teeth were beginning to loosen, shift & slide as the jawbone loss and gum recession worsened. There were tiny infectious, periodontal pockets/abscesses forming. This was paving a straight path to being toothless. My dental PTSD/Panic was escalating rapidly and severely. Sometimes mere finger touch or a piece of soft dental floss would trigger bleeds. The gums/jawbone were too severely damaged for traditional periodontal treatment-& that treatment would worsen & accelerate the teeth loss pathway. No grafting/regeneration/filler procedures were possible & no state-of-the-art LANAP laser was in Florida. Every 3 months NY treatment was no longer enough. My Cerebellar,

Ectodermal, Dwarfism, Alopecia, Autoimmune, Inflammatory Dental Ravage and Cerebellar Trigeminal Neuralgia were literally destroying me from the inside out both physically & mentally. How much more could I handle? I already had severe dental PTSD with dissociative features from my 1973 Anesthesia Awareness nightmare.

My dental PTSD panic terror was escalating rapidly. Although I had to take the "sudden middle of the night" emergency air flight to NY, I consoled myself with the belief that within a few weeks at very most, I would be heading back to the Palm trees & tropical breezes, all patched up like my prior every 3-month dental treatment trips to NY.

Nothing could have prepared me for what was to actually happen. It turned my world as I knew it, upside down & inside out forever.

At first, Dr Schamis & a local Long Island endodontist he referred me to both could not find the cause of my "face/mouth on hot fire" searing trigeminal pain, especially on the lower left side. Both dental professionals were beginning to think that my dental symptoms could be of psychiatric origin and Dr Schamis thought that perhaps a psychiatrist was needed. In angry furor & utter desperation, I begged for a 2nd referral. This time I hit "gold platinum and diamonds" the dental "treasure chest " with Dr Louis Siegelman & his associate Dr Danielle Currier and their phenomenal RDH Melissa, in NYC near Carnegie Hall. (see their website dentalphobia.com). Heart pounding panic intensely shook my terrified dwarf body as I trekked up to NYC by train & cab. I finally arrived & was welcomed with total, loving, compassionate and tender empathy & got to experience the

most incredible state of the art technology I had ever seen. Within a mere few minutes, the huge causal source of my agony lit up like a Christmas tree: it was a pile of twisted mangled broken bent razor sharp 1970's vintage root canal obturation metal silver points trapped and hidden to become like knife like razor blades tearing my flesh 24/7 & filled bloody infectious deep abscess debris. (See the chapter later in this book which explains all about this toxic metal "poison" no longer used in dentistry). It evaded detection twice on X-rays but the CT type extreme dental technology at Dr Siegelman's office spotted it in a few minutes. Arrangements were immediately made for Dr Siegelman to not only remove every last "crumb" of that metal, but also for him to do full mouth, LANAP, periodontal laser followed by Cavitron, electronic cleaning. Amazing Relief, the burning fire was extinguished. I thought this would cure my dental problems forever but that was NOT the case at all. My dental problems were headed into a larger dental nightmare nobody could have ever envisioned or imagined.

The dental pain of 1 tooth was conquered but the rest of my teeth became severely temperature hyper reactive-triggering cerebellar, trigeminal spasms that were agonizing and I refused opiates & pain killers as I did not want to become addicted.

The dwarfism dental ravage had irreversibly damaged microtubules & related dental features that process temperature. So cold, hot, warm were pain, pain, pain.

I discuss the anatomical/medical/dental stuff later in this book. I felt that you needed to have separate chapters explaining this extreme nightmare so that you could better understand my terror.

Also, for those of you not familiar with me, I also have Dyslexia, ADHD, Learning Disabilities, Aspergers (highest function autism), Irlen Syndrome, Panic/Anxiety, & dental PTSD. So, adding an experimental dental journey far from home indefinitely was a nearly unbearable herculean burden on me.

Isn't it ironic, amazing, & intriguing that God picked me a lifelong "hard core" dental phobic? My only guess is that God felt that I needed this experimental dental journey perhaps to "ease my dental terror pain by making me go the distance and doing the experiment"? My secondary guess is that perhaps God felt that if "Michael" built it (the experimental dental prosthetics) "people would come see " & then "believe " that dental miracles are for "real" and quite possible.

 This book is one that so many of you repeatedly asked me to compose, in order to provide a total, complete overview of my nightmare that led to my extraordinary and unique experimental, holistic treatment plan to save my teeth health and life.

I and my expert providers sincerely believe that this book will provide hope, healing, and happiness from the wonderful, experimental, holistic, and multifaceted treatment program I designed as it's so doable and filled with healing power. It not only restores teeth but heals body, mind, soul, and spirit. I also included a large chapter on the huge emotional/physical toll of relocating far from home and on the huge emotional/physical toll of undertaking experimental treatments and clinical trials.

One very unusual thing I learned from this unique, experimental, multi-faceted & holistic treatment program design I created from "scratch" is what Dr Harold Levinson(2019,pg 202) calls " enhanced emotional immunity" derived from surviving devastating and traumatizing conditions, including the ability to finely tune my survival "fighter" instincts despite what might appear to others as factors associated with traumatic "burn out"… the visual system, the endocrine system, the cardiac and respiratory system, so on and so forth.

I was faced with the nightmare split second, life changing and life altering decision that would forever turn my dyslexic dwarf world upside down and inside out, the hardest decision I would ever be faced with a decision that would change me forever, not just dentally but in every single aspect of my life.

The Drastic, Experimental Dental treatment was to try & stop my 24/7 pain by Root Canalling every single tooth in my dwarf mouth to destroy the nerve pain highway. The problem with that is it makes teeth as fragile as eggshells. The only possible solution was again Experimental and Dangerous & if it failed, I would be toothless forever. Dr Schamis invented the experimental procedures/experimental prosthetics needed to restore my dentition including the lost jawbone & wrecked gum tissue & stop the teeth from moving, shifting & loosening. I made the agonizing & terrifying, split-second decision to proceed with this dental experiment despite the horrific risks, nightmarish dangers & my dental PTSD terror.

One of the most horrifying things that had to be done was to drill down my already dwarfism damaged teeth to tiny pegs. That alone could have destroyed all my teeth. Just writing about it triggers panic for me. I really can't go into describing everything myself, so I chose to use an academic style approach to explain it impersonally to you. Hope you understand how this book writing actually triggers panic for me as I try my best to explain it. So please allow me to submit my story to you in that academic format so I don't relive the torment by having to go on describing it personally by myself. It literally anguishes me as I try to explain & re-explain by myself the terror/agony- which is exacerbating my cerebellar panic disorder. Please accept the way I chose to present my story in this book. It's not perhaps the "regular story book " way but I think you can follow my academic approach now that you have a clearer chronology of my story. The academic format allows me to not relive the agony panic & terror. Please respect & accept the academic approach from this point forward.

Special Introduction in Honor of Doctor Harold Levinson MD

Dear Dr Harold Levinson:

This book dramatically expands the heretofore myopic view of my rare medical based dental disease: Cerebellar Vestibular Hypopituitary Dwarfism Alopecia Ectodermal Autoimmune Inflammatory Dental Ravage with Cerebellar Vestibular Trigeminal Neuralgia and presents its real true "new" totality-providing a new greatly expanded view of my rare and extraordinary medical-dental case in an amazing and fascinating holistic manner. Throughout this book I tended to look at the "total medically based dental case picture largely" thru the "lens" of its underlying cerebellar-vestibular root causes, while mixing in an eclectic array of music, faith, psychology, sociology, religion, spirituality, hypnotherapy and even Tennis Therapy.

 I rapidly collected, collated, separated, summarized, and analyzed my rare and extraordinary case in terms of its underlying cerebellar-vestibular root causes and its heretofore hidden cerebellar-vestibular linkages, interconnections, and underpinnings. In other words, the common denominator of my experimental, dental, miracle story is the underlying cerebellar-vestibular medical root cause of my dental "nightmare", or more simply put, the defects in the cerebellar-vestibular roots that caused my "dental tree" to "go bananas" and "get scrambled". Much of the literature was and still is a bizarre "mishmash" of very confusing diagnostic terms and contradictory diagnoses. All failed to be unified, cohesive, connected and encompassing till my cerebellar based model was created by me thru trial and error, and then melded into a logical usable, practical, sensible, logical, and achievable form. Too often, the attitudes expressed in the literature were what I characterize as the " hopelessness excuse" such as " there's nothing that can be done, it's too risky, no proven scientific evidence. So on and so forth. I & Dr Schamis refused to accept this "cop-out excuse" and sought to find solutions and answers that the existing literature failed to provide. It took what I called "steely determination", "unrelenting fortitude", "raw courage", "gluey persistence " and "super focused, indomitable will".

Dr Schamis, Dr Levinson & I all felt that the "real truth" is what is experienced, tried and revealed", not what the experts previously loyally clung to- no matter how inferior their clung-to beliefs were. The experts too quickly gave up, " threw in the towel" and were too lazy to " stir up the bubbling hot cauldron" of symptoms. They preferred ignorance, confusion, and risk avoidance, they refused to take chances, they refused to explore trial and error, and refused to gamble, they refused to think creatively out of the box" and continued to refuse to do anything that could possibly fail. They hung tight to the status quo and forgot the importance of helping to alleviate suffering. Malpractice fears took precedent over patient suffering. Failure Prevention was their mantra & they refused to risk themselves by experimenting trial and error with new ideas. They remained frozen in place to what was scientifically proven… refusing to even consider new ideas. They also refused to consider experimentally tinkering with old inferior/abandoned ideas.

By comparison, Courageous Pioneers like Dr Schamis, Dr Levinson & I was filled with enthusiasm, curiosity, eagerness, and dedication, and we were all blessed with fresh eyes and open-mindedness to consider new perspectives that were not traditional…to look way outside the box and to experiment trial and error-while being proficient in understanding the harsh and "intimidating" clinical reality.

Dr Schamis & I started our quest from "ground zero" and were determined to understand and try what others were too terrified to even speak of. We had to take clues, symptoms, bits, pieces, and shreds and map out a dental-medical puzzle-maze framework for decoding the mystery dental-medical keys needed to open mystery dental-medical locks. We followed our "gut intuition" tempered with necessary caution, and we played amateur dental-medical detectives with enormous patience, fierce dedication, and unrelenting persistent determination, refusing to give up.

We analyzed, tested, re-analyzed, re-tested and sifted through piles of clues no matter how tiny, arcane, convoluted, and crazy they would seem to others. We needed to carefully identify each microscopic puzzle piece no matter how tiny to precisely identify each tiny microcosm needed to unlock the mysterious doors. It was to be a long, tedious process for both me & for Dr Schamis. We were driven to "unmask the bizarre and hidden dental enemies". We had to keep staying highly focused and extremely driven even when roadblocks, obstacles, unexpected detours and unforeseen twists and turns loomed ahead. We had to maintain our personal and professional determination to navigate through the perilous, experimental dental prosthetics journey to not only survive but to thrive victoriously.

 What made this also such a bitter struggle, is that we were facing a combined medical-dental bizarre and frightful nightmare that was unpredictable and which was affecting the "totality" of me. I found it often so painfully difficult to stay objective, professional, poised, and quasi-scientific, in order to control my often-overwhelming fear, panic and terror especially the horrifying past memories of Anesthesia Awareness & the fright filled, bad, lifetime memories of past failed treatment procedures with former providers. Despite it all I vowed to "set sail into uncharted perilous, dark, experimental dental waters" that could founder, capsize, and sink my rickety old vessel".

By myself, alone, despite my multiple disabilities and intense panic, I forced my brain to take often disparate, conflicting, bizarre, confusing, and contradictory data and try to give it a fresh, new interpretation, to update the old and obsolete, and to consider a new picture - filled with new ideas and new possibilities to explore. I often did rough drafts and scribbled furiously and kept updating, revising, and brainstorming. I jotted down symptoms, experiences, observations, findings and my questions, ideas, and thoughts.

In my hyperactive Aspie mind (I have Aspergers high function autism + ADHD + dyslexia PTSD), I kept thinking how my evolving-work-in-progress theory/model could become a potentially huge breakthrough for not just medicine and dentistry, but theology, spirituality, music & sports. Hopefully my innovative, multi-faceted model will provide new hope and new help. I hope that my model really captures the full essence and complete foundation for new therapeutic efforts, and I really hope that it brings a new, multi-disciplinary multi-pronged and multi-faceted, holistic, therapeutic, ''whole patient'' approach to treatment of rare and obscure medically based dental diseases.

I also laid out for you the twisted, turning, and detouring trial and error voyage I took including the "bread crumb trails" I sometimes encountered along the way. Basically, I created and solved the "mystery puzzle" by connecting each tiny, dot-like piece until everything "clicked in place logically" and I created structures like "literary walls" that "told my story". To date, no medical/dental professional has put together anything like my model. The seeds for part of it originated in the late 1960's-see my chapter on Psychological Iatrosedation to better understand the importance of a holistic body mind approach to dentistry. Sadly, its periodontist founder passed away & his latrosedation psychology model fell to the wayside & gathered dust until I resurrected & revamped it in this book.

In order to descramble the research literature "tangled mess" I first had to do " figurative exploratory dissection/biopsy surgery" on the research literature in order to create a new holistic medical-dental framework with its interconnections no longer hidden but finally exposed clearly for all to read, understand and learn. I had to show you the vast, diverse, and bizarre symptoms in a summarized yet comprehensive easy to understand "boiled down condensed totality"

and build my model upward from the "ground zero" symptoms "seeds" base. It was necessary for me to walk you thru the symptomatic, medical, dental foundation of diverse symptoms in order to show and explain to you the "dizzying" array of medical dental symptoms that were "intertwined and tangled" (what Dr Levinson called the "current scientific scramble") in the literature and needed to be broken down, explained, refuted by me if/as needed, and then I show you the new holistic Adjunctive Multi-Faceted treatment model that I created to connect & mesh with the Experimental medical based dental treatment model I explained. (Dr Levinson calls it a "new conceptualization") I walked all of you thru the paths I found & explored & also walked you thru the rocky, bumpy, twisted, confusing and unwieldy journey I endured to reach the "promised land" of Experimental Dental treatment including the experimental dental Prosthetics journey. (What Dr Levinson calls "scientific twists/turns.") My experience parallels what Dr Levinson calls "accidental succeeding in unscrambling.'".
 This journey is still ongoing as my rare medical based dental disease is incurable & chronic. The dental battle now continues every 2 weeks, So far So good. I walk you thru how I started with the symptom-diagnosis type beginning and how it brought me to Experimental Dental Treatment including Experimental Dental Prosthetics Treatment and the Experimental Cerebellar Trigeminal Neuralgia Full Mouth All Teeth Root Canal Nerve Removal, along with the Toxic Silver Metal Points Removal I endured, followed by Lanap Periodontal Laser Treatment & Cavitron Electronic Gingival Gum Curettage Cleaning-Scaling. I also explain how I created the needed holistic, Pastoral Clergy Music/Faith/Religion/Spirituality/Hypnotherapy/ Psychological Iatro-Sedation(non-drug) support model needed to make this Perilous & Scary Experimental Dental Treatment Journey into a really complete Healing of mind, body soul & spirit, instead of just a teeth treatment.

John Donne once wrote about how "No man is an Island" & Dylan Thomas once wrote about "a road less followed". Both are very relevant to the model that I created and Still Follow. I also walk you through how I went from Zero clergy to 3 pastors & a Rabbi, 3 churches & a Messianic Synagogue & added in 2 choral groups, bible related music therapy, dental PTSD hypnotherapy, and modified psychological Iatrosedation(non-drug) to achieve success in a highly perilous experimental dental prosthetics journey that I & Dr Schamis pioneered. I also included the story of how hidden pre-adult Metal Silver Point Root canal obturation filler material silently rotted infected & then nearly ended my life after evading dental x-ray detection & I Explain how Drs Siegelman & Currier & RDH Melissa worked hard to find/remove that destructive "teeth bone gum destroying" metal & then how they used LANAP periodontal laser & Cavitron to remove what I call "toxins". & and I included a chapter on my Tennis therapy as well, along with music/Spanish language therapies too. My exploration did not follow a straight path but rather a rutted, confusing, bizarre, scary, twisting, turning maze like form. Thus, this book format parallels that "awkward winding road" rather than the expected traditional points a to b to c. I tried to use a similar bizarre voyage path in this book, so you are in for a similarly circuitous and mind-bending experience.

See the "Exodus" Bible inspired information on Rabbi Rosenberg & the Shuvah Yisrael Messianic Judaism chapter to understand how I was "forced by emergency to suddenly & unexpectedly flee Florida" literally overnight, with no time to pack & how I had to make a split-second decision to stay in NY for experimental dental treatment that was & is perilous & of highest risk. I had no time to think or plan. All this was under herculean Olympic speed duress for the past few years. I had fled to save my teeth & life. The botched failed Florida surgical treatment & lack of any other treatment in Florida forced me to have to literally flee in middle of the night, like the Israelites fleeing Egypt & like Heroine of the Underground Railroad Harriet Tubman, whose 1st escape was in middle of the night-suddenly, without packing.

Thank God for Mercy Medical Angels for the airfare for my winged air flight to NY 4/1/2016. Thank You 'MMA' for being the powerful volition to spirit me like a bird to the "promised dental land up North. I would have died toothless in agony had I stayed in Florida. Unfortunately, there was NO treatment anywhere in Florida for my rare & severe condition. The attempted oral surgery in Florida was ultimately failing & I was out of options there.

 Nobody in Florida was/is familiar with my rare & severe condition. A cerebellar, hypopituitary, dwarfism, Ectodermal periodontal / endodontic dental ravage disease that had already left me bald from its alopecia defect. Bald is "yucky" enough, but bald & toothless is an unbearable nightmare. Meanwhile, this disease was destroying my teeth, my jawbone, and my gums. I refused to even consider Dentures (see my short chapter on this). My mouth/face were badly swollen/inflamed/infected and painful, and a simple brushing/flossing would trigger severe bleeds with blood spraying everywhere. The cerebellar, trigeminal neuralgia pain was worsening. My face, chin & neck were bleeding internally as well as very enlarged from the painful swelling. I looked & felt dreadful and even eating and drinking could trigger the pain. And my teeth were beginning to loosen, shift & slide as the jawbone loss and gum recession worsened. There were tiny periodontal pockets/abscesses forming. This was paving a terrifying straight path to being toothless.

My dental PTSD/Panic was escalating rapidly. Sometimes mere finger touch would trigger bleeds. The gums/bone were too severely damaged for traditional periodontal treatment-& that treatment would actually worsen & accelerate the teeth loss pathway. No grafting/regeneration/filler procedures were possible & no state-of-the-art LANAP laser was in Florida. Every 3-month NY treatment was no longer enough.   My dental PTSD panic was escalating rapidly. Although I had to take the "sudden middle of the night" flight to NY, I consoled myself with the belief that within a few weeks at very most, I would be heading back to the Palm trees & tropical breezes, all patched up like my prior every 3-month dental treatment trips to NY.

Nothing could have prepared me for what was to actually happen. It turned my world as I knew it, upside down & inside out forever.

At first, Dr Schamis & a local Long Island endodontist he referred me to as both could not find the cause of my "face/mouth on hot fire" searing trigeminal pain, especially on the lower left side. Both dental professionals were beginning to think that my dental symptoms could be of psychiatric origin and Dr Schamis thought that perhaps a psychiatrist was needed. In angry furor & utter desperation, I begged for a 2nd referral. This time I hit "gold platinum and diamonds" the dental "treasure chest " with Dr Louis Siegelman & his associate Dr Danielle Currier and their phenomenal RDH Melissa, in NYC near Carnegie Hall. (see their website dentalphobia.com).

 Heart pounding panic intensely shook my terrified dwarf body as I trekked up to NYC by train & cab. I finally arrived & was welcomed with total, loving, compassionate and tender empathy & got to experience the most incredible state of the art technology I had ever seen. Within a mere few minutes, the huge causal source of my agony lit up brightly like a Christmas tree: it was a sickening pile of infected corroded twisted mangled broken bent razor sharp 1970's vintage root canal obturation metal silver points trapped and hidden to become like knife like razor blades tearing my flesh 24/7 & bloody infectious deep abscess debris (See the chapter in this book about this metal "poison" no longer used in dentistry). It evaded detection twice on X rays but the CT type extreme dental technology spotted it in a few minutes. Arrangements were immediately made for Dr Siegelman to not only remove every last "crumb" of that metal, but also for him to do full mouth LANAP periodontal laser followed by Cavitron electronic cleaning. Amazing Relief, the burning fire was extinguished. I thought this would cure my problems forever but that was not the case at all. The rest of my miracle story would unfold slowly-a small bit at a time,

& sometimes it felt like it was moving at a snail's pace & as slow as molasses.

I felt that you also needed to have a chapter on Dwarfism Dentistry & a chapter on Obstacles/Risks/Challenges/Dangers of Experimental Dwarfism Dentistry to better understand how even so-called dental experts refused to even communicate with me and why they saw my bizarre case as a synonym for "dental malpractice liability".

Many times, I have had to teach my dental/medical providers how to handle my unique case especially where medical/dental overlapped & intersected like Venn diagrams due to its common denominator, a faulty defective and malfunctioning cerebellar-vestibular "system" that would require a simultaneous medical-dental cerebellar related approach. I used Dr Harold Levinson's books & articles as a springboard to build my model off of his models & am indebted to him for being my primary medical provider since Sept.1984 (note too that I am a patient of Dr Schamis since 1983). Please note too that like Dr Levinson, I too became a dyslexic, medical, dental researcher by necessity rather than by choice, and just like him, my ambitions and priorities were to relieve not just my own personal nightmare of suffering but to relieve pain & suffering of others with my rare and severe medically based dental condition.

One of the largest pieces of this huge Mystery puzzle solving was showing how my dwarfism alopecia and Dwarfism Dental Ravage (periodontic/endodontic) was connected by the "Cerebellar-Vestibular-Ectodermal" malfunction defect. I also mapped the total body effects of that Cerebellar Vestibular Ectodermal malfunction from head to toe to show you how this system is like a large tree with lots of branches & sub-branches that are interactively connected. When a provider is treating the dental ravage, they are indirectly affecting the entire cerebellar "tree". Dr Harold Levinson described the Cerebellum as a Giant Computer System. My own research corroborated that throughout this book. I also showed you how my cerebellar malfunction helped activate my trigeminal neuralgia & I showed you how the Dwarfism in my case is a cerebellar, vestibular, hypopituitary, ectodermal dwarfism with both dwarfism alopecia and its twin-like dwarfism dental ravage, their other major intersection point-autoimmune and inflammatory.

 I also included a chapter on the Experimental dentally Splinted bridge prosthetics invented by Dr Schamis for my dwarf mouth, so that you can better understand my experimental devices including the "downside" to it. I also included sections on Dental PTSD Hypnodontic Hypnotherapy, as well as a section explaining why Implants and dentures are virtually never the solution to this rare severe dental disease. And a section on Anesthesia Awareness Caused Dental Terror. I also included a section on why most people decline experimental treatment-& carefully explain why. I also added a section on why constant frequent dental treatment monitoring/cleaning is needed because these devices cannot be flossed.

Also, for those of you not familiar with me, I also have Dyslexia, ADHD, Learning Disabilities, Aspergers (highest function autism), Irlen Syndrome, Panic/Anxiety, & dental PTSD. So, adding an experimental dental journey far from home indefinitely was a herculean burden on me.

Isn't it ironic, amazing, & intriguing that God picked me to be a lifelong "hard core" dental phobic? My only guess is that God felt that I needed this experimental dental journey perhaps to "ease my dental terror pain by making me go the distance and doing the experiment"? My secondary guess is that perhaps God felt that if "Michael" built it (the experimental dental prosthetics) "people would come see" & then "believe" that dental miracles are for "real" and quite possible.

Dr Harold Levinson's admonition about holistically conceptualizing a complex multi-dimensional disorder under investigation became a crucial catalyst force for my decision to research and analyze my medical-dental disorder from the vantage point of cerebellar-vestibular disorder, following in the footsteps of Dr Levinson.

It is my hope that by participating in experimental care that it may eventually help loads of other suffering patients. It has certainly improved my academic ability to assess and quickly judge the significance of historical/subjective data.

 Dr Levinson was so spot on target that it is possible that a viable safe effective solution is often quite simple and readily at hand, and he was spot on target that though the theories abound, they are incapable of solving problems and correct that symptoms/signs exist but are overlooked denied or minimized. He was also so on point for mentioning the pursuit of unexpected, atypical, and paradoxical data. I and Dr Levinson & Dr Schamis definitely pursued where others were too afraid to even think of going.

Similar to Dr Levinson, Dr Schamis & I both hope that we are providing a groundbreaking new understanding to as wide an audience as possible, especially to concerned healer dentists, in order for rare extreme medical dental patients like me to obtain the best possible multi-disciplinary & multi-faceted holistic help and superior dental treatment results.

This book is one that so many of you repeatedly asked me to compose, in order to provide a total complete overview of the discoveries and diagnoses that led to my extraordinary and unique experimental holistic treatment plan to save my teeth health and life. This book writing process was tedious and time consuming yet so amazing and rewarding. I was able to identify the true underlying cerebellar link to the medically based dental nightmare I have been in. And now I know the signs & symptoms thoroughly. Many of them had not been realized before as connected. The careful analysis of the research literature data/findings allowed me to create a detailed and accurate "portrait" of this previously misdiagnosed misidentified misunderstood and non-understood dental-medical constellation syndrome to assist my team of providers so they could more efficiently help treat me. Many hidden clues were unearthed & carefully researched by me thanks to my precision research. I became proficient in reading, culling out, extracting and recording information from a very diverse and quite prolific body of literature from different fields and then cross-comparing and matching up the "pieces of this huge puzzle".

Along the way, my experimental and "controversial" treatments were often vociferously resisted and harshly condemned as well as denied and disbelieved. However, I and my team were undeterred by these negative critics and my devoted research more than validated the treatment pathways I and Dr Schamis chose & "designed".

I had reams of undeniable facts and convincing evidence and made crucial insights that would bring me stellar dental treatment results. My model truly encompasses the totality of my medical-dental disorder. My extremely dedicated research and my "street smart" practical experience combined with my unwavering faith and unbreakable conviction of beliefs would very slowly begin to chip away at the "granite mountain" of stubborn, arrogant disbelievers.

This book is filled with incredible findings, intriguing discoveries and practical solutions to this devastating medically based dental nightmare. I always focused on "connecting the dots and crumbs" in order to show the "co-occurrences" that up till now were thought of as separate and unrelated phenomena, such as the fascinating ectodermal cerebellar connections between alopecia and dental ravage. I also tried to show that what appears to be my having many different conditions is really one cerebellar ectodermal "tree trunk" loaded with hundreds of connected branches.

My extreme research unmasked the hidden underlying cerebellar related links to my rare dental malady. I think that you will find my insights have been presented here in a spellbinding and attention-grabbing manner. Many times, I felt like I was a dental explorer on a hunt for hidden treasure loads just waiting to be excavated and restored.

I and my expert providers sincerely believe that this book will provide hope, healing, and happiness from the wonderful experimental holistic and multifaceted treatment program I designed as it's so doable and filled with healing power. It not only restores teeth but heals body, mind, soul, and spirit.

I also included a large chapter on the huge emotional/physical toll of relocating far from home and on the huge emotional/physical toll of undertaking experimental treatments and clinical trials.

One very unusual thing I learned from this unique experimental multi-faceted & holistic treatment program design I created from "scratch" is what Dr Harold Levinson calls "enhanced emotional immunity" derived from surviving devastating and traumatizing conditions, including the ability to finely tune my survival "fighter" instincts despite what might appear to others as factors associated with traumatic "burn out".

I was very diligent in following Dr Harold Levinson's admonition about explaining all the relevant data both typical and atypical, in order to form an all-encompassing model and about carefully mapping the symptomatic overlaps.

Although I have ADHD/Dyslexia/Aspergers Autism, luckily the inner ear harmonizing medications from Dr Levinson combined with my IRLEN Color Tint dyslexia filter eyeglasses led to my " savant like" ability to over focus with razor sharp concentration for prolonged periods of time so that my attention is "super normal". This special ability has been a tremendous asset in writing this book. This is combined with what Dr Levinson refers to as "my significant determination skills. No matter how great the obstacles are, my stubborn determination (i.e. to see this book to completion). The mental challenges, the relentless need to tackle, simplify, explain and solve complex problems. Being tirelessly driven to solve complex problems, using street smart conceptual agility and sharp analytic skills needed to analyze everything for important clues and valuable correlations including identifying key characteristics along with underlying origins. It took enormous time, patience and determination for me to tirelessly read, write, collect, analyze, re-analyze, summarize and collate a huge amount of continually accruing data to find common points.

The more I researched the stronger my convictions grew about the connections I discovered especially in terms of the correlations I found between often seemingly unrelated impairments/symptoms. My confidence in my own findings steadily grew and more and more I began to seriously question the "expertise" of the professional providers. More & more I got to see that my "raw gut instinct" was right. Sometimes paradoxical findings would occur as I scanned the literature. It was thrilling for me to "clinically validate" my rare dental condition by combing through vast loads of research literature, looking for hidden clues, and overlooked evidence, much of which was overlapping (i.e. finding multiple impaired functions/disorders which overlapped with one another). It was exciting to find " new connections" & to identify common underlying cerebellar links. I felt that there would be significant therapeutic benefits of understanding the various mechanisms and how they could trigger things such as dental PTSD. It was incredible to read about cerebellar connections to the autonomic nervous system, the visual system, the endocrine system, the cardiac and respiratory system, and so on and so forth.

More on Why I am delighted that I became a Dyslexic ADHD Aspergers Autism PTSD LD Dwarf Test subject for the Experimental dental prosthetics April 2016-present:

I was faced with the nightmare split second life changing and life altering decision that would forever turn my dyslexic dwarf world upside down and inside out, the hardest decision I would ever be faced with a decision that would change me forever, not just dentally but in every single aspect of my life.

Within just a few minutes of looking at my reflection in a handheld dental patient mirror, my dwarf dyslexic composure was shaken to its core, as I almost didn't recognize my face, 'Amazing" isn't the only word to describe it-I was so stunned speechless and flooded with intense emotion to see my entire face so dramatically and miraculously altered. For the 1st time in my life. I no longer had severely buck splayed gapped upper front yellowy large teeth with a huge overbite. I had custom fitted experimental dentition that were pearly and straight.

Within seconds, I ran over & tearfully hugged Dr Schamis my " dental teeth saver angel" and he too was momentarily overcome with emotion as well, as I hugged him. A moment of mutual provider patient joy. Neither 1 of us had expected the miracle to be so amazingly perfect. No words can begin to describe the joy of having these truly, extraordinary, and miraculous, experimental, splinted, sealed dental bridge prosthetics so lovingly invented by this brilliant and artistic HypnoDontic dentist.

What also added to our joy are 2 other directly connected miracles: the incredible inner ear panic/phobia medication that allowed me to dentally succeed despite my terror of dental treatment and a unique dental phobia expert (see his website dentalphobia.com) Dr Louis Siegelman DDS in NYC, for finding and removing the hidden broken bent mangled and razor sharp 1970's vintage metal silver root canal points that had caused me agonizing painful harm and for his LANAP periodontal laser and Cavitron treatment on my gums. Thanks too to his associates Dr Currier & Melissa the RDH. for helping with that massive "dental mess".

Special Thanks to a Very Important Person in my Experimental Dental Prosthetics Journey: Patrick Hardison

The Miraculous face transplant Experimental pioneer.

He has been such a patient Rock of Gibraltar for me despite his own situation: Calming me Cheering me on Coaching me on. Motivating & Mentoring me. Guiding & Encouraging me. Keeping me strong. He shares his strength with me & helps keep good brakes on my tendency to rapidly panic.

He really understands my Dental PTSD intense pre-appointment panic & is a soothing calming reassuring & comforting person who TRULY understands the scariness of being an experimental pioneer. I love re-watching his videos before my scary experimental dental treatment every other week. It's like the lyrics of that classic pop song " Do I make you proud?"

Yes, Patrick, you make me so proud of you for keeping me strong by sharing your strength & supporting me when I often get very scared before my appointments. God Bless You, Patrick for being my courageous role model!

Full Mouth Root Canal - Validation & Support -A Brief Summary

Dr. Jayant Ambulgekar wrote that full mouth crown lengthening after *full mouth root canal* was selected as treatment of choice followed by prosthetic rehabilitation. See Full Mouth Rehabilitation of Mutilated Dentition. (Drs Jayant Ambulgekar Rizwan Sanad Manan Doshi Dr Subodh Gaikwad) Thus, the patient was 1st referred to Dept. of Endodontics for full mouth root canal treatment & then to the Dept. of

Prosthodontics for full mouth rehabilitation. Hence, full mouth crown lengthening after full mouth root canal was selected as treatment of choice followed by prosthetic rehabilitation.

The NYCdentist.COM section on tooth decay advertises the following: " Dental crowns on every tooth, **Root Canal Therapy performed on every tooth**. Avoiding potential painful root canal emergencies with preventative endodontics should be considered.

Best scientific clinical paper awarded at Tamil Nadu state conference was on **"full mouth root canal Endodontic Rehabilitation** in a medically compromised diabetes mellitus patient--A case clinical report "by Dr Vineet Vinayak.

Blind Men & Elephants: How it applies to my Dental Case

Lillian Quigley retold the story of "The Blind Men & The Elephant": To find out the whole truth we must put all the parts together". In an old fable from India, several blind men encountered an elephant & each blind man examined a separate part in an effort to determine what the creature was like...& afterward, each blind man described the elephant in radically different terms depending on which part each blind man examined. They all failed to see the big picture. Each man had focused on a limited narrow aspect while ignoring the other aspects.

In my own case, My Treatment providers initially were just like those blind men & it took some firm emphatic persistent demanding by me to get my providers to really look at the complete totality of my case. Hence, I was determined to create a holistic model for them to use in order to have a far more comprehensive panoramic view of me.

BRIEF HISTORICAL BACKGROUND OF DENTAL RECONSTRUCTION/RESTORATION

Thomas Berdmore wrote a Treatise on the disorders/deformities of teeth in 1768, & Simon Guilford wrote about Malposition of the teeth in 1889.

Research Methods Formats Styles Techniques & Strategies I used to design this book:

(Dr Lantz 's doctoral dissertation & the books by Dr Harold Levinson MD provided many different research methods. formats, styles, techniques & strategies that I combined to design this book.

I have listed the techniques and formats from Dr Lantz's doctoral dissertation to help walk you through my "mind processing" functions.

1) *Categorizing my findings*
2) *Identifying linkages between categories of data*
3) *Formulating explanations that could accommodate all the data.*
4) *Using a Theoretical framework based on social psychology Theoretical Analyses*
5) *Using Maximum variation*
6) *Separating similarities & differences linking similarities*
7) *Building theories*
8) *Considering alternative meanings*
9) *Combining systematic research with creativity*
10) *identifying building blocks that can form theories*
11) *developing concepts*
12) *abstracting data from small pieces of incidents, ideas, events, and acts*
13) *recording thoughts questions & impressions*
14) *naming categories & subcategories*
15) *identifying relationships and building explanations*
16) *explaining phenomena*

17) organizing around central concepts

18) identifying and building core variables related to social experiences

19) sorting information

20) trimming away excess information

21) expanding underdeveloped categories

22) identifying threads

23) creating foundational concepts

24) linking related data

25) constant comparative analysis -circular chains of thoughts

26) provide purposes + research questions.

27) identifying theoretical underpinnings

28) identifying gaps in the literature

29) identifying pre-conceptions

30) suggesting future research ideas

I combined the above strategies with what Dr Levinson described as:

1) correlation of the data derived from simultaneous paths of investigation.

2) a reconstructive analysis of the symptoms

3) highlighting the intuitive correlation between specific patterns of symptoms

4) developing associations between linkages

5) separating/dissecting/categorizing the myriad symptoms

6) Encompassing & explaining all relevant data both typical & atypical.

7) and identifying what the symptomatic overlapping is.

Some examples of dental prostheses include:

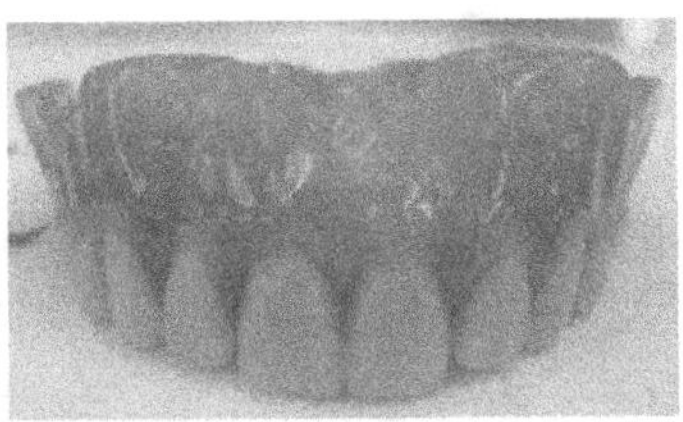

- dentures
- partial dentures
- overdentures
- dental implants SEE e.g. https://en.wikipedia.org/wiki/Dental_implant
- crowns
- bridges

Periodontal Splinting Prosthetics to stop Tooth Mobility/Loose Teeth Movement.

(Pidlisnyi) describes aesthetic periodontal splint bridges for use in dental situations such as dental trauma stabilization-in order to stabilize mobile loose and shifting teeth. In particular he refers to the use of dental adhesive and restorative ribboned fibers. (Strassler) is connected to Ribbond.com a periodontal splint product manufacturer, including both mandibular and maxillary splinting. It is represented as a strong durable bondable failure resistant periodontal splinting product.

(Dentistry today,) provided a very well-presented general discussion explaining the usage/benefits of Periodontal Splinting to save & stabilize mobile/loose/shifting teeth. A summary of their discussion is provided below to help you understand how this treatment saves teeth:

Periodontal Splinting refers to the stabilization of periodontally compromised loose mobile shifting moving teeth.ie with usage of materials such as fiber reinforced composite resin for example. When jawbone is lost or damaged, it will lead to lose teeth also known as periodontal mobility. Splinting improves long term prognosis of the affected teeth, as well as improving occlusion of the bite/fit of upper to lower teeth by stopping the movement of the teeth. The most common type of periodontal splinting historically has been the type that I have-namely cantilever splinted sealed connected crown bridges-where the crowns are joined together in what is often termed "full coverage cast restoration' where each tooth gets crowned with a cast acrylic restoration. The key disadvantages of this approach are the creation of a device that cannot be flossed, as each tooth/crown is connected & sealed to its neighboring teeth the need for all the affected/involved teeth to be drilled down to "peg like " form and the risk of loading strain stresses during chewing/biting/mastication which is sometimes referred to as torque force stresses on the teeth and the splinting material which can lead to possible fracturing and failure of the splinting and the affected teeth, the splint needs to resist occlusive/masticatory (bite/chew) forces that can lead to fracture failure. Strassler noted that a brittle resin/composite splint can crack within connector areas, leading to fractures in supporting pontics area, including the risk of catastrophic fracturing in the unreinforced composite area. The ideal solution is multi-directional reinforcement with crack stopping resin.

Another criticism of splinting is where excessive resin/cement over-reinforced material creates over contouring /overbulking of the splint. This causes the splinting to be difficult to clean & plaque accumulation to be rampant, especially where food particles can get trapped. Once Splinted, the interproximal surface cannot be perfectly cleaned. If there is excessive composite resin and/or excessive cement, access to those areas is extremely limited. Strassler noted that excessive resin/adhesive over the reinforcement material created overbulked restorative surfaces leading to hygienic difficulty, including plaque accumulation and trapped food particles.

Additional criticisms include the risk of exposed root surfaces, causing root sensitivity-the issue of splinting material thickness i.e. needing multi-directional reinforcement to prevent cracking- however advantages of the "historic' splinting technique include the use of prosthetic pontics to replace missing teeth which is a very huge "plus" in restoring the occlusive bite. Splinting can involve bonded adhesive resin. An example of splinting can also include a cast restoration on the lingual surface of teeth, aka pin splints.

Strassler noted that the clinical management of Hyper-Mobile Periodontally compromised teeth poses great challenges. Especially due to the jawbone loss, Mobility can be controlled/managed with Splinting Therapy to stabilize and connect teeth. The splinting stops the progression of teeth mobility/movement. 'Teeth Splinting is a Long-Term Commitment for both clinician and patient and he added that years ago, the optimal choice was full definitive coverage cast restorations using connected crowns, i.e. the fabrication of a multiple unit restoration to be placed on contiguous involved teeth, i.e. acrylic resin stabilization. Each tooth required preparation/restoration, i.e. teeth joined to cast porcelain metal splints and sometimes re-fabrication /re-cementation of the fixed splint was needed-i.e. with thicker connectors to avoid cracks and fractures. Especially at high loading stress areas such as areas with high load stress load from chewing mastication forces.

Rajaram & Mahendra noted that with permanent splinting, tooth resistance to an applied force is increased by joining it to neighboring teeth. It stabilizes mobile teeth, it forms a firm unit, improves occlusion and redistributes/redirects the forces, it preserves arch integrity and arrests mobility of teeth.

Lijiang & Lu noted that there is an improved periodontal condition after fixed splint restoration, including improved periodontal support.

 It helps control deteriorating periodontal condition via cementation of teeth to adjacent teeth. There can also be increased alveolar bone height after splinting due to bone infill.

Chee & Lee noted that there is high risk of decay when using splinted type dental restorations, including also with use of prosthetic over-dentures.

Grover & Mehra mentioned that dental prosthetic retention can be augmented by various attachments anchored to suitably strong teeth, and they also mention the use of rigid connectors.

Kumari & Kumar stated that rigid fixed prosthetics with rigid connectors can interfere with jaw growth in growing patients(non-adult). With removable prosthetics, underdeveloped alveolar jawbone ridges can create problems for prosthetic retention/stability. Ridge augmentation may be needed.

Meier, in his study of neural/cerebellar aspects of Dental Pain/Dental Fear, mentioned the use of experimental dental pain testing material that included Dental Splinting. Murthy, & Vaz mentioned that prosthodontists seldom use rigid connectors.

Warotayanont discussed a dental patient with a rare cerebellar disease called Dandy Walker Malformation: who presented a great challenge in dental management : presentation dentally included: fracture of prior endodontic root canal treated right crown tooth(maxillary upper right side) , coronal coverage a fracture of composite restoration that had become darkly stained, orofacial anomalies, childhood dental damage/trauma(age 10) concave facial profile, asymmetric face, chin deviation, malocclusion, crossbite/overbite/overjet, needing gingivectomy to increase crown length and needing posts, **&** Fiber Reinforced composite resin Periodontal Crown **Splinting due to loose periodontally mobile teeth**-there was also anterior teeth overcrowding, abnormal bite, a defective incisor needing restoration and gingival repair.

Strassler stated that Periodontal Splinting is a long-term commitment for both provider and patient. Li & Jiang indicate that the patient and provider need to agree on regular recall/maintenance after the splinted restoration is installed.

Dua, Singh & Aghi, 2011 stated that the foundation restoration of teeth is crucial and that it's necessary to conserve remaining teeth by reinforcing them with foundation restorations. Dr Michael Cone DMD stated that complete reorganization of occlusion may require splinted dentition with connectors/attachments to ensure retention.

Dental Clinical North America
https://www.ncbi.nlm.nih.gov/pubmed/3908166
indicated there are numerous factors that can have an adverse or beneficial effect upon the esthetic appearance of a ceramometal restoration. Some of these factors are beyond the influence of the

dentist unless he or she is aware of them. Knowledgeable practicing dentists have the ability to prescribe for their patients in such a manner as to achieve greater success and, in turn, greater patient acceptance and recognition. These are the rewards of a successful crown and bridge practice, and the ceramometal restoration is the basic state of the art prosthesis in present use. The type of alloy used in the ceramometal combination can have an effect upon the esthetic result.

One of the most important considerations in aesthetic ceramometal restorations is the correct anatomy, placement, and harmonious blending with the oral and facial features and coloring of the patient. It would be comforting if we could all agree on a definition of aesthetics. There is perhaps no more important aspect of marketing the ceramometal restoration to the patient than arrive, in advance, on a common ground and understanding of what the esthetic goals of the case are in realistic terms Planning and executing the restorative rehabilitation of a severely mutilated dentition is one of the most challenging tasks for the restorative dentist.

Musical Skills & Dental Prosthetics

Dr Donald Giddon noted that it is important to consider the effects of dental prosthetics on singing as well as on playing certain musical instruments that require use of the oral cavity, he views music as a biosocial aspect of the patient.

My experimental fixed permanent splinted sealed and Connected Dental Prosthetics: They fit over my severely damaged teeth & if/where I am missing a tooth, it provides a "fake replacement experimental tooth" called a pontic. Almost none of my teeth had to be removed. This is unlike implants which totally replace the teeth. Teeth extraction causes loss of jawbone & gum shrinkage-see my chapter on Teeth Loss.

Chapter 1A: Stress/Anxiety/Fear involved in an Experimental Dental Prosthetics Journey

Moon & Kim noted that emotional challenges exist before, during and after corrective orthodontic/orthognathic treatment.

Friedman, Landesman & Wexler felt that corrective prosthodontic treatment over a protracted period of time does include significant emotional involvement/investment -and can strain a patient's adaptive capacity to accept, triggering maladaptive responses including fear anxiety and depression that can impair a patient's quality of life. it can even include the risk of "emotional collapse" over feared loss of teeth.

General research has shown that such journeys can seem especially scary and filled with fear and anxiety. especially so in experimental treatments and clinical trials. And especially if one is the very first patient to receive such a treatment. Additional practical concerns can and do include travel distance, time commitments, protracted long duration of treatment and follow-up/monitoring/maintenance/exams/tests. Especially if the time parameters are not known and cannot be estimated. Impact on Finances, Family & Employment can be severe. Thus, psychosocial type considerations/planning are so crucial. Chamberlain stated that Depression awareness is important to consider in denture & prosthetic patients.

Falcon describes an 18 yr. old primordial dwarf dental patient named Hannah, mentions the following important items: Her fears about so many unknown factors, + the sense of there being no turning back. The article also mentioned that when she first saw herself toothless after her full teeth removal, she recalled "freaking out, feeling weird and kind of overwhelmed ' and she recalled that " her identity was in her teeth ". She also expressed that she wanted to wake up with teeth and go to bed with teeth.

Quinn terms the Experimental treatment patient's dilemma as the "Guinea Pig Syndrome' and states that patients have a fear of being a human guinea pig.

Although not a 'dental' situation, the following case of a young woman named Paige ,is very relevant to this section of the book, as I think you will agree after reading little bits and pieces of her Experimental Ulcerative Colitis Experimental Treatment Journey('Paige's Story-a personal story about her clinical trial treatment experience, shown by the Crohn's Colitis foundation) : She starts off by stating that enrolling in the clinical trial treatment was intimidating, I realized that I needed serious medical intervention to control my disease. This was not going to be a simple fix, it was rather an "end of the rope" strategy to manage this disease, I began the journey as a clinical trial patient with cautious optimism. She concludes by telling the readers that if they are a patient that is apprehensive about enrolling in a clinical trial, she hopes that you may have found something in her testimony that provided you with reassurance in your decision and optimism for your experience.

 Forster says that patients are very fearful of clinical trials, and they are especially apprehensive about having to travel far distances and potentially having to stay there for long indefinite stays in order to receive care. Tanner, BA wrote about the psychological aspects of Ectodermal Dysplasia). Naqash, mentioned the psychological trauma due to compromised oral health. Koob indicated the treatment is a protracted course into adulthood.

Gwendolyn Quinn poignantly describes how cancer patients' fears inhibit many from participating in experimental/clinical trials and why this is the case. Although not referencing the diseases covered in this book, I thought that some of the information was relevant & applicable to dental patients who hesitate to try experimental prosthetics/treatment: Quinn wrote patient related barriers have hindered patients' abilities to participate in clinical trials. Little is known about patients' emotional barriers of fear and how providers influence this barrier. She was researching the role of the emotional barrier of fear from reviewing patients' perceptions about participating in clinical trials and she was addressing the role of fear in patients considering participating in a clinical trial. Making a decision to participate triggers personal fears/anxieties, & the emotional barrier of Fear is the single largest inhibitor of decisions to participate in clinical trials and it often goes unaddressed. Many patients experience fear/anxiety/distress that can become overwhelming to them, and thus often leads to patients' difficulty in making a rational decision. Lessening that distress leads to patient empowerment as they can now better understand their treatment options.

 Personal treatment decision making requires supportive communication. And this supportive communication can serve to encourage patients to participate despite their fears of clinical trials and their fears of the unknowns and fears of risks involved. Patients have revealed that they are afraid, terrified, scared, overwhelmed, frightened, and some have commented that it was too hard to think about participating, and that they couldn't "hear" anything that was being said due to their feeling overwhelmed. Some noted that they really couldn't think about a clinical trial & had to first process and get through how scared they feel, some said that they couldn't think of anything except of their fears of death and dying, some are afraid of experimental testing, including fear of painful tests/procedures, some fear "not being in control and not having any control over what can happen-refusing participation in order to have control over the illness " "saying no one gave me some control over the disease" "it's like being a guinea pig" ,fearing negative outcomes-afraid to take chances with unknown outcomes-feeling if it fails they have no more hope-"it's going where no person has gone before and that is frightening, "feeling apprehensive over being experimented on, "you are a guinea pig-that's for sure" " a guinea pig to help find a cure someday" " fear of being a "guinea pig" is the major reason for declining to participate in clinical trials-scared to hear of a clinical trial as it sounded like there was no other options left...this may be our only hope? "last resort for people out of options" -very scary to hear there are no other options left-decision making involves strong emotional responses, emotion of fear was so overwhelming that patients cannot process thinking about alternative treatment approaches- distress hampers capacity to process info. -Patients face difficulties in making decisions to enroll in clinical trials without guaranteed outcomes, some patients perceive making trial decisions to be an oppressive burden...fear impacts cognition about clinical trials.

Chapter 1B: Teeth Health Affects the Whole Body!

Dr Gerry Curatola, aka the "RejuvDentist'`) stated that Teeth health is directly tied to whole body health and that teeth infections (i.e. periodontal/endodontic) can affect the " energy links' aka 'meridians' to various body organs. These 'meridians' can be a switch for the immune system. Dental Inflammatory disease can turn off the optimal immune function switch to multiple organs and increase one's risk of cancer, not just a risk of loss to the dental structural integrity. He also recommends the use of 3D dimensional dental scans, to supplement 2D dental x-rays. See his book "The Mouth-Body Connection". Watanabe indicated that Persistent periodontal bacterial inflammatory infections could spill over to the whole body including the brain and can lead to Alzheimer's Dementia.

Watanabe also reported that prefrontal cortical activation results from mastication and that mastication helps maintain cognitive function- Mastication causes fibroblast growth factors to be released into the brain- which promotes brain cell repair and learning/memory improvement including improved long-term memory. Mastication (Chewing) increases concentration as well as language processing speed and working memory task function. Periodontal disease can cause reduced cognitive function and increased amyloid protein in the hippocampus and in the cerebral cortex.

Mouth-Body Connection: Research studies show a connection between periodontal disease and other health conditions. Some oral pathogens involved in periodontal disease are risk factors, or are associated with systemic diseases, including heart disease, diabetes, dementia, and some types of cancer. Treating, and preventing, gum disease can help in the management of other illnesses.

Chapter 1C: Dental Provider Support is Crucial during a protracted treatment journey.

Chandrashekar noted the following: The merits of a tender loving care approach before, during and after treatment. including during planning/research/consideration/decision making preparation. He noted that the provider must " meet the mind of the patient before meeting the mouth " of the patient. Patient Mental Attitudes influence treatment outcomes. Patients can react strongly to "scary" treatment decision situations they are facing. So, winning and maintaining patient confidence and comfort is crucial. Helping patients develop acceptance of the proposed/planned treatment is crucial.

Patients have a risk of giving up if/when they feel overwhelmed by problems encountered. Provider assistance enhances patient willingness to tolerate and endure the prosthetics. Providers need to take into account the mental attitudes and psychological adaptive responses of their dental prosthetic patients. There is a relationship between psychology and dentistry-that requires proper consideration in dental treatment. The emotional/psychological state of the patient is an essential part of treatment and of the dentist-patient relationship. Success/Failure depends in part on the emotional state of the patient. There is a need to address negative psychological factors that can result in prosthetic failure, regardless of the technical excellence of the prosthetic. There can be maladaptive responses to treatment from things such as negative previous experiences, especially of traumatic bad past experiences. Additionally severe anxiety/depression can lead to low pain/anxiety tolerance levels. This is compounded when unfavorable biomechanical factors that can lead to maladaptive responses such as discouragement. There is a risk of the patient "giving up easily" if/when problems are encountered. Patient feelings that the problems are insurmountable and when patients begin to doubt the ability of anyone to help them. The provider needs to provide kind sympathetic help as much as they can, especially for new dental prosthetics.

 Fitting the personality of a patient can be more difficult than fitting the prosthetic to the patient's mouth. There is a need to fit oneself to the patient's psychological state. Koper divided denture patients into (3) different classes: Class 1: adapts physically but has psychological maladaptive distress such as anxiety, fear and or depression. Class 2: provider involved technically and emotionally for a protracted period of time because the patient is psychologically maladaptive/distressed. Class 3: The patient suffers "emotional collapse" including social withdrawal and personal suffering. Koper, & Chandrasekar both stated that patients can be made into excellent patients if handled properly, including extra time before, during and after each treatment appointment.

Krocha, stated that unfavorable anatomy may not always be a negative as provider support can help the patient to be willing to endure trial and error efforts.

Strassler stated that Periodontal Splinting is a long-term commitment for both provider and patient. Li & Jiang indicated that the patient and provider need to agree on regular recall/maintenance after the splinted restoration is installed.

Tanner wrote about the psychological aspects of Ectodermal Dysplasia.
Sherry & Aponte stated that understanding the patient is an important part of the puzzle. Naqash, mentioned psychological trauma due to compromised oral health.

Falcon, citing Dr Amirali Zandinejad as stating that regarding a 17 yr. old primordial dwarf dental patient Hannah) " If you have the knowledge and education to help others, you have a responsibility to use it'.

Koob mentioned that the treatment is a protracted course into adulthood. Therefore, it is important to provide support to the patient.

Linuma & Honnlee, describe Dr Honnlee, a military maxillofacial prosthodontist at the 59th Medical Wing-San Antonio Military Medical Center Joint Base San Antonio -Fort Sam Houston Texas, who stated that He can only imagine what the patients have gone thru, but their attitudes are so bright, it makes him want to be like them, be more motivated and have a better outlook on life.

Abbott, stated that a provider should "never treat a stranger" and that the provider needs to have a good awareness of

emotional/psychological problems of a patient which may relate to their dental situation. Gwendolyn Quinn wrote that little is known about patients' emotional barrier of fear and how treatment providers influence this barrier.

 Quinn also discusses the "Providers Influence in Clinical Trial Participation" -examining the role that providers play in patients' decision to participate in clinical trials- including patients accepting recommendations to enroll in clinical trials because of their relationship with and trust in the provider-One patient said she was scared to hear about a clinical trial because it sounded like there was no other option left for me-but she made the decision because she had faith in her provider and the provider told her that this trial may be her only hope-some patients make the decision to enroll in clinical trials based on provider recommendation-decision making involves strong emotional responses. It's critical that providers consider patient fears in efforts to develop therapeutic relationships with patients-providers need to dispel myths about being a "human guinea pig"...the provider needs to ease patients' fear/anxiety-and to help handle the patient's emotional needs.

Rodd & Noble, commented the following: The need for dental provider empathy/emotional support to traumatized dental patients, & improved dental provider awareness of dental patient trauma/distress/psychosocial stressors, and past history of unsightly unaesthetic dental appearance issues. Others can make hurtful comments or display unkind behaviors to those with unaesthetic teeth, adding to the dental patient's "social trauma". Rodd & Noble, added that dental patients do worry about the risks of a long term dental treatment plan-especially the high demands of prolonged treatment duration, especially in terms of long distance travel, the risk of dental emergencies requiring additional unplanned dental visits and the intense worry over dental risks of treatment on teeth that have a guarded or poor/long term prognosis and this can lead to treatment avoidance, for instance-fearing that the poor/guarded prognosis teeth could be ultimately and eventually lost despite the treatment.

Hickey & Salter noted that some of these dental prosthetic/prosthodontic patients are often coping with not just physical anomalies but also perhaps with impaired speaking /biting/chewing/eating/swallowing, unaesthetic unattractive appearance, pain/sensitivity discomfort, and impaired smiling. Prosthetics/prosthodontic treatment should also give these patients dental provider support. especially those with poor appearance and psychosocial problems, i.e. where a patient feels ridiculed by peers. Hickey & Salter also commented that each improvement can give the patient resolve to continue on with additional treatment.

Dr Kim Daxon, DDS prosthodontist at the Perio-Implant Advisory noted that the dental provider commitment needs to be for several years, including long term follow-ups, and which may include modification/replacement/repair of the prosthetics and years of dental rehab.

(Allison Thompson, stated that the dental provider-patient relationship is what makes the crucial difference-The best way to overcome fear is a very strong sense of trust in the dental provider. A strong patient/dental provider relationship is really the best way, rather than "gimmicky" amenities such as spa treatments, scented gloves, flat screen TV's, massage chairs, aromatherapy meditative music, flavored gels and fragrant candles. Thompson adds that it doesn't matter what the spa treatment is if the dental patient doesn't totally trust the dental provider. Thompson adds too that it's crucial to take plenty of time with patients, including rest breaks, to allow for longer appointments. and do anything to help strengthen the dental provider/patient relationship trust...and need to try to help these patients as much as possible.

 Mike Mcbride expresses the following important related and relevant considerations: Traumatized Dental patients need a dental provider who knows, understands and accepts my past and has a plan for treating me. The dental provider needs to understand that these aren't your teeth, and my past is not your past. The dental provider must understand that I know that I am doing what I have to do in order to deal with a problem. That is strength, not weakness. The dental provider needs to understand and accept that reliance on medication to prevent panic attacks is simply what I need to do. It's simply doing what I need to do so you can do what you have to do. The dental provider must accept being a team member and must understand what I am dealing with...the dental provider needs to support me in doing what I need to do,

Jeff Elder, and Philip Weinstein, Clinical Psychologist at the Dental Fears Research Clinic, at the University of WA @ Seattle) believes that with genuine dental provider support for traumatized/terrified dental patients, these patients not only can, but will go back for dental treatment, and that can have a profound impact on someone's life, (citing Weinstein) The key to it is the crucial importance and vital need for repeated encouragement and emotional support from the dental provider, and the absence of "provider shaming (of patients) " - Dr Lori Pappert says that someone who's coming back already feels embarrassed.

(Blomqvist, Dahllof & Bejerot report that dental providers need to slow down the pace of their speech when dealing with autism spectrum adult patients in order to facilitate patient comprehension, tolerance, acceptance, and comfort. These adult patients are very afraid, fearful, frightened, anxious, and panicked. Supportive dental provider communication is crucial for adult autism spectrum dental patients. Milgrom, Weinstein & Getz, & Blomqvist, Dahllof & Bejerot both suggest that teaching /training adult autism spectrum dental patients BEFORE treatment is very important, e.g. what to expect.

(Weissenberg, (Appukuttan) (Deva Prya) Brodsgaard. Moore Eli and Armfield, all indicated that Dental providers need to understand and support the Odontophobia dental patient, even when/if the patient presents with what can seem like very psychoneurotic behavior: Odontophobia refers to those with persistent irrational phobic fear of dentistry.

These patients perceive a dental setting as threatening, and they tend to have very low tolerance for pain. They are also known to exaggerate their memories of past dental pain and are often filled with irrelevant anxiety in response to dental pain. Such patients react very stressfully to perceived threats. They have increased perception of pain including longer lasting perceived pain. This in turn causes reduced cooperation & can even lead to misdiagnosis. Dentists tend to see these dental patients as highly stressful to manage, and these dental patients are often perceived as "hypochondriac" and are perceived as uncooperative, and as requiring more time/resources to treat, & are viewed as unpleasant by dental providers. This can often

lead to strained dentist/patient relationships. Eli added that these patients' extreme dental phobic anxiety can even cause misdiagnosis of endodontic tooth vitality. (Armfield, added that painful traumatic emergency dental procedures exacerbate/reinforce fear-often leading to complete avoidance in the future, creating a vicious cycle of dental fear.

Botto described chairside techniques for dental providers to use to reduce dental fears of patients-I have briefly summarized them below for you: Listen to what is being told by the fearful patient. Take their words seriously. Show empathy and provide sensitive sympathy. Provide repeated reassurances & be honest, provide moral/emotional support & validate their fears/concerns/feelings.

(Samantha Lile, Samantha noted that the dentist needs to use psychology to get you in the door and put your mind at ease, getting dental phobics to come in even for a check-up is like "pulling teeth". The dentist needs to put people at ease before and after they sit in that "dreaded recliner' 'the late periodontist Nathan Friedman indicated that 57% of dentists cited "difficult patients" as the most stressful factor in their practice.

Armfield noted that very few dentists take the time to really talk to patients during treatment appointments. It's easy to miss non-verbal signs of fear such as perspiration or watery tearful eyes. An appointment can be very traumatic. Without communication, the dentist may never know how the patient is feeling. A soothing calm voice filled with compassion, empathy, kindness, and patience is crucial.

Chapter 2: The Experimental Dental Prosthetics "Nina Pinta Santa Maria" Dental ship's maiden voyage sailing into uncharted dark stormy waters:

Dr Schamis & I was faced with an agonizing set of decisions on whether or not to gamble with and on the "high stakes low probability of success casino dice down a perilous dental casino gambling table. "This would lead to a monumental ongoing uncharted experimental dental prosthetics maiden voyage into rocky stormy and perilous waters with no lighthouse or beacon light in sight and no compass or GPS nor onboard navigation technology guide. This would be Primitive style exploration like none other. Extreme Exploration Experimentation with no backup plan, no fallback plan, no safety net, no rescue sailors, no lifeboats, no life preservers, no rescue plans. The stakes were grave and there was no turning back nor mind changing "escape" options.

 It was an all or nothing gamble that even hardened veteran casino gamblers would find "bone chilling". There would not be cadcam technology or any cybertechnology to guide us through the waters and no dental coast guard emergency rescue if this experimental dental ship foundered on the rocky shoals nor if it capsized and sank. It would involve drastic risk taking that could destroy my teeth and cause irreversible and uncorrectable harm or that could even leave me for dead, toothless, bald, and dead.

Still, we were undeterred given my dental pain and teeth mobility (loosening teeth). So, this "all or nothing" bet was "off the Richter scale" of grave risk. Among the grave risks were the risks of worsening my already loose teeth. And this terrifying venture included the unavoidable extraction of at least a few teeth that could not be saved/salvaged. The severe gum recession and severe jawbone loss would also be severe danger risks, especially given the already loosening teeth. The Experimental Extreme prosthetics would require very extreme experimental splinting in order to stop the looseness or "periodontal mobility " caused by the weak gums/jawbone. I have included in this book a detailed chapter explaining dental splinting. The splinting would create a solid connected strong set of teeth; however, it would prevent me from flossing anymore. Copious & profuse amounts of permanent dental cement material would be needed including repair material. The latter was to be powerfully tested when 1 of my prosthetic gadgets cracked open from me crunching on hard thick Bavarian pretzels. Luckily Dr Schamis's " witches brew" tough cement patched my prosthetic.

 The copious quantity/thickness of the permanent cement would pose the risk of exacerbating the periodontitis by creating a thick irritant to my weak and already inflamed recessed gums. And there was a risk of rejection of the non-biomaterials & No grafting/rejuvenation were possible. So, at every turn, dangerous perils abounded. And, as time would keep moving ahead, so too my disease could accelerate its fierce angry resistance to this dental experimentation and the disease could also be exacerbated by the experimental treatment.

Drilling on already enamel eroded teeth and placing tools there could have had disastrous outcomes. And my old painful dry sockets could decide to pain me again. It would be an ongoing scary experimental journey for years with no end in sight. An ongoing experimental exploration the likes of which had never been carried to this extreme. Drilling on enamel eroded weak teeth could also cause fatal teeth fractures, forcing gadgets into tiny spaces could cause breakages and further damage. It could also 'resurrect' the dry socket problem caused by prior extractions as aforementioned. Disaster risks loomed and threatened at every step…keep in mind my severe dental PTSD with dental panic/terror, that had to be factored into this unprecedented experimental dental voyage.

Despite my emotions running very high, I had to remain focused on the miracle prize type outcome of full mouth fixed permanent experimental splinted sealed and connected dental prosthetics, with splints that would stop my loose teeth from moving and which would also have the jawbone loss controlled. There was no opportunity to change my mind and quit, everything had to be done steadily without interruption. So, it was full steam ahead for our little old rickety boat.

Sounds easy enough to you. It was anything but easy given my multiple disabilities and the PTSD with Panic/Aspergers/ADHD.

Staying constantly focused on steaming ahead, was going to be a herculean challenge for me. It would require treatment visits at least a few times a week, despite my full-time job and other responsibilities especially musically. Before long, I was to rapidly & painfully discover that I could not handle it all by myself, that my emotional spiritual burden had begun to feel like a heavy albatross like stone noose around my neck, weighing me down, even with the frequent hypodontia hypnotherapy. I could not depend on my dental/medical providers for more emotional/spiritual support & I was heading into silent but intense crisis mode.

Keep in mind too that in 1973 at the age of 10, I had suffered severe maxillofacial dental surgery anesthesia awareness with cardiac arrest hemorrhage and NDE Near death experience, which left me with severe Dental PTSD Post Traumatic Stress Disorder with panic attacks. It was an unbearable pain torture experience that would be forever seared into my lifetime memory. I could hear & feel everything yet be unable to move or communicate as hours of excruciating surgery continued.

Therefore, it was imperative & urgent to create a pastoral faith/ religious clergy/ music therapy support system, an interdisciplinary team to keep me peaceful and stable and help me with the coping and healing I needed. The stress on me was taking a heavy toll, overflowing me with intense panic anxiety and fear. I was feeling very overwhelmed and very overloaded. So, building such an unusual multi-disciplinary team from scratch was itself going to be a herculean struggle loading me with even more panic anxiety & fear. However, I knew there was no procrastinating & time was of the essence. I far under-estimated initially how treacherous it would be to create such a team for me. See my chapter in this book-that explains how crucial it is to have a team that includes religious faith & spiritual healing & music therapy.

I began getting intermittent episodes of what was to be eventually determined to be Cerebellar Vestibular Trigeminal Neuralgia or "CV TN" for short. Once more, I was on my poor dwarf knees begging for help. Hot & Cold temperatures & even things like toothpaste mouthwash & toothbrush bristles were enough to trigger the "TN" pain. The pain would migrate all over my teeth, gums and jaw. And before long, it felt like my teeth were loosening & shifting and my bathroom sink started to be filled with blood from simply brushing my teeth. More & more, my terror was escalating rapidly, & I was filled with intense panic and heightened desperation. My desperate online research also enabled me to uncover underlying reasons for my temperature sensitive dental pain agony:

Temperature Hypersensitivity Dental Pain/ Painful Hyper-Reaction of Dwarf Teeth

Kantaputra. and Terlemez, noted in a study of Dwarf teeth that there is a loss of dental microtubule integrity and defective microtubules. Kantaputra further hypothesized that this may be possibly caused by a defective PCNT gene that plays a crucial role in tooth development, notably in permanent teeth. Sosa & Burke noted the case of a 20 yr. old young dwarf female patient with damaged/defective microtubules, causing pain. Huneycutt observed the following: impaired temperature regulation, and sensitivity to temperature changes.

Although not specifically referencing the rare conditions in this book, the following might be useful in better understanding the Hypersensitivity/Pain issue provided above. Central NJ Prosthodontics piece on Tooth Sensitivity) explains the situation quite well: Dentin (calcified living issue) sends sensitivity sensations to nerves deep in the inner core of the teeth. The dentin is covered by hard enamel on the visible part of the teeth (the visible part is called the crown of the tooth). The dentin also covers soft cementum on tooth roots below the gum line. Dentin contains many microscopic tubules/canals. If gums are shrinking/recessed, then pain/sensitivity may result. For instance, as the gum shrinks/recesses, root surfaces get exposed, leading to pain/sensitivity. This becomes even worse if the tooth roots were not totally covered by cementum during development. Tooth decay there causes pain/sensitivity, as decay exposes dentin. The decay can move down to nerves and trigger pain, The pain then begins to increase. Bonding of the outer teeth surface may possibly help with reducing discomfort. The damaged dentin/enamel/cementum can end up with cavities, teeth fractures, exposed roots, and gum recession. The enamel layer protects the crowns of the teeth above the gum. Under the gum line, cementum layers protect tooth roots. Under the cementum is dentin. Dentin can lose its protective covering of enamel/cementum, then the tubules/canals allow hot and cold temperature to reach the nerve cells in the teeth, triggering pain/sensitivity.

(Dr Jeffrey Chirilio DMD) wrote about Tooth Sensitivity Pain, generally without referencing the diseases discussed in this book, but I felt the information was important to share here. (Chirilio) cites how a gust of wind can cause some patients to grab their jaws during a change in barometric pressure. He adds the following important material: A periodontal infection can cause mouth pain due to inflammation and swelling. A periodontal gum infection can lead to bone loss extending to the root tips of teeth and its delicate sensitive nerve endings can react in pain, loose, mobile teeth resulting from periodontal bone loss can also cause pain. The movement of loose teeth causes pain. Chirilio notes too that as decayed diseased pulp tissue dies. There can be decreased sensitivity. It can spread to the periodontal ligament that encases the tooth & attaches it to the jawbone and to the surrounding! In overwhelming terror panic, I had begun to plead with Dr Michael Schamis DDS PC to stop my agony or at least decrease its "angry red hot " pain by doing this highest risk experimental full mouth all teeth root canal nerve removal to "cut off the nerve pain superhighway filled with trigeminal neuralgia "burning fire pain', However such extreme root canal would cause my already weak sick damaged teeth to fracture & die unless all the teeth were crown capped/bridge. The problem with that is due to my severe jawbone loss crown caps & regular bridges wouldn't be an option because they would be as loose as the teeth were becoming & implants/grafts/regenerations were not an option for me due to the dwarfism and severe jawbone loss.

In other words, I was out of options, The experimental total mouth root canal would make my teeth like porous eggshells ready to fracture & be destroyed as a result, Therefore the experimental prosthetics were my only choice to save my "salvageable teeth and replace my missing teeth after the total full mouth root ***canal. Root canals save teeth from decay, but they can also weaken them.***
***https://www.colgate.com/en-us/oral-health/root-canals/what-is-root-canal-treatment* When the pulp inside a tooth is infected or no longer living, dentists can treat the tooth through a root canal by removing the pulp and apply filling to replace it. When performing routine root canals, however, dentists drill through the tooth and then remove infected and decayed enamel, dentin, and pulp.**

Full mouth Root Canal treatment is rare but not unheard of. What Dr Schamis & I came up with, was to change the course of my entire life again-in a way nobody could have ever predicted, envisioned, or imagined, an experimental plan so bold and daring and never successfully carried out before. Dr Schamis & I agreed on this new plan that was fraught with dangerous risks and potential dangers. There was no guidebook nor road map or any other literature to navigate us through this most perilous and brave experimental dental journey. He & I would be world class dental pioneers, embarking on a dental mission the likes of which had never been successfully done before. It would require me to stay put in NY until further notice and would require a huge amount of time, work, effort, trial and error guessing, and total healing- as well as boat loads of faith and support. So, our "little old rickety dental ship" embarked on its maiden voyage into uncharted rocky stormy waters.

Chapter 3: My Silver Point Root Canal Dental Nightmare

Who would have thought that an old fragile thin delicate broken corroded metal "wire" could cause burning teeth agony & evade detection by a few dentists? It only appeared on a CT scan, & on state-of-the-art special dental x rays. Thank God for Dr Louis Siegelman DDS for finding & removing the jagged broken metal wire "point" & for re-treating that infected tooth that was torturing me in April 2016 until Dr Siegelman "cured" the tooth. (3) Dentists, including Dr Schamis first suggested it was my imagination, & that I needed psychiatric help not endodontic dental surgery as it failed to appear on bunches of dental x-rays, including x-rays by an endodontist. In my own case, (2) Dental offices using 2D type dental failed to detect the broken jagged corroded razor-sharp twisted metal silver points root canal obturation filler material. Luckily & miraculously, the state-of-the-art dental technology allowed Dr Louis Siegelman DDS to find & remove this dangerous & infected metal from my mouth in April 2016.

I owe Dr Louis Siegelman DDS a million accolades & a million medals for finding the hidden "torture metal pile " and excavating it out & for re-doing the root canal there, in order to save the lower left side posterior back tooth.

I decided that you folks need to have a better understanding of the AGONY created by these " vintage" metal wire root canal fillers also known as '' obturations", This material was from my childhood/preteen years & was silently festering near my chin. If not for Dr Siegelman I & the affected tooth could have both died. Once the Silver point torture wire was removed, and LANAP Laser + Gutta Percha root canal retreatment was done, the hot searing 24/7 burning toothache was finally over for good. I decided that you readers need to better understand the history of silver points & why they have not been used in many years, yet countless adults like me had to contend with the dreadful aftermath of these archaic and obsolete root canal "filler" type material. Thus, it's really important that the readers get a lesson about this dreadful material.

Chana, Briggs & Moss wrote an excellent article on this very matter & I "dissected' the most salient information to share here: They discussed how degradation (i.e. corrosion) of silver endodontic points cause painful infection, abscessing, & ultimately Endodontic Root Canal tooth failure/tooth loss: These thin metal points become separated from the main body & displace apically. The Silver Points deteriorated significantly with a surface coating of silver chloride salt. There is microleakage with infection and galvanic reaction. Silver Points originated in the 1930's as endodontic root canal obturation "filler material" for use within root canals. The Radio Dense silver wire ended up moving through the root canals.

Ruddle wrote that the rigid round wire was used to seal irregularly shaped endodontic root canal systems. Problems included under filing, chronic leakage, and the issue of thorough cleanliness of the wire-teeth tended to become stained from the metallic corrosion byproducts- chronic leakage greatly reduced the seal and reduced lateral retention. The metallic points caused argyrosis and periradicular inflammation of the unshaped canals. The Silver point cones would split into sections and would rapidly show erosion during mechanical manipulation.

Langley wrote a fascinating historical background piece on these silver endodontic points. I have summarized the most salient information herein for you to peruse: Langley described how in Israel, an ancient skull was found in the Negev Desert with bronze wire inside a maxillary cuspid tooth. Anthropologists believe that this wire signifies early primitive techniques to treat infected root canal systems, Langley continued on to describe the following: the problem of poor apical seal, difficulty with fit in the apical terminus, the problem where a large portion of the irregular canal remained unfilled or only filled with cement, as these metal points failed to create a reliable long-term seal both apically and coronally. These silver points also created a great problem with being an obstructive impediment to placing a post/core/build-up. These silver points corroded from saliva/oral fluids, causing inflammation. These silver points also posed a great difficulty in extracting them from sub-orifice/coronal orifices. Often there would be no "tail" to grasp onto in order to remove them. They caused chronic apical periodontitis and endodontic lesions. These points failed to create a seal at the apical terminus of the canal. It was also found that upon removing the points, unfilled lateral canals would appear, and this too contributed to silver point failure.

Gulati noted the following problems with silver points: They fail to produce a 3-dimensional seal of the endodontic root canal system, they compromise apical seal, they show poor adaptability to root canal walls, they fail to seal the accessory canals that are often present. They corrode over time due to saliva and oral fluids. They cause chronic apical periodontitis. They lack plasticity to flow and conform to the shape of the canals. They create difficult root end prep in canals filled with metal. They cause inflammatory root resorption. They led to failure to properly clean/shape the canals. They caused extensive corrosive micro- leakage & caused irritation. Their corrosion makes them fragile, causes them to turn black & tarnish, they are easily fractured and quick to shred. They corrode spontaneously in blood/serum due to unstable electrochemical behavior. Their corrosion byproducts can cause irreversible staining of tooth structure and surrounding tissue (argyrosis), the corrosion products cause periarticular inflammation and inflammatory root resorption as well as endodontic pathosis.

Post/Core/Build Ups are impossible with intact silver points, thus making removal and alternate material replacement. Apical surgery becomes more complicated due to difficulties encountered when attempting a root-end prep in canals filled with the silver points. Their soft smooth and slippery texture didn't bind well in canals, their fragility caused them to sometimes shear off, they can be accidentally severed, their removal can sometimes be impossible, especially as they tend to migrate into very hard to reach spaces. They fracture easily and are easily drilled thru. Even worse, if the points are packed with amalgam, it becomes like reinforced concrete and needs special solvents to help with removal.

Again, A trillion medals to Dr Louis Siegelman & his associate Dr Danielle Currier & Dear " Melissa' the RDH for all you have done especially that silver point removal & the Lanap laser /Cavitron. Thank You for believing me when nobody else did & for finding & removing all that "toxin" material that was destroying my teeth. And thank you for being a role model in helping extreme "aspie" dental phobics like me! Everyone should read your website www.dentalphobia.com Thank You for stopping the torture pain & for helping save my teeth when nobody could find my torture pain. Hugs to you & your staff. I love all of you! Especially Melissa! (Note: Sadly, Melissa tragically passed away not long after she helped treat me)

Full Mouth Root Canal - Validation & Support -A Brief Summary

Dr. Jayant Ambulgekar wrote that full mouth crown lengthening after *full mouth root canal* was selected as treatment of choice followed by prosthetic rehabilitation. See Full Mouth Rehabilitation of Mutilated Dentition. (Drs Jayant Ambulgekar Rizwan Sanad Manan Doshi Dr Subodh Gaikwad) Thus, the patient was 1st referred to Dept. of Endodontics for full mouth root canal treatment & then to the Dept. of Prosthodontics for full mouth rehabilitation. Hence, full mouth crown lengthening after full mouth root canal was selected as treatment of choice followed by prosthetic rehabilitation.

The NYCDENTIST.COM section on tooth decay advertises the following: " Dental crowns on every tooth, Root Canal Therapy performed on every tooth. Avoiding potential painful root canal emergencies with preventative endodontics should be considered.

Best scientific clinical paper awarded at Tamil Nadu state conference was on **"full mouth root canal Endodontic Rehabilitation** in a medically compromised diabetes mellitus patient-A-case clinical report by Dr Vineet Vinayak.

Chapter 4: Experimental Dental Prosthetics for Ectodermal Dental disease /Dwarfism Dental

A comprehensive & thorough search of the literature on Experimental Type Dental Prosthetics for Ectodermal dental disease yielded almost no findings. One intriguing case deserved mention: Rockman describes a Magnetic Retention Dental Prosthetic to restore form and function. This technique uses magnets to enhance retention of the dental prosthetics. It was considered an alternative prosthetic design and was done at the Dept of Pediatric Dentistry at the School of Dentistry-Medical College of Georgia, Augusta GA c/o Drs Rockman & Hall together with their prosthetics laboratory technologist.

Grover & Mehra, refer to Rockman regarding the use of magnets to enhance retention of dental prosthetics. Grover & Mehra also mention that in some cases, dental prosthetic retention can be possibly augmented by various attachments anchored to suitably strong teeth.

Regarding the Benefits of Non-Denture Dental Prosthetics in the Correction/Rehabilitation of Dwarfism Dental Pathology and also of Ectodermal Dysplasia Dental Disease Dalkiz & Dalkiz noted that these positive dental prosthetic benefits and favorable effects include increased vertical jawbone height, improved lip support, and improved maxillo-facial prosthodontic relationships.

Bani et al indicates that dental prosthetics may improve masticatory (chewing) muscle and may help compensate for reduced vertical alveolar jawbone height dimension. and can improve facial expression, as well as improve speech. (Bani) also noted that permanent tooth forms are selected to provide better occlusion, both dynamic & occlusion. (Bani) also noted that dental prosthetics can increase occlusal vertical height dimension as well as improve sagittal and vertical craniofacial features.

Grover & Mehra, discuss the benefits of prosthodontic dental prosthetics as follows: improved alveolar jawbone vertical height dimension + increased vertical height dimension of occlusion, improved muscular-cutaneous profile and dento-facial appearance, reduces risk of resorption / atrophy of alveolar jawbone ridges that are severely affected by missing teeth, restoration of esthetic facial appearance, corrected mandibular posture, minimizes antero-rotation of mandible that otherwise would cause an upward and forward displacement of chin/lower jaw, increased height of lower 1/3 of face. reduced risk of class 3 malocclusion, provides favorable backward downward rotation of mandible, allows normal spatial positioning of the chin, restoration of hypoplastic teeth-restoring normal size/shape/dimension morphology of hypoplastic teeth, improves alignment of teeth in proper position, modifies abnormal patterns of dentofacial development and improves sagittal/vertical dento-facial esthetics.

Omo & Ennibulele state that dental prosthetics may aid in jawbone development improvement. They add that there is a need for well fabricated dental prosthetics for these special dental patients.

Shin states that dental prosthetics reduce cognitive decline, and these dental prosthetics can include bridges and crowns.

Okubo, Fujinami & Minakuchi, did a study of how dental prosthetics affect postural control as well as affect walking and standing, standing stability and gait stability, they concluded that the dental prosthetics yielded increased gait velocity, and may be an effective aid to maintain and improve balance control,

Watanabe, noted that in a study of 218 elderly people, those that were toothless and did NOT use dental prosthetics scored lower on the mini mental state exam. Those with dental prosthetics showed higher cerebral blood flow (cbf) and the toothless "edentulous" patients showed lower cerebral blood flow (cbf).

Rodd & Noble, cite the positive psychosocial outcomes following dental prosthetic restoration of teeth such as brighter outlook & improved social life. Hickey & Salter noted that often patients feel more positive after dental prosthetics treatment, and the dental prosthetics intervention can be beneficial for the patient's well-being. Hickey & Salter also noted that maxillofacial dental prosthetic/prosthodontic treatment offers improvement in esthetic appearance, function & overall health as well., & can lead to renewed self-confidence. Improved appearance can also enhance employment opportunities. Each improvement can give the patient the resolve to continue on with additional treatment, benefits of such treatment can give the patient psychological support, The treatment can assist a patient in being more socially outgoing and in enjoying life and the prosthetic treatment can have an enormous impact on personal lives and serve as a wonderful sense of "reward".

Dr Donald Giddon studied the psychological benefits of dental prosthetics and mentioned that the prosthetics can make the continuation of musical skills/abilities possible, such as restoring the ability to sing and/or play a musical instrument that is dependent on the mouth/jaw. Dr Kim Daxon DDS a prosthodontist at the Periodontal Implant Advisory states that there are psychological benefits to having fixed permanent dental prosthetics. Dr Patricia Nihill, DMD says that for her 21 yr. old female dwarf dental prosthetics patient "Tina;" along with the functional benefits of an overdenture, the esthetic results appeared to improve 'Tina's " self-esteem and overall appearance, as well as improve her posterior function. The esthetic results appeared to improve the patient's self-esteem and overall appearance, a satisfactory functional result with a significant improvement in esthetics was achieved "Tina" took quite a different view of her personal appearance, seemed much more sure of herself, began using makeup and jewelry, and was pleased with compliments about her appearance. Stock anterior pediatric teeth were reshaped to eliminate the bulbous teeth shape and to develop a more feminine and adult tooth shape and appearance, posterior teeth were waxed and processed to provide a customized balanced occlusion.

Cariati notes that corrective dental treatment can improve psychosocial wellbeing-dento-facial deformities can cause psychosocial issues including insecurity about one's appearance.

 Even More on the Use of Dental Prosthetics for Ectodermal Dysplasia Dental and Dwarfism Dental Disease - Vallejo, discusses treatment with removable dental prosthetics), Grover & Mehra, and Lomuzio discuss the need for complex prosthodontic prosthetics treatment of children with ectodermal dysplasia dental disease. Pigno and Vieira, Yenisey, Nabadalung, Hickey & Vergo, Kaul & Reddy all wrote about the prosthodontic management of ectodermal dysplasia dental disease. Suri wrote about the simultaneous functional fixed appliance therapy for dental alignment prior to prosthetic habilitation of Ectodermal Dysplasia Dental disease. Ferrante & Blasi mention the use of functional dental prosthetics in Dwarf Dental patients. Ferrante & Blasi recommend the use of a 5-tooth fixed bridge supported on a 6-fixture zirconia substructure for the mandibular arch. Naqash, recommends the use of a 6-unit fixed bridge prosthetic for the maxillary arch.

(Dr Patricia Nihill, wrote up a fascinating dwarfism/ectodermal dental disease prosthetics case story called " Esthetic overdentures for a patient with possible Seckel Syndrome (Dwarfism) which I have summarized below for you: Dr Patricia Nihill DMD, treated a young 21 yr. old woman who I will pseudonym for you as "Tina". She has a rare form of Seckel dwarfism + Ectodermal dysplasia dental disease. I too have dwarfism but of another rare type & have cerebellar ectodermal dental disease, so this case was fascinating for me to read and summarize for you.

Tina presented with the following dental history:
micrognathia(undersized lower mandible jaw bone, aka mandibular hypoplasia), microdontia (tiny teeth),severe bony undercuts, retrognathic lower mandible jaw bone, with abnormal posterior positioning with overbite of top (maxillary) teeth, high flat palatal arch, overcrowded teeth(due to undersized jaw bones) hypoplastic alveolar jawbone loss, short roots, simplified single roots on molars, reduced number of cells in dental pulp, dentin dysplasia, enamel erosion, taurodontism (*taurodontism* is a condition found in the molar teeth of humans whereby the body of the tooth and pulp chamber is enlarged vertically at the expense of the roots. As a result, the floor of the pulp and the furcation of the tooth is moved apically down the root) widely spaced teeth, lips with inadequate support, very small upper/lower jaws, 6 missing teeth. bilateral mandibular tori, with buccal and facial undercuts of both upper/lower jaws, short conical shape roots, inadequate jawbone support/vertical height, single rooted molars, malformed roots, horizontal impacted teeth. and very severe periodontal disease with severe advanced periodontal mobility of Class 2 to 3, causing very loose teeth at high risk for falling out.

"Tina" also presented with a reading/learning disability, along with sparse thin hair, hypopituitary growth hormone proportional short stature dwarfism, and was receiving post-secondary school vocational work-study-training in clerical tasks and was considered to be an "underachiever",

The advanced severe periodontal disease caused several loose mobile posterior decayed teeth to be extracted. Occlusal sealants were placed on remaining teeth. The mandibular tori & the horizontal #7 tooth were saved to preserve bone for potential future implant surgery. An immediate transitional denture was fabricated with anticipated replacement in the future. Treatment complications include small jaws requiring use of pediatric trays...there was a problem making dental impressions, and with initially fabricating the overdenture. A custom tray was border molded with a chairside resilient denture liner followed by a polysulfide wash.

Once jaw related records were made, shade and tooth selection were performed. Stock anterior pediatric teeth were reshaped to eliminate bulbousness and to develop a more feminine and adult tooth shape and appearance. Because of the minimal space available over occlusal/buccal surfaces of the flat plane retained premolars as well as the extremely short arch lengths, posterior teeth were waxed and processed to provide a customized balanced occlusion. An initial trial pack with tooth color resin for the posterior teeth was followed by injection molded acrylic processing of the rest of the denture. Extractions of remaining mobile loss periodontally damaged anterior teeth were done, immediate overdentures were placed with chairside tissue conditioner. At later appointments, the tissue conditioner was changed to promote stability as healing progressed. A satisfactory functional result with a significant improvement in esthetics was achieved. The use of a resilient soft denture liner was helpful in obtaining a good border seal despite severe saved bony undercuts, facilitating retention, and avoiding surgical intervention. This unique situation for a 21 yr. old young woman dental patient required improvisation of existing dental materials such as reshaping stock pediatric anterior teeth, and heat-processed posterior teeth for the overdenture, along with the functional benefits of an overdenture, the extraction of periodontally damaged mobile loose decayed teeth provided better posterior function.

Note: Restoration leading to a natural and attractive appearance is important for the normal mental and future social development of patients. Prosthetic treatment methods using partial removable dental prostheses or dental implants are the primary treatment options for the prosthetic rehabilitation of these patients. Hypodontia or total anodontia is often associated with underdeveloped alveolar ridges which bring about less bone volume for the support of conventional removable dental prostheses or implant placement. When determining the most favorable prosthetic approach, the patient's age, dental and skeletal maturity, bone volume, and patient's cooperation must be considered. Therefore, partial removable dental prostheses sometimes can be a more advantageous option in growing patients than partial fixed dental prostheses because jaw growth necessitates prostheses adjustments. Removable dental prostheses require follow-ups and management. They should be replaced or adjusted when decreased OVD or mandibular posture displacement are observed due to growth. Without dentures, the anterior rotation of the mandible may cause an upward and forward displacement of the chin, leading to shortening of the lower third of the face and a Class III malocclusion tendency. With dentures, the mandible is rotated into a backward-downward position and the chin can maintain its normal position. Due to the growth and development of the patient, lack of occlusal contact of the posterior teeth may need to be managed.

Chapter 5:   How Cornerstone Church rescued me from the stormy spiritual waters.

First let me tell you about the dark, stormy, spiritual, waters and how my little "boat" was being knocked into by "waves" as my "faith navigation compass" was failing badly, my faith rapidly depleting as it was being shaken by very rough winds with no lighthouse beacon of illumination to guide my " battered little rickety dental boat". Within a matter of weeks of starting very intensive, experimental, dental, prosthetics preparatory work, my religious/spiritual faith was being knocked and rocked about tumultuously like a tiny boat being trapped caught up in dark, stormy, wavy waters. It often felt like I was trapped on a lone, little ship in the darkest of night in increasingly, stormy, rainy, wavy waters with nobody to guide me into a well-lit safe calm and peaceful harbor marina to rest at. In my mind I kept thinking of that old pop tune "Bridge over troubled waters". Meanwhile I was struggling to keep my rickety, old, little boat from drifting further into the stormy, wavy, dark waters. The further adrift my little vessel became the more weary, exhausted and frightened I was becoming, and I felt increasingly abandoned.

Yet I knew there was no turning back and heading toward southeastern tropical waters, no changing course, no escape, no rescue in sight, and my mind was drowning in terror.

In my total despair, an idea popped into my dwarf alopecia head. I needed to create a religious spiritual faith-based support team with music therapy " built in", in order to replenish, restore and re-energize my very depleted religious/spiritual faith. I was about to find out that my idea was actually going to make me.

Feel even more depleted and discouraged than I had been before. My rickety, little boat was about to get knocked into even harder than before, further exacerbating my panic terror and further depleting my already exhausted state. A dark night of depleted faith, an increasing nightmare of faith, rocking my weary soul to its lowest inner core. and rocking my frail boat to and fro in dark, stormy waters and I feared that my frail, little vessel could end up crashing into the rocks at the shoreline.

My Faith get rocked to its innermost core:

It seemed like such an easy idea that popped into my dwarf alopecia head- contact over 30+ local churches/synagogues & send them the articles/links to my case along with a "query note/letter" asking them to help be part of the multidisciplinary team approach I envisioned wanted & needed. I was certain they would respond happily & be willing to be part of my team. Nothing could have prepared me for the devastating response I got. I had sweetly, compassionately & kindly contacted 30 churches/synagogues in the local area, brimming with self-assurance and poise, sending emails and phone messages explaining my situation and including links to my articles. Begging & pleading for rides to/from churches and synagogues. One by one they figuratively slammed the door at me and refused to help me and they gave flimsy excuse after flimsy excuse. No, we're sorry we can't we don't we wouldn't, no, no, no, no, no, some didn't even want to answer my impassioned pleas… My soul felt like it was 'dying of despair" and my self-confidence "was torn to shreds".

Finally, a local church I will call "VYC" contacted me. They offered a 1 time only situation for Christmas Eve 2016 & told me nobody there was willing to drive me Christmas day to/from their church. As soon as I returned to my humble rented room on Christmas Eve 2016, slushy sleety rain began to drizzle, it was dark dreary and bitterly cold, as well as silently quiet and lonely.

Tearfully I asked God why I was brought here but rejected by 30 congregations? Why & what was wrong with me? I must be truly worthless to be rejected so many times. None of them cared to offer any help & were aware I couldn't afford repeated taxicab rides or to ship my car from Fla. Why has compassion disappeared? What would Jesus think of this? The clock continued to faintly tick as minutes and hours passed, as I was overflowing with the worst despair-thinking-what a way to spend Christmas-alone in my room, I had nowhere to celebrate Chanukah either. Over the past weeks, my elderly mom repeatedly begged me to throw in the towel, quit treatment & go back to Fla. That was not a sensible thing to do unless I wanted to be toothless permanently.

Finally,12:30 am arrived that sad Christmas Eve now turned into Christmas Day 2016. Tears were running down my face as I realized that my Christmas would be like my Chanukah-a lonely non-celebration spent alone in my rented little room. I struggled to regain composure and pulled out my tear-stained crumpled up handwritten list of the 30+ congregations I was refused by. As I re-read the list, Suddenly I noticed that I never contacted the 31st congregation listed. I had accidentally missed contacting them. Mind you it was 12:30am on Christmas Day… The Church was Cornerstone Christian Church in Hicksville NY. I figured that most likely the phone # was an office number & expected to reach an answering machine voicemail with a pre-recorded generic Merry Xmas message and leave your number at the sound of the tone, Instead, a very warm, compassionate, gentle & tender-hearted man answered the phone-I had reached his home-Pastor Phil Alba & his wife Peggy. **(side note: one of the reasons too for my despair is I had no church music opportunities here since I arrived months prior-this "broke my tender heart')**

Within minutes, he was calming me down and began to contact and mobilize others from Cornerstone church to become my "team". I was no longer isolated, rejected alone & unwanted. I was never going to be churchless again here, He even agreed to let me play piano at the church starting that very Christmas Day & ever since! They even bought a better piano that they let me select! Within minutes, rides were set up& I had the Best Christmas Day Ever !!!!! It was amazing & my heart was overflowing with joy & gratitude -& he even gave me a Bible & his wife donated me many many things including my beloved "furry soft" bathrobe. (Then others there donated me things as well). I have had weekly rides to/from Cornerstone Church and I love playing the Krakauer piano there (see my YouTube solo church piano video), Christmas Day 2016 was freezing temperature wise but that was more than offset by the incredible warmth of Pastor Phil, his wife Peggy & the wonderful members there who embrace me with open arms, It replenished and restored my depleted faith -God had finally answered my prayers. I didn't know much bible at all so Pastor Phil & others there began teaching me. I was no longer alone & no longer drowning in my frail little vessel in stormy, dark, wavy water, & no longer in darkness. In fact, one of the very first things I immediately noticed at Cornerstone church is the magnificent hanging wall tapestry there of a beautiful lighthouse with beacon adjacent to a rocky shore. Indeed, my boat and I was finally safe & situated at the lighthouse beacon. The beautiful hanging wall tapestry really spoke volumes-it was a perfect depiction of my craving a " bridge over troubled waters" to keep me steady on my experimental dental prosthetics treatment journey.

What's even more intriguing is this past spring I was asked to play solo piano at a messianic synagogue talent show.

 I asked them what I needed to play. To my utter amazement, they responded " Cornerstone" by Leon Patillo, whose theme included the phrase " a fine stone, a precious cornerstone". I don't think it's a coincidence, I think it was verification from God that Cornerstone is where I belong!

This is what the Bible says about <u>**Cornerstones & its related literature:**</u>

Psalm 118:22 "The stone which the builders rejected has become the cornerstone."

(New International Bible).,'

Matthew 21:42 " Jesus said to them "Have you never read in the scriptures: The stone the builders rejected has become the cornerstone."'

Luke 20:17 But Jesus looked directly at them & beheld them -Then what is the meaning of that which is written: The stone the builders rejected has become the cornerstone".

Acts 4:11 He is the stone you builders rejected which has become the cornerstone.

1 Peter 2:7 To you who believe then, this stone is precious, but to those who do not believe, the stone the builders have rejected has become the cornerstone.

Isaiah 28:16 (see also the Cornerstone song by Leon Patillo with these words) So this is what the Lord God says: See, I lay a stone in Zion, a tested stone, a precious cornerstone, a sure foundation, the one who believes will never be shaken."

Matthew 21:42 Jesus saith unto them: Did ye never read in the scriptures: The stone which the builders rejected the same is becoming the head of the corner.

"He is the stone which the builders refused: they would go on building without him, this proved the ruin of those who thus made light of him." See Biblehub.com/psalms/118-123.htm Matthew Henry Commentary.

Chapter 6: Coming to Grips with Forced Relocation-I cannot go home to Florida.

Kate Jackson, Tracey Greene-Mintz, Kim Warchol, Kim & Tach Branch-Dogans, all describe how Sudden Unexpected Forced Relocation can cause severe emotional trauma, including irritability, anxiety panic depression self-isolation, fight or flight cardiac anxiety attacks, tachycardia rapid heartbeat, and insomnia, When a move is initiated suddenly, the symptoms can multiply rapidly, when the person realizes that they cannot go back, the symptoms exacerbate, If unaddressed, the consequences can be severe, and can even negatively impact cognitive function and physical health, especially for those who already have difficulty assimilating new information.

It triggers fear. loss of the familiar, confusion, and overloading, and they cannot adapt to the new changes. This erodes their self-confidence and removes their comfort-the anxiety/fear can be long lasting until they can begin to forge new relationships and get better acquainted with a different physical environment. and gradually begin adjusting, the symptoms are worse in those with cognitive challenges, they feel helpless and can't deal with the loss of personal autonomy, and deal with the loneliness/isolation and they despair that they don't feel a sense of belonging. and they feel unwelcome, rejected, isolated and alone,

Operation We Are Here Ministering to Military personnel-US Army

affected by Deployment, Clergy Resources describes the emotional stress of military deployment and the importance of having chaplains/clergy ministering to military professionals.

When dealing with relocation for military deployment. Douglas L Carver Chaplain Major General, US Army Chief of Chaplains, states that there is an uncertain world of global challenge & there's a need to provide more effective religious faith support. Their clergy resource manual is intended as an information resource to guide religious organizations who wish to reach out and support these military persons. Deployment commitments have increased worldwide. which has led to increased anxiety/stress/ uncertainty. This manual has broken down the emotional effects of deployment relocation as follows: Stage 1 Anticipation of Departure & Anticipation of Loss, Stage 2 deals with Detachment & Withdrawal: the hurt of separation, creation of emotional distancing, gradual shutdown of emotion, feelings of numbness, lack of emotional connectivity which leads to relationship difficulties. Stage 3 Emotional Disorganization-burnout fatigue and feelings of being overwhelmed, Stage 4 Recovery & Stabilization: Resilience & Coping, increased confidence, positive outlook, emotional strength, and use of supportive resources. Stage 7 deals with stabilization and Reintegration, stabilized relationships, and the risk of instability from excess stress,

The info. manual proceeds into Chaplain/Clergy Religious/Spiritual Faith Support: including nurturing pastoral counseling, pastoral education, trauma management and sustaining of spiritual fitness thru ministry support, and relationship strengthening programs, to help build more effective relationships, and it may include off-site retreats. The religious/spiritual faith support can help with coping with unexpected challenges and offer multiple options for reach out services/programs.

It helps strengthen emotional safety, builds friendships, validates and shows appreciation and honors these personnel who loyally serve our country, it acknowledges their dedication, provides enrichment, and classes/courses/training/seminars and stress management assistance, as well as bible study, and helps people get re-settled in their new areas, assists with forming fellowship groups, meetings, mutual support, practical help such as with finding living quarters, aids with errands, child care, transportation, errands, discussion groups, provides safe sanctuary for prayer, etcetera.

To backtrack for a bit now, I have included some bible verse excerpts for you to help you see more clearly the biblical aspects of my own forced sudden unexpected relocation from FL to NY 4/1/2016. Let's take a trek backward in time to EXODUS: Ancient Egypt & The Israelite Slaves: Moses reminded his enslaved people the Israelites that they had to leave in a hurry-hastily, Exodus 12:11 mentions "dressed to travel" and "you are to eat in haste." The Israelites were told by God to dress to travel and were finally told that this is the time of their Exodus from Egypt. Imagine how frightening it must have been to hear. (see bible.org regarding the Exodus Passover Escape from Egypt) Imagine waiting and how it felt when the time suddenly arrived very late at night, God set the Israelites free from bondage.

Also see a "paralleling" note in the New Testament :1 Corinthians 10:13 about God providing "a way out" Think about the following concept: Sharing God's provision of a way out, an Exodus, a Deliverance, Exodus 12: V31 explained how Pharoah summoned Moses & Aaron in the night & said for them to get up & out, go as you've requested & leave. The Israelites were pressed to leave Egypt before anything else awful happened to them.

The Israelites loaded wagons, pressing clothing into their hands. Imagine if you had to make a sudden and significant change in one's life, which imbalanced you for a while, and sometimes longing to return although it was so unpleasant there, imagine anticipating a change for a while but circumstances forced you to wait, and then how it felt when the time suddenly arrived very late one night, unexpectedly. God finally set you free, Imagine the Holy Spirit is about to show you where change is suddenly coming into your life, it's called " stepping out of your comfort zone in faith, making whatever change the Lord asks, not looking back longingly on what you are leaving, but looking ahead to what God has prepared for you in a new place far away. Exodus 12:48-49 mentions " the foreigner who lives among you" (and wants to observe) Exodus 12: 51 The Lord brought the Israelites out of Egypt. Exodus 13:8 refers to what the Lord did for me when I came out of Egypt, with a mighty hand the Lord brought the Israelites out of Egypt, God set them free, guided & protected them with his love, and hoping that they never forget what he did ...as the Israelites left Egypt, they were ill-equipped for a nomadic life nor prepared for conflict-

God knew their faith was weak & God didn't want them retreating back out of fear, The" symbolism" of the "return home" facing danger & trial, being brought through a time of change, The Lord provides guidance, helping them to not be distracted from what he had set before them. One needs to be attentive to God's direction including knowing ways to avoid and not retreating from the right path, you may not be prepared emotionally to "deal with it" but the Holy Spirit/Lord God will guide and prepare you...You might feel that you are wandering around confused, lost & frightened. Moses (Exodus 14:13) told the Israelites not to fear & told them to stand firm & see that God will provide, The Lord will fight for you, protecting you from danger & trouble, you are faced with a challenge -only to

recognize that the Lord God is protecting you. Moses & the Israelites created a song of celebration of God's liberation & protection.

You might feel as though you were in an Emotional/Spiritual desert, without hope. but God will heal the situation. (see David Colburn for example) Roy Yanke wrote about the effects of forced exits in the Ministry, the spiritual/emotional trauma, the deep distress, It can overwhelm a person's ability to cope, and cause intense fear, feelings of danger, anger, anxiety, fatigue, panic, loss of self-esteem and deeply wounded trust. The person begins to see themselves as "damaged goods'', they feel a loss of spiritual connection, a sense of emotional loss, and they despair over the loss of fellowship, support.

The support relationship that would help someone through a transition is suddenly & traumatically ended.

Where can the person go, and who can they talk to in order to process the grief/loss from a forced exit, it can carry very long-term effects, See also Deanna Harrison, Deanna) -her book about moving on and surviving the grief of forced exit, the trauma of an abrupt halt to life as one has known it up to the point of sudden and abrupt forced exit, they can be plunged into a grief so deep, Roy Yanke, indicates that a traumatic exit can create an emotional/spiritual "toxicity" that can be carried into the next role in their life, if not addressed and resolved, a forced exit can be packed with a tsunami like force,**40% of those who undergo forced exit never return to church!**

Roy Yanke also noted that the affected persons need to have their wounded hearts healed. They need to accept & resolve the "harsh" reality of their spiritual upheaval. The next step is to connect with those who can help them navigate through the "dark waters" after a forced exit, Ministries and clergy need to offer hope & healing when all seems lost ...during the "victim's season of grief" following forced exit. Lisa Ferentz wrote that Congregations need to offer people a way to heal by re-connecting to new religious groups after the forced exit. These people were robbed of their spirituality & of the religious activities that used to bring them comfort. (Umcom.org United Methodist Communications) wrote about tips to help people who are relocating (" on the move").

Susan Miller started the "Just Moved Ministry" which is spiritually based & non-profit, for women who are uprooted and gives them tools to help them embrace new lives. She now leads relocation classes in churches and military installations. She tries to help people who want to move on to a new church faith community. She cautions about "spiritual strain and overload factors", & states that moving is a tangible loss, you will grieve, and go through stages of grief from losing close touch to the church you once loved. It can be even more traumatic when you move to a new place where you may not have a support system in place. There is also loss of personal identity in a move, it can be huge loneliness is a bigger issue than many people realize. Let the new congregation be a part of your "new family", Don't isolate yourself.

Circumstances may force you to hit the ground running, find time to settle in, start putting down new roots, communicate, share, and pray. The greatest adventure is building the Kingdom of God ...you are doing God's work and God has you right where you are to be. Churches need to put out the welcome mat in meaningful ways. Coordinate with teams of volunteers to help with things such as providing transportation. Offer acts of kindness such as giving others rides, invite them to participate in fun activities and church events that they might not be otherwise included in. Give them calls, send them emails, drop them notes, be an "encourager", help others to get settled in& to take time to rest and reflect. Providing time/place for a little rest and relaxation, invitations to others' homes are great way to socialize, Justmoved.org offers Christ centered books/materials related to moving, as well as weekly words of encouragement emails, newsletters to encourage women in transition, prayer support teams, tips and encouragement. Be proactive to help prevent burnout crises and to prevent feeling disillusioned, Also see Susan Miller's book After *the Boxes Are Unpacked: Moving on After Moving In*

Marsha Wiggins-Frame wrote about Relocation & Wellbeing -What pastoral counselors need to know. She mentioned the following: the increased difficulty adjusting to multiple successive relocations, (also see Anderson & Stark) and the stresses of job/employment problems during relocation. Over 20% of Americans move each year as per Hazler & Nass. Each year Over 1.5 million Americans over 65 relocate per Marsha Wiggins-Frame, and she also mentions mobility syndrome aka Relocation Stress Syndrome or "RS", that includes disruption of routines, severance of support networks, and the difficulty of establishing oneself in a new area.

(Dr Lantz, Cheryl M Dr PhD, RN BSN) did her doctoral dissertation on the role of Spirituality/religious faith during stressful relocations by older adults. Her doctoral dissertation included the following useful information: Negative responses to Relocation Stress, Spiritual Assessment Tools, Religious Affiliations, Extra Personal Spiritual Resources, Spiritual Blessings, Spiritual Influences within older adults undergoing relocation-she stated that nothing has been done to qualitatively study the spiritual aspects of relocation. Lantz noted that The NANDA North American Nursing Diagnostic Association Model did not incorporate the spiritual stresses that older adults experience during relocation.

Then NANDA North American Nursing Diagnostic Association Model was amended in 2007 to reflect the addition of RSS Relocation Stress Syndrome: Disturbances (physical psychosocial including loneliness & isolation) from a transfer from 1 environment to another. (see Mallick & Whipple regarding Validation of Nursing Diagnosis of RSS Relocation Stress Syndrome). To holistically care for older adults, research is needed to reveal the spiritual influences and stressors during relocation...and the use of spiritual/religious practices to cope with relocation stresses, The spirituality models address end of life issues & the dying process, but they don't address the role of spirituality during relocation, i.e. the spiritual aspects of re-adjustment during transition and relocation, including spiritual coping mechanisms as per Lantz. Lantz noted that little is known about how older adults use spirituality as a coping mechanism during transition & relocation. Relocation is a major life stressor affecting and involving physical, emotional, social and interpersonal cognitive factors The Lantz study is also significant in providing information that reduces this gap in knowledge. It facilitates understanding the implications of the spiritual domain in relocation situations that were almost non-existent until the Lantz study. Lantz's findings give direction as to how to assist those traumatized by transition-relocation- by providing spiritual care to them during the relocation process. Please note that Lantz's study focused on the 1st 6 months of relocation.

(Berube, & Devinne, indicated that Relocation =Establishment in a new place.

Lantz and other researchers have added the person whose experience it is -at the center of the relocation process. In other words, Human beings are really the heart of the relocation experience.

Scocco, Rappatoni & Giovanna, wrote about the "eustress of distress- eustress meaning moderate or normal psychological stress interpreted as being beneficial for the experiencer. Decreasing distress and increasing eustress will help you, Relocation stress alters homeostasis, causes suffering, disrupts life, and can precede psychiatric illness,

(Richard Schulz, & Gail Brenner, did a study on Relocation of elderly people including nursing home residents. They noted that involuntary forced relocation can cause feelings of loss of control- which led to their study using a "Predictability Control Model" as part of their control factors.

Lantz indicated that Holistic health includes the role of the spirit in relocation/transition.

Betty Ackley, Betty & Gail Ludwig, Nanda, Jackson, Lantz. Castle, Mitchell Smith & Crome Brugler, Titus & NYPaver + Jackson all discusses more on RSS Relocation Stress Syndrome: The symptoms can include loneliness, depression, anxiety, panic, alienation, anger, insecurity, dependency, worry, withdrawal, frustration, loss of appetite, low self-esteem, self-doubt, fear, despondency. becoming reclusive/phobic, nervousness feeling

frightened, fatigued, unable to concentrate, learning impairment, memory difficulties, impaired learning, self-doubt insecurity, obsessive thoughts, confusion, disorientation, spatial impairment, getting lost a lot. unable to trust, having no friends, sadness, vertigo, dizziness, impaired learning, social withdrawal, being uneasy, jittery, loss of autonomy/independence, loss of self-worth exhaustion palpitations, loss of identity, lost confidence, feelings of injustice, fear of people, introversion -see Oswald & Crane,

Another reason that can cause distress is that often older adults who move often need accommodations & assistance & they fear having difficulty getting that help for their special needs-They often struggle with inadequate support as per Jackson, Relocation Stress Syndrome disrupts homeostasis and spirituality, spiritual aspects of this syndrome must be studied if healthcare providers are to provide holistic healthcare. Relocation Stress Syndrome can be helped by sensitive holistic healthcare coupled with improved physical /psychosocial environment: Washburn, Ramey Cress, and Lantz, all added that no studies have addressed the positive side of relocation from the perspective of Spirituality. Lantz indicated that no studies had been made of the processes used by older adults regarding their spirituality during relocation. Mallick & Whipple call for more research to continue validation of the Relocation Stress Syndrome + Oswald & Rowles suggest studies that would reveal subtle dimensions of the relocation process for older adults. Thomas Coffman examined Relocation & Survival of elderly people -from forced relocation: he cited " Disintegrative deterioration" caused by the loss of key support people, a " serious deterioration/loss in the person's support system, if sufficient replacement support is not immediately provided for, the negative effects/risks can be overwhelming & catastrophic, this mirrors a finding by Dr Harold Levinson MD about Catastrophic anxiety from feared loss of somatic stability...

Cari Shane spoke about Transitional Trauma: ' moving is so much more than just moving', a loss of control, emotions involved in forced moves can actually trigger real physical reactions especially in aging adults, a physical/emotional toll. effects can take years to recover from, including isolation trauma & feeling like a prisoner in your new place & not seeing others for days and often having nothing to do but wait...

Susie Danick, of TAD Relocation Washington DC. indicated that when there is no real professional plan to minimize trauma, the trauma is very real, the enormity of emotion of saying goodbye,

Julyne Derrick, talked about transfer trauma -anxiety-loneliness -after a move, she interviewed Social Worker Tracy Greene Muniz, a Nationally recognized expert in Relocation Stress Syndrome-& Muniz commented that when you yank people out of what their concept of home is, it can be very traumatic...moving is one of life's most stressful moments for anyone, In 1992, the North American Nursing Diagnostic Assn added Relocation Stress as an official diagnosis. It can create a new sense of insecurity and distrust and can trigger great distress as the patient tries to recreate their old home in a new place, Donna Morse, BSN RN says that Relocation Stress Syndrome is for real. The trauma is compounded when the move is forced & unanticipated, and it can trigger severe loneliness, anxiety & grief.

Amber Williams did a University Educational Thesis study on Relocation Stress Syndrome & here is a summary of what she found & discussed:

The trauma can be severe when the move is sudden and unanticipated (also see Morse,2000, pg. 24aaa). The patient can feel powerless, lacking in ability to control, angry, lonely, anxious, frightened, fearful, scared, sad despondent, with a devalued sense of self- socially isolated/alone, helpless, unable to socially function, dependent, feeling of loss of independence and autonomy. threatened, unwell, fatigued, exhausted, depressed, filled with procrastination and dread, overwhelmed, confused, lost. worthless, and infantilized (treated as a child). It can also include an unplanned for response of panic to unexpected diagnosis of illness/disability...it can trigger homesickness for loved one's relatives and family, especially if the move is a far distance away, the abrupt transition is a shock to body, mind and spirit, which exacerbates the existing medical condition due to severe stress of relocation "under duress".

The patient often feels abandoned rejected unwanted devalued and deserted and feels being treated unfairly and unjustly, discriminated against, punished, ganged up on, picked on, treated in a discriminatory way, picked on, singled out, being spitefully treated, feeling cruelly treated. and struggling to understand grasp and accept the forced move, desperately seeking return of lost control, sensing loss of personal identity, fearing loss of connection to family friends' relatives and care providers, especially where the patient is already grappling with cognitive impairment. and fearing that nobody is willing to help them after they relocate. They are filled with emotional crisis, struggling with accepting the transition (also see Kao et al), Amber Williams also mentions that removing patients from strong trusted beloved bonding attachment support figures in their lives can cause Relocation Stress Syndrome to be severe.

Despite the now prolific evidence proving the seriousness & severity of Relocation stress syndrome, there are still many that stubbornly disbelieve & even cruelly deny the evidence & arrogantly try to invalidate that evidence, including some Courts.

Terri Keville, cited the heartbreaking legal case of Reed vs Hurley Medical Center 395 nw 2nd 12,14, Michigan Court of Appeals)Regarding a patient with muscular dystrophy who alleged that he would suffer transfer trauma if his care was transferred from a hospital to a nursing home -The Michigan Court of Appeals disagreed with the patient and responded that "the evidence did not show a sufficient likelihood that the patient would suffer transfer trauma" DESPITE the patient showing the Appeals Court the devastating effects of transfer trauma-including severe emotional/psychological/physical hardship that the transfer would cause him, (447 US 784 NOTE 16 US Supreme Court) & The court averred that the patients could be legally forced to relocate (447 US 793 US Supreme Court). Borup, Gallego & Heffernan noted that some view transfer trauma as an unproven myth.

Recovering from Relocation Stress Syndrome:

Delgado indicated that Inner peace, wellbeing, and tranquility is necessary for people in order to have goals and hopes, dreams and aspirations-Inner peace/tranquility & comfort =success in coping with stressors.

(Narayanasamey stated that Energy is strengthened from a strong sense of spirituality within their being.

Sacred Music can be part of the therapeutic healing process- (see Kirkland & Mcilveen) the feeling from the music is a vital element in group religious settings. Lantz shows that Music Therapy for strengthening spirituality is very important, church music supports the person's need to connect to a higher power,

Kirkland & McIlveen, mentions " Spiritual Therapy" as a way to facilitate healing and as a way to feel joyous and whole and enriched by the sacred.

Koenig & Lawson, mention the benefits of developing connections with congregations as support networks -this is a positive impact churches have. & Mackenzie, Bergland & Kirkevold, explain how attending church services increases opportunities to socialize with others of similar beliefs, and it supports a person's inner spirit(see also Ai & Mackenzie) ,(Lantz states too that religious socialization at church is very important in a therapeutic way, for these older traumatized adults, many turn to faith beliefs as they age ,growth in faith occurs as a person faces challenges, difficulties & problems in life,(Seymour, 1995) found that as people age their religious practices may be limited by physical/cognitive/psychosocial deficits yet their personal spirituality deepens. For example, (Ross, 1996) found that hospitalized adult patients sometimes need religious services-and that they would have benefitted spiritually if they had been transported to church services, these patients were not provided the spiritual support of being transported to church services.

Lantz, explained that older adults rely on and strengthen their spirituality beliefs and practices as they lose physical abilities and suffer other life losses, church attendance and religiousness supports their spirits, hospitalized adults would have attended to their religious practices and ceremonies if they had been told of the spiritual supports available at the hospital.

Lantz added that isolation supports dysfunctional emotional states such as depression-those that relocate risk isolation if they don't adjust to the new location, social interaction is needed. Church attendance supports their spirits. Lantz, suggests that it's important to ease stressful situations for older adults during transition/relocation, i.e. enhancing holistic care such as assisting patients with meeting spiritual needs-when a patient and their caregivers work toward the optimal outcome of the relocation-spiritual needs will be met and Relocation Stress syndrome will be decreased & the patient will adjust well to relocation.

Lantz says that when patients draw upon their spirituality to assist them in adjusting to relocation, their spirituality flourishes after the relocation, closeness and desire for God grows within their holistic being, spiritual influences alter their religious/spiritual feelings, After religious services, patients are at peace and feel spiritually fulfilled, and researchers began to question 'what happens in the time between the arrival at their new home and adjusting to it, to gain peaceful states and a sense of the sacred from spiritual practices'.

(Lantz also suggests that these people try to maintain some ties to people from their past location such as family relatives and friends -it's significant to maintain helping relationships as those were/are core relationships in their lives.

Lantz adds that patients drew upon their spirituality to assist them with their relocation adjustment. Their spirituality flourished after the relocation. Closeness and desire for God grew within their holistic being, spiritual influences altered their religious/spiritual feelings.

Lantz described Spirituality=intrapersonal relationship with God. One can grow spiritually during relocation-there are blessings in spiritual lives during relocation ,increased desire/time for spirituality, a new sense of time to focus on their spiritual life after they relocated, the relocated person continues to search for spiritual guidance, there are blessings in spiritual lives during relocation, Their health status becomes a spiritual opportunity, a new sense of time ,to focus on spiritual life ,more time to study bible and to attend services and more time for spiritual practices,

Eldon Killian, described a sample of medical patients surveyed -where over 90% indicated that the care/treatment they were receiving/experiencing at their new location was better/improved than the care at their prior location.(Eldon Killian, also noted that those people who kept busy with activities had less time to negatively reflect to others about their relocation, and that those who were busy with activities at their

the new location made better adjustment than patients who had plenty of idle time to negatively reflect on their despair. Similarly, (Borup & Gallego,) asserted that traumatic effects of forced relocation can be prevented minimized or ameliorated through activities and programs. Eldon Killian wrote that Relocation stress can be controlled by social intervention.

Richard Schulz, & Gail Brenner in a 1977 study of relocation by elderly people, including nursing home patients- noted that the people who recovered from the relocation trauma were the ones who got opportunities to be independent at their new location, and who were given the chance to have decision making control regarding their time/space usage and who were given access to trying out new skills in the community. Those that were denied/deprived of those favorable conditions exhibited deterioration and withdrawal whereas those afforded those benefits thrived from increased sense of control over their new environment. Terri Keville noted too that the person's subjective feeling of disruption and its related stress-is decreased when patients are not separated from familiar caretakers/providers aka when patients are not separated from their support system. Coffman noted a significant correlation between staff morale & patient success in a new location (of the patient). Coffman, 1981 noted too that patient interaction and Activity involvement is crucial for recovering from relocation stress.

Claire Kowalski interestingly noted the following unusual factor in adapting successfully to forced institutional relocation of the elderly : (ibid, pg. 512): Elderly patients may still perceive the locus of control as still being in themselves if they have voluntarily entrusted their care to others whom they trust, and if those to whom they voluntarily entrusted their institutional and related care behave so as to merit the trust placed in them by the elderly relocated patients.

 Amber Williams, wrote about environmental factors that alleviate relocation stress syndrome, as her University educational study thesis: She recommended creating a healing environment, and providing coping resources(see also McKinney & Melby She researched what methods/solutions can be developed to reduce the effects of Relocation Stress Syndrome...Her hypothesis was that the occurrence of this syndrome can be reduced thru environmental actions. (Citing Castle, she states that a single new room may constitute the equivalent of a home- and the new room becomes a new place imbued with meanings and significances nearly or somewhat equivalent to those that evolved in their prior residences, bringing beloved and cherished possessions/belongings helps keep some of the attachment bonds intact and boosts self-esteem and personal pride. (also see Golant, SM 2003)

(Amber Williams, and Dr William Thomas) & (Weinstein) each refer to the concept of an "Eden alternative'- a "habitat" that is nurturing to personal growth and which helps people to thrive, & not just merely providing treatment. Such a "habitat" recognizes, appreciates & promotes each person's capacity or growth ,cares for each other's needs & capitalizes on each other's capacities,(see e.g. Weinstein),It is also characterized by stable, steady, reliable, dependable & predictable regular, ongoing long term care, Weinstein notes that socially diverse location is important-with a devotion to harmony & tranquility.(see Williams) People who interact with their surroundings are more engaged & continue to thrive in their new environment-(Dr Thomas Williams, and Amber Williams, explains that it's a basic human need to give as well as receive(see Weinstein, 1997,pg 4) People enjoy caring for others-the need is always there,(ibid), Dr Thomas adds that this requires a change in attitude, more change in your heart than change in your pocket-(See Weinstein, Spiritual wellbeing includes comfort & meaningful activity in a healing environment (see Williams. When a patient is in such a healing place, there is measurable improvement in physical & psychological health (also see Hamilton & Watkins, The environment has a measurable impact on humans (Williams Also see Looker PA & Stichler, regarding Healing Environments, and see Weinstein, regarding The Eden Alternative: Activities Adaptation)**Learning about the need for Coping Skills/Abilities** Amber Williams Kao Describe coping as a function of personal and environmental characteristics for the purpose of regulating emotions. When a person is coping with a situation they are trying to regulate/control their emotions, a coping strategy is a process that changes over time and often includes problem solving to deal with unexpected transitions/changes. Schwarz describes coping in terms of needing to compensate and adjust, in order to reduce stress and to adapt to new conditions.

Chapter 7: I Never Expected to get (2) More Pastors onto my "team"

I was so grateful to get Pastor Phil Alba to join my "team" then I found out that Pastors Juan Reyes of New Generation Church & Pastor Fredy Sermeno of Ministerio Emanuel were going to be sharing the premises with Cornerstone Church. Pastor Phil introduced me to both pastors & they too welcomed me into their church & provided rides to/from church & allowed me to share my music skills. Amazing how after 30 congregations rejected me, not only did #31 embrace me & welcome me into their awesome Cornerstone Church, but I also now had 3 pastors on my "team', Totally AMAZING & I am so eternally grateful for these 3 incredible pastors & their lovely church congregations. I needed & still need all the Pastoral support as my experimental dental treatment journey continues very actively!

Dental stuff is still quite scary & panic/fear inducing for me. I am still very much the dental "scaredy cat fraidy cat". What makes this add-on of (2) churches is that they are "Hispanic" (aka Spanish) churches AND I had earned my 1st BA degree in Spanish from Hofstra University in Spring 1983(my 2ND BA was in Music also from Hofstra University, Spring 1984). I was not diagnosed with the learning disorders till a few months after struggling fiercely to earn my (2) BA degrees, & I had vowed to eventually resume both my Music & my Spanish studies once the medications & Irlen color tint eyeglasses would restore and normalize my learning ability.

I especially love Spanish Music as well & wanted to re-learn that too. This time I would not be struggling severely, thanks to the medicine/color glasses & thanks to people re-teaching me. I was never able to afford to travel & stay in a native Spanish speaking country- that would have really helped with learning by immersion. However, God didn't forget how I had wanted such an opportunity & this time God sent the Native Spanish speaking world to me & I would be able to immerse myself in it several times a week at no cost to me. How miraculous is that? Isn't God great? The 2 Spanish churches allow me to fully immerse myself in the Spanish language I craved for so long & they are helping me to greatly improve my non-native but increasingly Spanish proficiency. It allows me to hear, speak & read Spanish, & that is so joyful & so is my trying to learn advanced Spanish music too. I even have a great little Spanish restaurant across the street from Church. How awesome is that?

I was also able to take bible studies at the 2 churches & learn the Santa Biblia-Bible in Spanish too, I even took the Discipleship classes at "NGC" New Generation Church with Pastor Reyes & his wife Evelina. Pastor Sermeno at Ministerio Emanuel is helping me with tackling the Santa Biblia-totally in Spanish-which is very challenging yet rewarding for me.

And what was REALLY REALLY SPECIAL is that during June 2018, Pastor Reyes had me fully immerse in the waters at Sunken Meadow Beach in Suffolk County LI NY. My joy was & is indescribable. It was yet another step forward for me in my extremely unique Faith thru/with Experimental Dental Prosthetics treatment journey here.

Please note that some Messianic Jews view water immersion as a "rite of passage"
 (see e.g. Cohn-Sherbok, "Messianic Judaism'‘) My experimental dental prosthetics journey is also kind of like the theme of the song about "You raise me up to more than I could be” and that "rising up" is also connected to water immersion in a faith journey.

For example, Christian theologian writer John Piper has mentioned " the rising of faith" and Colossians 2:12 refers to "raised with him thru your faith in the power of God & walk in the newness of life..."Some Christians see water immersion as a declaration of new faith & trust, arising to a new life.

Chapter 8: Messianic Rabbi David Rosenberg & Shuvah Yisrael -The Messianic Rabbi part of 3 Pastors & a Rabbi: Healing My Body & Mind Thru Embracing Messianic Judaism as part of my Experimental Dental Prosthetics Treatment Journey Miracle:

In my Religious/Spiritual Faith Mind Body healing part of my Experimental Dental Prosthetics Treatment Journey Miracle, I was blessed to meet & get to know Messianic Rabbi David Rosenberg & his incredible congregation Shuvah Yisrael in Plainview NY, & that is how "3 pastors" became transformed into "3 Pastors & a Rabbi". He & Shuvah have become a huge vital and crucial part of my Experimental Dental Prosthetics Miracle Journey. It however was a "circuitous and anguished path" that led me to find him & Shuvah. Let me give you a brief glimpse into that path for a moment.

I was having enormous difficulty finding a synagogue willing to help me. This had added to my sense of personal failure and personal rejection. Finally, a Messianic Synagogue in or near Holbrook NY steered me to Shuvah. I was really scared that they too would refuse and reject me but found the courage to contact Rabbi Rosenberg & Shuvah despite my fears and self-doubt. To my amazement & delight he & Shuvah welcomed me immediately, with open arms & welcoming embrace. It's now my 2nd High Holiday season with them & I truly love it there.

And what's also remarkable is that I found a "new" therapeutic healing modality there. I had never expected to find there a most incredible and very unique " therapeutic style " tennis teacher who has been working very hard with me to improve on my multiple disabilities and the tennis is great for helping my jaw/face/shoulders/neck to adapt to the experimental dental prosthetics including the experimental splints that compensate for my lost jawbone. Tennis is improving flexibility thus helping my body to adapt well to the experimental dental prosthetics reconstruction.

As a result, I added a Therapeutic Tennis chapter to this book to help explain the therapeutic role of tennis in my healing journey and how tennis helps others with disabilities similar to mine.

Thank You Again Rabbi "David" & Shuvah for welcoming & embracing me & for the support friendship & prayers & I LOVE LOVE LOVE the music there.

Lastly, it was wonderful that they had me play "Cornerstone" by Leon Patillo on their piano for their Purim Talent show. That so overjoyed me!

Now for a more formal connection to Messianic Judaism I want to share this with you:

In my repeated online search for solace, I often thought of Israelites in Exodus having to flee Egypt in minutes, similar in a way to my suddenly having to flee Florida in the middle of the night. When I began to finally try and recover from the overwhelming shock and heavy stress of my sudden forced fleeing in the middle of the night from Florida, my mind kept recalling how the Israelites had to flee Egypt in the middle of the night, and then one day over 3 yrs. Later, I found an intriguing Messianic Judaism article online that really comforted me greatly called "I am the Lord, your Healer". (As per Aaron Eby, Director of Vine of David) .I condensed its key points & summarized them for you here: I am the Lord your healer (Exodus 15:26),The journey from Egypt to Sinai involved a physical and spiritual transformation ..Embarking on a long journey thru the desert

,finding oasis on a long journey thru the desert...and finally the Israelites receiving the Torah at Mount Sinai were healed(Exodus Rabbah 7:1) ,the Israelites who left Egypt were broken and battered victims of appalling slave abuse, beaten, & ruthlessly forced to work, their lives and their bodies were treated as worthless.,. and God tried to comfort them by telling them " I will put none of the diseases on you that I put on Egypt for I am the Lord your healer" (Exodus 15:26).

 The long journey through the desert was from darkness to light, a transition from bitterness to sweetness, The Israelites reached an oasis pool of bitter water called "Marah" which means bitter just like the maror eaten at the Passover Seder where we re-enact the Israelites' suffering, but through a miracle, God changed the bitterness of the water into sweetness., Healing is God's signature. Those who administer treatments & alleviate suffering & increase life, are truly walking in the ways of the Creator, They are his agents in the world, God granted some people exceptional skill in healing people, leading them to discover powerful treatments, God's healing power, healing from God, God's compassionate care every moment of our lives , sustained by the compassionate King, each time we arrive at a significant moment we bless God who has kept us alive, upheld us and let us reach this time, God heals the body, Many Jews also recite a prayer before taking medication

or treatment," let it be your will, O Lord, my God and God of my fathers -that this endeavor will result in my healing for you...for you freely heal... (see e.g. James 5:14)

The Apostles taught us that when a person is sick, they should apply both prayers and medicinal treatment, Judaism teaches that physical ailments have a spiritual counterpart, this means that a complete treatment will account for both. Yeshua performed both spiritual and physical healing for the people he touched, Ask God to regenerate us as God can regenerate us spiritually so we can stand, behold, see and hear... (note: there were also disabled Israelites who received the Torah at Mount Sinai-see Exodus Rabbah 7:1)

Embarking on a journey into Messianic Judaism can be daunting but every journey begins w/ a small step. All healing comes from Hashem including miracles of healing. See also (James 5:14) let them pray over him, anointing him with oil in the name of the Lord. (that was how medicines were applied in the 1st century) The article also mentions " Blossoming" (1 Kings 6:1) Jews for Jesus wrote that The Messiah would perform signs of healing. Also see Extraordinary Miracles of the Messiah by Messianic Bible.com and see the Holy Spirit's gift of healing(Learn Religions.com) Gifts of his glory described the healing power of Messianic Judaism as follows: a journey of faith, God's healing touch, God miraculously appears throughout life, even in the times of dark valleys and dark times in life, bringing healing restoration, an intimate relationship with Yeshua -filled with sweet tenderness and affection, his arms are always outstretched waiting for you to come back to him, God is with us even during the storms in our lives, find healing, discover God by reading about faith,

David Yonke wrote how one needs to strengthen their relationship with the Lord, in order to be healthier and more stable, and strengthened ,Yeshua is like a place of refuge/sanctuary, one needs to meet and accept Yeshua , he is like a place of healing intercession ,he helps calm people and gives them a sense of peace- as soon as one enters a messianic synagogue, one feels God's presence and gets a real calmness and peace, when you are there you never want to leave, there's such a peace in there, There God can start working in you, as you strengthen your relationship with God, and you will have an increased sense of peace and clarity-a connection where you talk to the Lord -you sit there and sort out your thoughts, when you're in that kind of atmosphere, you're able to focus a lot better ,it's a good place to relax and sit before the Lord, to steady your mind and focus on what's meaningful, a house of refuge, people can sit and let the Lord minister to them ,and help them to seek intimacy with God,(Adat Adonai Messianic Synagogue, Rabbi Kirt Schneider, Ottawa Lakes Mi)

Jewish Voice Blog -Miracles describes Miraculous Healing thru Yeshua the Great Physician who heals ,healed bodies, healed minds, healed souls ,come to experience the love of Jesus, The functional truth is that God will heal & save, God is not only willing but eager to share his great love with people in need...especially when we are faithful ,he wants us to partner with him...in the generous release of his healing power...Jesus wants care and love for all people, he wants to share physical healing with people,(as per Kehila News).

Yeshua performed his miracles as acts of compassion, Yeshua strengthened the sickly, and healed the diseased...King Yeshua is a shepherd you can trust with your problems. JewishVoice.Org writes about the following: Is anyone among you sick? Let him call for the elders of Messiah's community & let them pray over him, anointing him with oil in the name of the Lord, They hoped for a miracle & Yeshua didn't disappoint, prayers and sharing of Yeshua, power of prayer...professing new faith in Yeshua as Lord, miraculous blessings God has poured out, giving miraculous evidence of his presence, eternal differences for a person who desperately needs to hear about Yeshua,

Mark Ellis, Mark describes how miracles unfolded after an Orthodox Jewish man found Yeshua in Israel. Yeshua is part of God's plan for restoring people, this man was praying to God for deliverance from the turmoil in his home and family, he prayed too for healing in his body, God heard his prayers and orchestrated the kind of answer only God could bring ,God's miraculous answer...He now has the opportunity to share the miracle that God brought to his life, the fact that God used him despite his weakness is miraculous...and he feels that more miracles are on the way to him...

Marsden describes the miracle story of LEGALLY BLIND Messianic
Rabbi Jeff Grillo, at Rock of Israel Messianic Congregation Clover
SC-who has been legally blind since age 5 from Retinitis Pigmentosa.
He is also a cancer survivor and an ordained minister.

Sid Roth, & Rabbi Eric Carlson describe Miracles of Yeshua,
salvation thru Yeshua delivers people from sicknesses, Rabbis 2000
yrs. ago knew that only the True Messiah would heal -Yeshua even
healed lepers,(see Luke 17:12-14) Yeshua performed many miraculous
signs-See John 11:45-47.

<u>Healing Aspergers Autism Thru Messianic Judaism (I have Aspergers)</u>

Kerry Magro, & Louisa Wuethrich described how Kerry Magro was
diagnosed with Aspergers autism as an adult at age 34 and her new
journey is her plan to go to college- Kerry found a new home at
Restoration, a Messianic synagogue. She was longing to connect with
people and to share herself and share with others- and never
understanding how to accomplish that. She felt like an outsider
looking in, and longing for church related activities where she could
be immersed in things of life that she really cares for ,the things that
she really wanted ,longing to fit in, she grew in her Christian faith and
slowly began to find places where she would fit in, such as moments
of time with small groups, God "maneuvered" her to Restoration
Synagogue ,the joy of diving into Messianic Judaism, messianic
worship with music and dance, diving into learning about the Jewish
roots of her faith, and becoming part of a congregation that really drew
her in, received her and accepted her, nothing was wrong with her
churches but she began to experience community on a whole new
level, the leader treated her in helpful ways ...never judging her
,understanding her, helping her to understand other perspectives, She
met amazing people by how quickly she read books and articles,
including reference materials. She felt like she was part of a team, a
team that helps with services, a volunteer ministry, She began hoping

for new ways for her to be part of service at Restoration Synagogue, hoping to open up new ways to help herself overcome her Aspergers difficulties that made it difficult for her to minister to people in the way she had always longed for ,

<u>Healing thru Messianic Judaism -A recent resource that may be helpful to you is:</u>

Congregation Ruach Israel, Needham MA. Refuah Shlema Healing Prayer Conference Unite Boston Rabbi Nathan Joiner. Healing Prayer from the Messianic Jewish Tradition- A life transforming journey. office@ruachisrael.org

Chapter 9: Dentistry & Religious Faith

Lidia Jordao examined the relationship between rates of attending religious services and oral health, by doing a sample study of adolescents in Brazil. The statistical dental variables included cavities and periodontitis and the independent explanatory variable was the frequency of attending religious services. Attending religious services was positively significantly statistically associated with oral health behaviors such as faithfully attending dental checkups and dental hygiene appointments.

Leroy Gatlin examined how dentists can work with their Christian Science patients to respect their faith while providing treatment. I have summarized his ideas, opinions, findings and conclusions for you as follows: Prayer helps patients to get thru dental treatment procedures especially in terms of coping with pain, the patients use prayerful thoughts and focus on the spiritual aspects of coping, these patients are committed to spiritual healing thru prayer, they often believe in faith healing including spiritual study, prayer, and growth in grace, feeling & thinking about their heartfelt inner communion with God before during and after the dental treatment, They believe that healing is connected to engaging with the divine, even for cavities ,Faith is integral to restorative care, effective healing thru prayer,

Olympia Union Gospel mission has a dental clinic and the reason for it is this: A trip to the dentist might lead to someone's salvation -when a dentist eliminates dental pain, hope and confidence return, creating an open door for the Gospel Message.

Jewish Voices Outreach in Ethiopia/Zimbabwe/ Mudanda provided dental care to over 8,071 people. They described their dental mission as follows: Together we have done miracles ...helped bring miracles of spiritual and physical transformation to hurting people, brought spiritual hope and healing care and relieved pain...witnessed healing miracles, the Lord touched people in supernatural ways as well as thru compassionate and skillful attention of dedicated dental professionals, God was able to do beyond what we asked and prayed for,

Carolyn Henderson wrote a humorous and satirical piece called "God the dentist" and I have paraphrased & condensed it here for you : Going to the dentist is a lot like submitting myself to God...trust/dependence on someone other than ourselves, like a dentist, God sees cracks we don't see that could lead to greater damage that will hurt more to fix, doesn't seem like a problem to us ...but God is the dentist. God wants to know when you have pain and provides comfort, we can't assert much independence over a dentist's judgment, expertise, and skill, yet we do this with God, convinced that we know more than God knows regarding our lives, God's spiritual dental work in our life is free for us to accept,

Manya Brachear-Pashman, writes a heartwarming piece on how a dentist, Dr Patrick Blaney, Westmont IL, treats clergy for free : Suddenly every filling, every dental bridge, have become acts of ministry, Each morning he and his employees pray before seeing the first patient, my patients should feel like God is loving them thru me, well done good and faithful servant, as per one of his patients retired priest Rev. Gerald Tivey & Tivey says regarding Dr Patrick Blaney, 'his spirituality and Christianity

are just part of him and they boil over in everything he does, and Rev Patricia Handley says that 'his journey has really been putting one foot in front of the other, as God has opened doors for him,

Pastor Ezekiel Bathfire wrote " God's approach to Toothache-prayers required". I have selected some of it for inclusion here in summarized form: Proverbs 25:19 Confiding in an unfaithful man in time of trouble is like a broken tooth, Jeremiah 31:30 every man that eateth the sour grape, his teeth shall be set on edge, Song of Songs 4:2 teeth like flocks of sheep, Bathfire adds that it would have been very useful to those who preach the Gospel to have Jesus do "The Miracle of the Toothache"...and Bathfire goes further to say : And there was, at that time, in Judea, a man who was a rich man, and who was seized of toothache with a great ache-ance and the aching was great-and the man came unto Jesus and said " Lord, Lord, I cry out with pain and woe , there is great pain, whereas I may be rich, my riches are as naught when set against this pain, it is very much of this world, I would give those riches to be free- Jesus then poked his finger in his mouth and all the teeth became like a flock of sheep, and the rich man would give all his treasure to the poor and go to heaven ,yours in pain & Christ...Bill Gaultiere wrote about fear of the dentist & religious faith : Based on Ephesians 2:6, He realized that going to the dentist is a chance to practice living from the heavenly realms where I am in Christ. Exodus 21:21-25 refers to " tooth for tooth". (See also Burns 1786, Address to the toothache)

Chapter 10: Anesthesia Awareness-A Real Life Waking-Awake Nightmare

A HUGE component of my severe Dental PTSD Panic Terror was the Anesthesia Awareness I experienced in 1973 at the age of 10 during pre-orthodontic, maxillofacial, oral-dental surgery. It left me with a lifetime legacy of TERROR associated with Dentistry.

The Information Below Helps Explain Anesthesia Awareness.

 Please see LI herald.com/bellmore/stories/a-dental-miracle which is a fabulous article about me & Dr Schamis, written by Brian Stieglitz.

Robson speaks of the 'utter horror' of waking up during anesthesia & says it's more common than you think. Robson also talks about the Donna Penner case as follows: lying awake, unable to signal her distress, unable to signal that anything was wrong, frozen helpless with indescribable agony..."this is how I am going to die" right here on the table, nobody even noticing what's going on, left with lingering trauma, the resurfacing of these memories, never fully escaping the effects of this "life sentence" feeling powerless, unable to move or to even utter a sound, unable to open one's eyes, unable to breathe and thoughts of death, out of body experience, felt the presence of God, absolutely helpless, hearing voices/sounds," they seemed to be panicking .,heard them say they were losing me ,searing burning pain ,pain unlike anything I thought possible...too horrible to endure, screaming silently don't they know I'm awake, unable to move, fearing that I'm dying, the distress amplified by the lack of understanding by others,

The Patient Safety Institute also discusses the Donna Penner case as follows: Donna Penner from Altona Manitoba Canada, has PTSD Post Traumatic Stress Disorder from Anesthesia Awareness, 'I thought I was going to die", the pain was horrific, no words to describe how much it hurt, thinking I wasn't going to live through it. I could do absolutely nothing, fully aware, feeling excruciating agony, racing heartbeat, the terror was overwhelming, fears of suffocation ,stunned by the cold response, devastated, a life altering emotional wound, triggering terrible memories, left with difficulty focusing/concentrating, anxiety attacks, broken trust, and she concludes by saying that her mission is to tell her story as often and as widely as possible -she needs people to learn, to know, that this thing can happen to others, and does happen, and she finally adds that "If I can make a difference in 1 person's life, I will gladly retell my story a thousand times". Also see the NY times feature " Awake on The Table;" Despite the foregoing, some scientists recently opine that "paradoxically" anesthetics may have the ability to actually weaken PTSD Traumatic Memories.

Dengler described how some research scientists have recently found that sometimes some anesthetics can actually weaken PTSD Traumatic Memories: Dengler notes that some memories can leave people emotionally scarred for a lifetime-and added that there is new research now suggesting that perhaps routine surgical anesthetics may have the ability to weaken emotionally traumatizing and disturbing memories ,citing the recent findings of Dr Bryan Strange, a neuroscientist at the Technical University of Madrid Spain. Dr Strange believes that some surgical anesthetics can reduce emotionally traumatic past memories. He adds that these anesthetics can reduce brain activity in areas critical to emotional memory formation. He suggests that using such anesthetics may pave a new way to treat anxiety disorders in the future.

McDonald did research on the issue of pain flashbacks in PTSD with a focus on Anesthesia Awareness patients. McDonald explains that pain flashbacks = somato-sensory multi-sensory memories where the "encoded past pain '" is re-experienced in the present time. Patients with Anesthesia Awareness who had regained consciousness during surgical anesthesia later re-experienced that pain they felt during the surgery-a multi-sensory re-experiencing of the pain, somatic flashbacks of the burning searing pain. With "elevated somatic focus" and hypervigilance, the pain serves as a somatic reminder of the past trauma. This results in cognitive/physical/behavioral effects including increased attention to present and future pain/pain stimuli and hyperarousal, which is "self-amplifying", and the past pain is felt during flashbacks, the flashbacks represent the trauma history that causes the re-experiencing of pain and other bodily sensations as well.

ANESTHESIA AND COGNITIVE LEARNING MEMORY DIFFICULTIES: CEREBELLAR ASPECTS

Dina Maron described Anesthesia as a "dilemma" due to long term effects on memory/brain function. She opined that being "put under" with anesthesia early in life seems related to future cognitive problems. She adds that anesthesia exposure in animals is linked to long term learning & memory problems for almost all anesthetics. Ketamine given to monkeys was shown to cause lasting damage to the brain, including learning impairment and worsened color discrimination skills.

The monkeys who were given the ketamine were unable to select as many levers per second as the monkeys who did not receive the ketamine. Years after ketamine monkeys exposed to ketamine still show below normal brain function, citing Merle Paule at the FDA, director at their division of Neurotoxicity-FDA National Center for Toxicological Research. The ketamine monkeys had more neuron death than non-ketamine monkeys. Primate monkeys with isoflurane/nitrous oxide mix for 8hr one time use showed long term developmental learning problems. Dina Maron noted that showed that children with multiple anesthesia exposures prior to age 2 are twice as likely to be learning impaired and children under age 3 with 1 surgical anesthesia event are more likely to have difficulties with abstract reasoning and expressive language skills by age 10 & showed that children under age 4 who had a surgical anesthesia event later showed lower scores on listening comprehension and abstract visual spatial perceptual IQ scores. Lastly, Dina Maron also wrote that cognitive deficits were found in kids who had anesthesia 2 or more times-and exhibited brain changes in the occipital cortex and in the ***CEREBELLUM***. Lizette Borreli also wrote about how general anesthesia may impact cognitive function.

<u>The Cerebellum & Anesthesia/Anesthetics</u>

After my 1973 "NDE" near death experience caused by an hours long Anesthesia Awareness during Oral Dental Maxillofacial Surgery at age 10, 11 years passed & I was diagnosed in Sept 1984 by Dr Harold Levinson MD with Cerebellar Vestibular disease, The diagnosis & my curiosity & intuition " came together" & I decided to use my "freedom to be dyslexic, dysmetric and dyspraxia" (see Levinson, Harold)to explore my "hunch" that indeed the cerebellar disease was involved in my bizarre anesthesia failure that triggered my lifelong cerebellar dental PTSD. Once again, my hunch paid off nicely. Although there was a paucity of information to be found, pertaining to my "hunch" I did find a VETERINARY research article that supports my hunch. I am currently researching the Cerebellar-Anesthesia connection further. However, I felt it was important to share that Veterinary article as it is relevant to my "hunch".

Shamir, Goelman & Chai did a research project at the Koret School Veterinary Medicine Teaching Hospital at Hebrew University, Jerusalem Israel on the topic of Post Anesthesia Cerebellar Dysfunction in Cats. It was a study of 11 long -haired Persian Cats. The study occurred between 1998-2002. The study topic was regarding the acute onset of cerebellar dysfunction following uncomplicated general anesthesia veterinary medical procedures. All 11 cats had developed diffuse cerebellar disease which had started acutely after brief and uneventful general anesthesia. All 11 cats developed acute cerebellar signs immediately upon recovery from brief and uneventful general anesthesia. 1 of the 11 cats had surgery for mandibular jaw fracture repair.

 The Cerebellar Neuro Deficits testing revealed: ataxic gait(ataxia), hypermetria, wide stance, tendency to fall over, discoordination, tremors, delayed hopping, and lack of a menace response ocellary. The anesthetics used were ketamine, diazepam (valium) xylazine, acepromazine & halothane. All 11 cats presented with a new form of cerebellar disease that followed brief general anesthesia with ketamine being the only anesthetic common to all 11 cats. The cerebellar damage was non-reversible. There are binding affinities of ketamine to cerebellar receptors (CNS) possibly causing cytotoxicity and cerebellar cell death. The ketamine may have also caused ischemic insult to the cerebellum during the anesthesia.

Xiao did research on cerebellar damage from propofol anesthesia on very young lab mice still in their development state. He determined the following: propofol anesthesia exposure in early life of lab mice induced developmental impairments in the mice cerebellums. The exposure to the propofol anesthesia was associated with decreased Purkinje cells and their cellular activity and decreased protein levels in the cerebellum, impairing Bergmann glia development leading to cerebellar developmental defects, neurotoxic damage effects on the cerebellum, causing cerebellar movement disorders. and even led to suppressed hippocampal neurogenesis.

. Lastly, Dina Maron showed that cognitive deficits were found in kids who had anesthesia 2 or more times-and exhibited brain changes in the occipital cortex and in the ***CEREBELLUM,*** and Lizette Borreli stated that general anesthesia is linked to decreased cerebellar density.

As a result of reading this paper, I started to wonder if the ETHER I received in 1973 at age 10. caused my cerebellar disease or whether the disease pre-existed prior to the anesthesia. There is no way to know for sure.

<u>Cerebellum & "NDE;" Near Death Experience</u>

In 1973 at age 10, My Dental PTSD was largely caused by Anesthesia Failure/ Anesthesia Awareness during several hours of invasive maxillofacial-dental surgery that culminated in hemorrhaging and Cardiac arrest "coding. " Over 20 years later I was diagnosed with the rare Cerebellar-Vestibular disease. Since that diagnosis, I have studiously been searching the literature to see if and how the Cerebellum was somehow involved in my NDE "Near Death Experience" as I was greatly motivated from my dedicated review of the outstanding Cerebellar research of my brilliant neurologist Dr Harold Levinson MD, who is literally the pre-eminent Cerebellum Expert in the world. There sadly is a paucity of published work on this unique Cerebellum-NDE Near Death Experience. However, I did find very intriguing & quite fascinating related research that helped shed a new light on a very old "NDE Near Death Experience" close to 50 yrs. ago, a memory forever seared indelibly on my mind for my whole life ever since that "nightmare reality".

(Strubelt Maas and Schulter each have some incredible published research that is truly intriguing and quite relevant

regarding NDE Near Death Experience & The Cerebellum. It confirmed to me that my NDE was so connected to my Cerebellar disease. Below is a brief overview of the Strubelt & Maas findings: They were found in NDE patients following incredible "traits" as follows: Enhanced Synaptic Excitation in CEREBELLAR Purkinje cells. through the glutamatergic pathway and they also noted that Glutamate, an excitatory neurotransmitter, can produce excitotoxicity in Purkinje cells. Similarly, Schulter wrote about a case of illusory own body perceptions after transcranial magnetic stimulation of the Cerebellum.

Chapter 11: Abusive Dentists can cause a lifetime of traumatic flashback memories

Ming Kurtis discusses the use of trauma inducing restraints on children and Ming also mentions that an abused dental patient can be left with a lifetime of traumatic memories-dental PTSD- lasting scars you can't see-and some of these severely terrorized dental victims can feel that they are not dentally treatable by others, these patients fear being hurt, misunderstood. rejected and re-traumatized. Ming mentioned too that the new provider could have rejected this patient as had the dentist before this one-and this new provider could refuse urgently needed care to them now. This intense and extreme fear can cause not just dental PTSD but also a paralyzing lifelong panic associated with dentists and dentistry, especially if coupled with horrific and abusive past dental experiences that resulted in dental PTSD traumatic memory flashbacks. One patient had even mentioned that this intense emotion overloaded recall can even make a patient want to leap out of the dental chair to flee the office.

Mike McBride in a poignant piece called "Sometimes it takes a Root Canal" described the problems as follows: He commented that: Many child abuse survivors have problems going to the dentist, they can even re-experience feeling dental pain just by writing about past dental pain. Many abuse victims recall how sadistic dentists drilled and pulled teeth with little or no numbing at all.

Terrance Heath wrote about a person who was physically assaulted by their dentist when the person was age 6. The horrific experience left that person with dental PTSD that makes dental visits terrifying. As an adult, that person rarely visited the dentist -only going when emergencies occurred & the person required Valium in order to go to the dentist.

(CBS News 5/18/2016) in a feature on pediatric dental restraint devices, described the horrific and traumatic suffering experienced by some kids with whom dental restraints were used : Some parents claim that their kids were tortured and traumatized by these restraint devices...a horrible nightmare experience with long lasting traumatic effects...terrified...nightmares at night ...couldn't get the child back to another dentist for quite some time ,seemed like torture to the kids-the psychological ramifications included dental PTSD, psychologically harmful/harmed, a horrific experience that left emotional scars that are still present years later...it will live on with the kids forever...

I was actually molested & "tortured" by some dental/medical providers during my childhood & it left me with tremendous fear & mistrust of other providers.

Chapter 12: Risks Obstacles Challenges Dangers & Impediments

Dr Schamis and I felt that you really needed to understand the extremely severe Obstacles Challenges Dangers and Impediments that he & I faced regarding my Experimental Dental prosthetic rehabilitation.

(Bani) indicated that often there is little or no alveolar jawbone ridge upon which to construct & noted that jawbone atrophy may be present in alveolar jawbone deficient patients and that bone grafting may be needed, and noted that reconstruction efforts are at great risk of failure-especially due to prosthetic infra-occlusion and insufficient alveolar jawbone support.

Ferrante & Blasi state that with Hypopituitary Dwarfism there are multiple dental anomalies & that there is the problematic dilemma regarding the use of functional dental prosthetics to treat the multiple abnormal defective dental teeth/jaw/gum anomalies, including the difficulty in using dental prosthetics without surgical intervention: Ferrante & Blasi also note that the ideal resolution involves fixed permanent dental prosthetics, i.e. zirconium sub-structured dental prosthetics.

They cite as an example the use of a 5-tooth fixed ceramic prosthetic on a 6-fixture zirconia substructure for a mandibular arch. They further explained that "dental tooth stumping" via cutters is often needed in order to fit the prosthetics, as well as chamfer of affected teeth and that hypopituitary dwarfs have abnormally small maxilla/mandible and they also noted that physical changes from tooth eruption can lead to malformed teeth. They also stated that prosthetic rehab is especially challenging in cases where there is growth hormone

dysfunction. The zirconium resists corrosion & is lighter than steel. &
has the hardness of copper. The zirconium is usable for creating
prosthetic substructure for fixed prosthetics i.e. good fixity to
underlying teeth. They do warn that root canal procedures could
compromise the stability/aesthetics of dental prosthetics.

Aydinbelge notes briefly the challenge of fitting/designing dental
implant prosthetics in ectodermal pediatric patients. Grover & Mehra
discuss the risks/obstacles/problems/difficulties and significant
challenges in prosthodontic dental prosthetic usage in both dwarfism
dental disease & ectodermal dysplasia dental disease. (Note that in my
case, I have both diseases as they are related to each other.) Their
discussion includes many valid points, important considerations and
risk factors as follows: Difficulty in achieving stability and retention,
which may require regular adjustment-replacement may be needed if
there is a decrease in vertical height dimension of occlusion and/or the
presence of abnormal mandibular posture, usage of prosthetics to
minimize/prevent anterior-rotation of mandible that could otherwise
cause upward and forward displacement of the chin, as well as
otherwise causing reduced vertical height of the lower 1/3 of the face
and an otherwise tendency toward class 3 malocclusion.

 The prosthetics need to allow for a backward and downward rotation
of the mandible and need to provide normal spatial positioning of the
chin. Underdeveloped maxillary tuberosities and underdeveloped
alveolar jawbone ridges are problematic factors for the stability of the
prosthetics. The prosthetics specialist must take care to obtain a wide
distribution of occlusal force load & in some cases, retention of the
dental prosthetics can be improved by the use of various attachments
anchored to available suitable teeth. The prosthetic could create a
problem if/when it crosses the midline and there is a problem with
short tooth crown heights during correction of hypoplastic teeth.
Treatment may be needed to align the teeth into acceptable position
before the prosthetic can be fabricated. Ortho type appliances may be

needed to modify the abnormal dentofacial area and to align the teeth
there. Sagittal/Vertical dentofacial areas may need special correction.

 Suri wrote about the need/use of simultaneous functional fixed
appliance therapy for dental alignment prior to the use of
prosthetic/prosthodontic rehabilitation of Ectodermal Dysplasia Dental
Disease. Kumari & Kumar state that teeth reduction may be needed in
order to get fixed dental prosthetics. Britto cautions that growth
hormone deficient dwarf adults are at high risk of periodontal disease
if they undergo prosthetic dentistry. Jain noted: problem of
support/retention/stability of dentures,
including little resistance to lateral forces on dentures. Naqash noted
that Crown Build-ups may be needed.

(Falcon) wrote about 17 yr. old primordial dwarf Hannah McCain-
The obstacles were/are "herculean'`; All of her teeth had to be
extracted as they were loose, rootless and defective. She lacks the
jawbone needed for implants. While major bone grafts
mature/strengthen, she has to wear pediatric starter dentures for about
6 months. The provisional dentures will be converted to fixed dentures
while her final prosthetic is being fabricated. Inesp Alves wrote fixed
dental appliances can aggravate the dwarfism dental deformities.

Omo & Ennnibulele describe dental Prosthetic rehabilitation of
Ectodermal Dysplasia dental patients present a unique challenge. They
have a great need for well fabricated dental prosthetics however they
present major unique challenges and problematic factors in terms of
the resistance forces/ retention and stability of the prosthetics.

It is much more difficult than in normal patients. Masoumeh
Rostamzadeh states that rare dental syndromes such as Papillon-
Lefevre Syndrome are very difficult to treat especially due the poor
periodontal condition where alveolar vertical jawbone height support
is lost as the alveolar jawbone supports the teeth. Jokstad mentions the
dilemma of choosing best care when a disease is poorly understood,

especially if there are many different strategies to choose from. (citing Abraham Flexner, Abraham) Jokstad also mentions that there are uncertainties to deal with.

Dr Kim Daxon, prosthodontist with the Perio Implant Advisory notes the "challenge of treatment planning for a long term multi-faceted case needing treatment that can take several years, including long term follow-ups, and repair/modification/replacement of the prosthetics. the dental rehab. can be very long-as long as several years, many treatment decision dilemmas, prosthetically challenging but ultimately a very happy patient. Dr Arlen Meyers MD + Dr Jeff Burgess DDS advise that dental patients with neurological diseases require special management in terms of dental treatment planning.

Dr Patricia Nihill, DMD, described the challenges of treating a 21 yr. old dwarf woman with ectodermal dental disease, as follows: Treatment complications included small jaws requiring use of pediatric trays, the problem of prosthetic retention, the severe bony undercuts posed a problem with making impressions, and with fabricating the overdenture.,, minimal space available over the occlusal/buccal surfaces of the retained premolars, coupled with extremely short arch length, extractions of severely periodontally mobile loose posterior teeth, difficulty with retention/seal, unique situation required improvisation of existing dental materials such as reshaping stock pediatric anterior teeth , the need to extract severely mobile loose teeth caused by advanced severe periodontal disease… the need to reshape stock pediatric dental prosthetics ,

Ambulgekar, Sanadi, Doshi & Gaikwad wrote a case report about a rare unusual and severe dental patient in India who had what they called Mutilated Dentition which is severely worn dentition that is often challenging to manage due to loss of vertical dimension, loss of tooth structure, and the uneven wear of teeth that creates an uneven plane of occlusion.

Singh Dua &Aghi, described the functional rehab. of mutilated dentition. Obstacles Challenges & Difficulties included: severe attrition of dentition that causes depressed facial appearance/look, loss of VDO Verticalook, lossn of Occlusion, the need for foundation restoration of dentition with final rehab. via fixed prosthetics, unfavorable coordination of stomatognathic system, teeth fractures, enamel erosion, the need to conserve remaining teeth by reinforcing them with foundation restorations, treatment of stubborn periapical infections, and the risk of failure from multiple fixed prosthetics. Bell noted that Multiple fixed prosthetics also enhance the chances of failure, i.e. ceramometal bridges. Harold Preiskel commented that the problem of restoring mutilated dentition challenges the skills of even the most experienced prosthodontist. Paranhos, Kanda,Ghalili & Kotick, discussed the reconstruction of worn mutilated dentition in a patient with multiple obstacles/risks including : enamelerosion/deficiency/hypoplasia , occlusal discrepancies, non-restorable teeth, repeated teeth fractures and problems with maintaining roots in the anterior region of the mandible and a goal of trying to preserve jawbone. Gurav, Ram & Khanna, discussed the occlusal rehab. of severely mutilated dentition : this case involved severe attrition of posterior teeth, enamel erosion, eroded teeth, loss/decrease of occlusal vertical dimension-the patient needs to have an increase in the occlusal vertical dimension via careful methodological alteration-in order to prevent TMJ joint problems and to prevent masticatory muscle chewing impairment - there is insufficient space, the occlusion needs to be stabilized, the tooth surface loss is severe, lost muscle tone, decreased masticatory muscle chewing function, loss of anterior guidance due to anterior teeth degeneration. There are also unnatural oblique forces on the posterior teeth & TMJ joint problems- Management of this with fixed prosthetics is complex and among the most difficult to restore. The OVD occlusal vertical dimension & interocclusal rest spaces need precise measurement, need to restore the loss of OVD as this affects the entire face, not just the perioral areas- and there is temperature hypersensitivity, severe caries/cavities on most teeth, a deep bite and decreased facial height at occlusion due to the lost OVD occlusal vertical dimension caused by the severe attrition of posterior teeth and there is severe periodontitis and inadequate height of mandibular anterior teeth, the teeth are too small for crowns, posts/cores and crown lengthening are needed, gingival gum recontouring is needed, need to reposition gum tissue, need to overcome posterior attrition and lost anterior guidance, and there is loss of posterior dis-occlusion. Posts are passive metal posts which strengthen the tooth at the cementoenamel junction, and they match the canals of the tooth.

Bilodeau noted that in a patient with mutilated dentition, her dentition could not be restored with prosthetics alone. Dua, Singh & Aghi described the abnormalities as " Mutilated Dentition". They noted the presence of Severe dentition attrition, loss of vertical dimension of occlusion, depressed facial appearance, unfavorable coordination of stomatognathic system, teeth fractures, increased temperature sensitivity, enamel erosion, and non-resolving periapical infections. Patel, Jayanti 11/30/2018) also described the abnormalities as " Mutilated Dentition". Patel defined it as grossly weakened, severely worn, badly broken down and added that it includes the fact that the amount of remaining tooth structure is less than the amount of tooth loss, meaning that the teeth lost is greater than the number of remaining teeth left. They also added the following other traits/symptoms: loss of occlusal vertical dimension aka lost vertical dimension of occlusion, lost teeth structure, uneven teeth wear, uneven plane of occlusion, poor esthetics, reduced chewing ability, centric defects, and abnormal occlusal contact patterns- posts and cores may be needed in order to use full coverage porcelain fused to metal fixed restoration of the entire dentition.

Daing, Singh & Dixit noted the following obstacles/risks: the possible need for full mouth crown lengthening, the surgical removal of hard/soft periodontal tissues to achieve increased tooth length, the surgical repositioning of periodontal tissues apically and the need to correct reduced vertical dimension, worn out dentition, collapsed bite-the collapsed bite prevents prosthodontic rehab until crown lengthening is done. The bones may need re-contouring to harmonize with tooth surface topography, short teeth make crowns problematic-i.e. short crown height due to loss of tooth structure. There is also the issue of uneven gingival gum contours.

Wankhade, Lokade & Rajguru, described the severe difficulties in prosthodontic rehab. Of mutilated dentition as follows: severely worn excess wear completely worn dentition-especially challenging due to loss of occlusal vertical dimension aka vertical dimension of occlusion, loss of teeth structure, uneven teeth wear, uneven plane of occlusion, damaged tooth cusps, flattened occlusal teeth surface, loss of anterior guidance function of anterior teeth that is needed for aesthetics-the restoration of anterior teeth is thus necessary, severe attrition of teeth, collapsed facial appearance due to loss of vertical occlusal dimension that needs to be restored, need to correct the occlusal plane and need to restore aesthetics ,prosthetic rehab. of severe loss of vertical dimension of occlusion or "vod" is risky and pronc to problems because of the complex structure of the stomatognathic system, and if the teeth are "bruxed/grinded" loss of anterior guidance occurs and posterior interferences occur, and the posterior interferences can trigger excess activity of the masseter/temporalis muscles-allowing generation of more forces to grind the teeth even more *aggressively.*

Ambulgekar, Sanadi Doshi & Gaikwad, also described the risks and obstacles of full mouth rehab. of mutilated dentition as follows: Surgical crown lengthening may be needed to ensure retention and form ,restoration must be performed on a periodontium free of inflammation for a good functional restorative result, and biological width needs to be preserved...Gingivectomy may be needed to eliminate periodontal pocket tissue and or sulcus wall tissue ,may need to remove overgrown gingival/periodontal pockets that could interfere with restoration, Bone margin removal may be needed -where tooth supporting bone is removed (ostectomy) the part of the tooth coronal to the alveolar crest may need lengthening, there can be issues with required bio width-the physical dimension of junctional epithelium and attached connective tissue, crestal bone may be lost to re-establish bio width. There needs to be at least 3 mm between restoration gingival gum margins and alveolar bone crest, there needs to be that 3 mm between that margin and bone crest to preserve attached gingival margins ,there may be collapsed bite, there may be a need for full mouth root canal before prosthodontic restoration is started, gingival gum recession is a risk after bone removal-thin gingival gum tissue is prone to recession, and there is a problematic risk regarding bio width-imposed by a restoration i.e. prosthetic device placed there in the bio width zone, which can cause gingival gum inflammation, periodontal pockets to form, and alveolar jawbone lost, gum/bone surgeries may be required ,i.e. osteoplasty/gingivectomy(tissue removal), the smile line has to be established ,need to evaluate occlusal planes both anterior and posterior in order to keep harmony and balance vs gingival gum contours, collapsed vertical dimensions/bite may require surgical crown lengthening, tissues may need elevating and/or repositioning, osseous bone resection may be needed to achieve proper distance between gum restoration margin and alveolar jawbone crest, restoration may need to be extended gingivally(gums) to create enough resistance and to protect retention form, gum contour alterations may be needed if the teeth are deficient, the restoration interface may need masking, and if the prosthetic restoration margin is placed too far below gum line, it can impinge on gingival gum attachment and violates bio width-osseous reduction jawbone material may need reduction/removal to keep bio width...and may need dental bond core/cast post if tooth structure is inadequate...

Jaafar Abduo mentioned occlusal interference that causes insufficient space for a prosthetic, and insufficient bone/gum support, for a porcelain fused to metal prosthetic. Dr Miles Cone DMD wrote that Obstacles & Risks include shortened dental arches, impaired masticatory chewing function, undulating occlusal planes, over-erupted opposing dentition, tipping, mesialization of freestanding teeth, and potential collapse of occlusal vertical dimension.

Chapter 13: My Dental Terror/Dental Panic

For many patients like me, going to the dentist is truly terrifying, panic filled and "white knuckling". A huge overwhelming frightening and terrifying experience. A monster sized and very dreaded ordeal, Even with Nitrous Oxide sedation. One that sends the heart racing and pounding into tachycardia, Shaking Tremors & Hyperventilation, as well as hot/cold flushes-the "fight or flight" reaction running on overdrive. **I also urge the readers to visit the website Dentalphobia.com and I urge the readers to read Phobia Free by Dr Harold Levinson MD.**

Dr Harold Levinson explains that cerebellar patients like me are prone to catastrophic anxiety, and rapid buildups of anxiety & are frequently found to have feelings of being alone, off balance, and having nothing and no one to hang onto emotionally, and that can trigger severe catastrophic flooding of cerebellar circuits and a cerebellar failure to inhibit/neutralize anxiety/panic. The patient will have difficulty breathing, tachycardia, heart pounding/racing, and dysmetric disinhibition of vital reflex functioning and catastrophic anxiety responses with rapid dysmetric heartbeats/pulse rates, feelings of overload and flooding, a need for familiar faces/persons-that symbolically represents the need for stable electromagnetic reference points.

Feelings of rejection can trigger flooding of cerebellar anxiety/panic circuits, feelings of being trapped, rapid buildup of paralyzing and terrifying emotion, disinhibited responses. severe anticipatory anxiety, emotional volatility, feelings of dying, powerful escalation of emotions, fear of losing emotional control, hypotensive cardiac reactions, dysmetric heartbeat with rapidity, fainting, vertigo, nausea, retching gagging emesis, racing heart/pulse, hyperventilation.

 Hambridge talks about the "terror of the dentist's chair".., "huge hurtful needles" ..."the whole dental experience terrifying me" the acrid antiseptic smell, the fear of being trapped, unable to move or escape, "an emotional wreck before an appointment", unable to sleep, the feeling of being physically sick before the appointment ,"prolonged agony" the sense of "dread" ,the procrastination of putting off the appointment as long as possible" the desperate wish for a calming influence, the having to be in absolute agony to make the appointment,42% of people are dental phobic from traumatic past experiences,38% of people are dental phobic due to fear of pain, and 20% of people are dental phobic due to a terror of needles, Not only do they risk unsightly deterioration of teeth, such intense terror level fear of dentists can have extremely tragic consequences ,Hansen describes how going to the dentist "makes her neurotic" : here are excerpts/clips from her WordPress blog to give you a poignant overview of what she terms as "neurotic" and it is really heartbreaking and heart rendering. Although some readers may see it as comical/humorous, it's anything but comical/humorous:

Hansen writes: an entire life terrified of dentists, constantly battling encroaching dental terror, needing/wanting a compassionate understanding of my traumatic childhood dental experiences, a lifelong dental terror, a world of dental terror, a major pronounced fear of dentists, dental terror from childhood dental trauma, countless terrorizing dental visits, no longer just words of dental terror.

Going to the dentist makes me neurotic, after all the dental terror I've been thru, it takes weeks just to get up the courage to phone for an appointment, dentistry=the topic at top of my mind, my biggest fear= going to the dentist.,, You would think that by now I would easily sail thru the dental appointments like a pro-but it's not so ,my dental avoidance behavior in full force, a sad pitiful case, they hate to see me coming because I'm so neurotic about the whole thing, they poke me with that metal death hook, they're gum sadists, other people who like dentists don't have to go very often. I'm crying like a baby for the nitrous oxide gas, they speak to me like they would to a cornered animal. I need to get the torture over with. I hate/dread the wicked metal dental prod. I'm like an elephant when it comes to dentistry. My memory for dental torture is detailed and long.,

After reading her dental story, I know that she is a kindred spirit, my clone, my duplicate, my doppelganger, my twin. It all describes ME perfectly and exactly.   It's almost like she voiced the very words I'm thinking of 24/7, my dental "obsession". Ulrich Klages described dental terror/panic with the following 'mini-vignettes" : Breaking into a cold sweat cowering in the corner ,butchery with no regard for patient suffering barbaric providers/procedures being filled with great mental pain a nightmare forever etched in my mind ...never again went near a dental office for a decade-remaining a slave to one's dental fears for life- until my teeth condition got progressively worse-deeply rooted convictions about dental suffering my heart in my throat, my fear of unbearable pain

 Susan Zakin described the dental experience as "Odontophobia" or "extreme dental fear/anxiety and I have summarized her observations as follows : So terrified of seeing a dentist that the patient refused to get his teeth cleaned for 9 yrs. although the patient is a tough Master Sergeant in the US Air Force & a veteran of Operation Desert Storm and is football player as well., this patient said to the dentist that the dentist could send the patient to Operation Desert Storm, or to Iraq, and added that the dentist was welcome to have people shoot the patient but pleaded and begged not to be sent to the dental clinic-the patient added that the patient can die or get blown up, but the patient prefers to do that rather than sit in the dental chair.

The patient also noted that he would rather endure danger or throbbing dental pain rather than be forced to visit a dentist. Susan Zakin added that these sorts of terrified dental patients anticipate and predict dental pain before the dental appointment even takes place. She adds that these terrified dental patients tend to report the following anecdotal traumatic past dental histories: dentists who ignored their protests of pain, dentists who held them down against their will, feelings of panic/helplessness, terrifying childhood dental visits, patients contemplating running out of a dental office at the prospect of even a simple dental cleaning. feelings of loss of control, feeling trapped in the dental chair, terrifying memories of sharp painful dental picks jabbed into tender gums, worrying/panicking if they feel that the dentist is not taking the time to listen, answer, explain, reassure and calm them, especially triggered if they feel the dentist is rushed/rushing…fears of anesthetics wearing off/failing to numb, past episodes of physiological " fight or flight" panic, especially if they feel the dentist was not responsive/sympathetic about the fear and pain,. and she noted that some terrified adult dental patients even whimper before any work is even done, many even have full blown panic attacks before any work is even started.

Jeff Elder described dental terror/dental PTSD as follows:

-when it comes to dental work, the patient just freezes up (in terror)... the treatment so terrifying that the patient stayed away for decades, and ended up with loose teeth and bad gums ,the patient held off until the toothache became unbearable-the patient commented that the dentist hurts you more than the toothache, he cited the research of Dr Philip Weinstein, clinical psychologist and co-founder of the Dental Fears Research Clinic, University of WA at Seattle. Dr Philip Weinstein, studies why people don't go to the dentist until advanced severe unbearable dental pain occurs and that severe pain reinforces the fear and adds to the problem of dental avoidance.

Stefan Bracha, wonders " Post-Traumatic Dental Care Anxiety"-is Dental Phobia a Misnomer? He explains the following " equation": Panic attacks + Phobic Avoidance=PTSD Post Traumatic Stress

Disorder + Traumatic Memories of highly Traumatizing Past Experiences + the memories of the Pain. Stefan Bracha, goes on to add the following additional information in further support of his "equation: Individuals who experienced painful dental treatments and perceived a lack of control in the dental situation -were 14 times more likely to also report higher dental fear and 16 times more likely to report being less than willing to return to dental treatment. He then posits that this should be conceptualized as PDTA Post Traumatic Dental Care Anxiety & should be classified as a form of PTSD in the DSM Diagnostic & Statistical Manual.

 DeJongh, & Fransen, & Dejongh examined psychological trauma phenomenon exposure and trauma symptoms in dental patients with dental anxiety. They concluded that horrific dental treatment experiences cause Dental PTSD. DeJongh added that 76% of anxious dental patients suffer from traumatic dental event memories and traumatic symptoms arising from it. Dejongh also noted that anticipatory pre-treatment anxiety is caused by high levels of intrusive past dental trauma memories from prior dental trauma events. Dejongh also noted the presence of recurrent intrusive dental trauma memories arising from horrific past dental experiences and patients struggling to find ways to avoid the recurrent "bad" memories. Jerry Bernson states that the higher the level of dental fear, the greater the desire to avoid dental treatment. She also said that the "'avoiders " tended to resort to "catastrophizing", self-distancing, self-distraction and desperate prayers filled with despair. She called these " self-reported dental coping strategies among fearful adult dental patients".

Cohen described "dental fright" experientially as follows: severe enough to cause feelings of exhaustion after the appointment, panic from smell of eugenol/cloves/cut dentine, panic from sensations of high frequency vibrations...feeling powerless trapped & vulnerable from laying back in the dental chair, gagging, bleeding, recalling traumatic past dental memories, out-of-body detachment, tremors, shakiness, sweating perspiration, intense galvanic skin, showing fear.

Kindism described dental terror in terms of "curled up in tears, crying because of being terrified' 'a well-established terror of dentists, panicked and frozen in fear as they laid in the chair." Kindism also described the terror as follows: attempting to pray away the cavities, envisioning hard x-rays cutting into tender gums, panic simply telling me to relax sets off alarm bells, total state of terror, massive anxiety attacks, sobbing in irrational terror like a child, filled with terrorizing fears, dentists are scary people known for terrorizing patients.

Dr Michael Breus describes dental terror in a unique way : dreams of teeth falling out, scary dreams, scary nightmares, he adds that the ancient Greeks tried to divine meaning behind teeth falling out dreams, Other cultures saw teeth falling out dreams as a foreboding of death,39% of participants in a study experienced teeth related dreams ,in 2018, Israeli scientists investigated theories about teeth dreams, using a sample of 200 undergraduate college students, psychological distress can manifest in dental discomfort symptoms, Reus refers to Coolidge & Bracken's study on recurrent teeth loss dreams, a sample of 28 undergraduate college students, those with the recurrent teeth loss dreams are more anxious/depressed, showed lower ego strength, were less satisfied with their lives , felt less control over their lives, were more concerned about death, and felt more hopeless. Breus also noted a " mouth tension link" to teeth loss dreams.

Holly Woolard, and Dr David Blende describe the dentally terrified as the toughest dental patients with multiple problems ,They would rather ride out an earthquake than visit the dentist, The mere thought of sitting with someone prodding in their mouth is downright terrifying, many have not been to a dentist in decades, they cannot bring themselves to go to a dentist, Some need several glasses of wine in order to get up the courage to make a call to a dentist, to them the hardest and bravest step is to pick up the phone to call a dentist, they feel helpless ,they are terrified of the thought of being in extremely close proximity to a dentist, Katherine Foley states too that 10% of the population is extremely dental phobic, filled with acute & intense fear of dentistry, and since 1969,there have been approx. a dozen dental phobia anxiety questionnaires/surveys, including Corah Dental Anxiety Scale(1969), Kleinknecht Dental Fear Survey, Stouthart Dental Anxiety Inventory, Weiner Dental Fear Questionnaire, Fear of Dental Treatment Cognitive Inventory, Modified Dental Anxiety Scale, & Index of Dental Fear/Dental Anxiety(2010 IDAF4CT) & the BMC Oral Health study -a sample of 6,000 people, cited by Armfield.

 The BMC study showed that 33% of the sample avoid dental care and have poor dental health. The 33% blamed it on past painful experiences and feared anticipated pain in the future. The BMC study quantified dental anxiety in the general population (see Poorsattar). There was also the Champong Sedation Anesthesia Progress on Dental Fear published study. The Champong study showed that a "half sample" avoided dentistry, and it examined dental phobia through the lens of need/demand for sedation dentistry. & there was also the Maggirias study on psychological factors and pain perception vs dental anxiety/phobia and the Mehrstedt study on oral health quality of life vs dental anxiety/phobia.

Randy Fiedler described dental terror in 'almost humorous poetic" form & I have extracted the most salient verses for you to ponder mental nerves are so sensitive as those in the mouth-pump them full of enough happy gas (nitrous oxide) to make having a cavity filled feel like winning the lottery. My childhood dentist was DR Iwilldrilldeeper, and he had excavation talents. pain=megaphone, poke around with power tools, dentist quickly finds bad teeth by determining which ones provoked the loudest screams, sadistic drug-free dentistry, interrogation while hitting nerves, could no longer be dragged to the dentist against my will, habit of avoiding dentists continued for many years, intense pain rendered me helpless, molars turning into barnacles, grisly ordeal, dentist looking down on me with disapproval.

Jill Alexandra describes her own battle with dental terror as follows: (
I have selected and summarized key items from her published story
about her dental terror): terrifying tornado of apprehension, drowning
in anxiety, a lifetime of horrific experiences caused me to avoid
dentists as much as possible, thereby destroying my teeth, my panic
and hyper-awareness, bad experiences, death grip of panic, terrifying
instruments of torture, I am one of the worst dental patients you could
have,

I can't breathe. Everything about it is a trigger for me, a relentless
bombardment of sensory overload and terror, shaking so badly from
panic, paralyzed with terror, terrified to even complain, the patient
from hell(me) had arrived, confessing my terror to him(dentist),dental
is the enemy, it terrifies you, my panic makes it so difficult to reveal
my terror, I keep my eyes closed the whole time…. I can disappear
into my own world, I tend to hyperventilate and need times for him to
stop, he knows it's far more than just average dental phobia, he knows
that my "tough as nails act" is superficial and transparent facade hiding
my intense fears, panic attacks, traumatic memory recalls, nervous
meltdowns, the mere sight of the office sends me into tailspins, my
constant struggle, I still get panicky and terrified every time I am
about to enter his office, my breathing gets constricted, my heart
pounds and I fight off the urge to flee...panic battle, my body goes
wrong, severe anxiety and panic is the enemy you do war with, it's an
enemy you can't do war with alone, Like me, she too has
ADHD/PTSD/PANIC !

Chapter 14: My Dental Anxiety/Panic/Phobia/PTSD

Ulrich Klages wrote about dental anxiety, dental sensitivity, and dental pain in which he viewed dental anxiety/ dental sensitivity as a predictor of dental pain in patients undergoing restorative dental procedures & his research found that high dental anxiety amplifies the perception of dental pain. My research has shown intriguing things like "Nothing Personal Doc but I hate dentists" (citing comment of Dr Mac Lee, dentist in Edna Texas. My own research has also shown issues like "insensitive comments by a childhood dentist that were carried over into adulthood traumatic dental memories-and my research has also shown that the imagination can send anxiety levels soaring, due to an innate fear of suffering pain while consciously aware. Samantha Liles says the whirring of the drill and the giant painful needles cause plenty of people to be too afraid to see a dentist. Some dental phobias are extremely intense-and getting some patients to come into a dental office for just a checkup is like 'pulling teeth". Daniel McNeil, l & Randall, Cameron, state that almost 50% of the population fear the dentist, and 10% avoid the dentist altogether.

ADHD and Dental Anxiety

Blomqvist & Holmberg did a research study on Salivary Cortisol levels & dental anxiety in kids with ADHD. They determined that the ADHD kids, especially those with severe hyperactivity, have a different stress reaction (as measured by salivary cortisol) during dental visits and are more dentally anxious than those kids without ADHD. Those without ADHD show lower stress reactivity. There is however very little research on Adults with ADHD in terms of Dental Anxiety.

<u>ADULT Autism/Aspergers/ASD and Dentistry and dental anxiety/panic/phobia</u>

Adult Autism/ASD/Aspergers is known for cerebellar caused anxiety/panic/phobic behavior in dental settings, and I have Aspergers (highest function Autism).

Blomqvist, Dahllof & Bejerot published a research study on Experiences of Dental Care & Dental Anxiety in Adults with Autism/ASD/Aspergers, at the Karolinska Institute in Sweden. I have summarized their findings for you, as follows: The Autism/ASD/Asperger Adult Dental Patients complained more about dental pain/discomfort than "normal" adult dental patients, and the Autism/ASD/Aspergers Adult patients felt that they were more "forced" into dental treatment than "normal adult dental patients. The authors state that more methods to support these "special needs" adult dental patients need to be developed in order to reduce the negative dental experiences and dental anxiety in these "special needs " adult dental.

patients. 5% of these special needs adult population avoids dental treatment due to anxiety/panic/phobia-as they regard a dental setting as a danger.

These "special needs" adult dental patients complain of feeling helpless, and they report a history of past pain/trauma/negative dental experiences. Many of these "special needs adult dental patients are phobic of needles, syringes and injections and have an intense terror of dental pain/discomfort/dental bleeding.

Their perception/hypersensitivity to dental pain is fueled by their extreme degrees of anxiety/fear and by their hyper-reactive and hyper-sensitive sensory mechanisms. They have an intense fear/panic about dental pain being uncontrollable and unbearable & show unusual sensory sensitivities/responses to stimuli. They tend to be over-reactive to sound, light, visuals, and even to tastes, scents, and textures. They tend to be flooded with unusual and extreme reactions to even mild benign stimuli. They show abnormal responses to dental sensory stimuli and over-react. Over 40% of these special needs adults show dental over-reactivity. The authors of this study commented that there are very few dental research studies on these special needs adults.

 The authors of this paper also commented that these special needs adults are difficult to utilize in dental research due to their "impaired prediction of pain/distress, their difficulty with wrongful expectation of pain and their "highly unpredictable inner autistic world", as well as due to their difficulty with new unfamiliar sensory inputs/events, their impaired perception, their inflexibility, and their extreme anxiety. Blomqvist, Dahllof & Bejerot used the following format for their research: a double cohort adult group arrangement of both special needs adult dental patients and control group members without special needs. It took place in Stockholm Sweden in 2008, 47 special needs adults vs 69 normal controls. Those with neurologic diagnoses were excluded and so were intellectually disabled persons. Some of the special needs adults were selected at a neuropsychiatric clinic in Stockholm Sweden and others from an Autism community facility group home in Stockholm Sweden. The 69 normal controls were 34 men and 35 women from 6 dental clinics in Stockholm Sweden. and all were screened for autism symptoms. The special needs adults were often found to generate complaints of insufficient numbing/anesthesia and excessive pain, and many griped that they were forced into dental treatment.

 The following statistically based testing/diagnostic models were used to measure anxiety/panic: Corah Dental Anxiety Scale (1969) the DAS Dental Anxiety Scale that includes measurement of anticipatory waiting time anxiety, and the Revised Dental Beliefs survey that includes perception of dentist behavior and how the dentist delivered care (performed) & it includes perceived dentist attitudes regarding dental care. Blomqvist, Dahllof & Bejerot also explained that these special needs adult dental patients (on the autism spectrum) report recurrent dental pain, insufficient numbing anesthetic, and feelings of being pressured/coerced/forced into dental treatment that they were not prepared for nor expecting.

Their scores on these areas were statistically higher than those of the "normal controls" group. These "on the spectrum' patients were also noted for "griping" that the dentist seems hurried and, in a rush, therefore the care must not be very good, and they also state that they feel helpless in the dental chair and feel that they cannot have a brief rest break where the treatment is briefly interrupted, when they feel a need for the rest break. These "on the spectrum" dental patients also claimed to feel rushed and hurried by the dental provider, and so they begin to worry about receiving less than competent skilled care, that is not high quality and not being performed properly and they also worry that the dentist might not be skilled enough to deal with their fears, sensitivities, discomfort, pain and the dental problems needing treatment. These " on the spectrum" dental patients also reported that there was more pain than expected. and that they were suffering from the pain, and it made them feel that they were even "more forced" into receiving the treatment. They reported repeated instances of insufficient numbing anesthetic.

They react intensely to insufficient numbing anesthetic levels, and to the resulting pain. Those on the autism spectrum reported insufficient numbing pain twice as often as the non-ASD control subjects. ASD (autism spectrum) tends to have a very low pain threshold limit tolerance and exhibit a greater need for anesthetics likely also due to their sensory over-responsivity and over-reactivity and tendency to sensorially overload. They report more instances of sensory "overload" from the pain/discomfort, and they appear to have a lower pain tolerance limit than the control group, and a greater need for more frequent re-numbing and a need for higher total doses of numbing anesthetic, i.e. more propofol was needed. The "on the spectrum" patients also showed heightened stress from dental pain and their anxiety reinforces their pain, their pain/anxiety/stress levels are very high during dental treatment. They complain repeatedly of pain even with re-numbing, and report "sensory overload" caused by their over-responsivity and over-sensitivity, visually olfactorily, auditorily, tactilely, and kinesthetically and they process noxious stimuli differently especially visually.

Sewell says the dentist/hygienist/assistant need to be aware of the following: unusauditorily, itivities including sounds of drills/suctions/visual/auditory/tactile/olfactory/taste/color/texture oversensitivity very low pain tolerance/pain limits tendency toward inflammatory and autoimmune issues and caries and xerostomia sleep apnea is common… so is bruxism/grinding fear of opening the mouth acute anxiety/panic over-reaction to toothpaste/prophy paste oral burning sensation difficulty with brushes/floss i.e. over-reaction to bristle texture tendency toward gingivitis/periodontitis, gum recession, gum overgrowth difficulty and chewing/biting/swallowing. (Blomqvist, Dahllof & Bejerot say that training on-the-autism-spectrum adult dental patients BEFORE treatment procedures can be helpful, e.g. what to expect, and how, why, when, and where.

Leah Stein & Jose Polido, Shulamite Green, & Ayelet Ben-Sasson, state that the autism spectrum population is at high risk for oral disease and that they are known to have significant sensory processing difficulties that pose a challenge for dental providers. They have a unique sensory over-responsivity and sensory hyper-arousal and sensory defensiveness across all sensory domain, and this even affects their dental hygiene home care, making it difficult, especially with regard to intraoral hyper-sensitivity, for instance difficulty tolerating bristles of a toothbrush, due to texture which triggers tactile over-reaction for them.

Shulamite Green, & Ayelet Ben-Sasson found that 70% of kids on the autism spectrum have sensory over-responsivity, compared to 10% of non-spectrum kids. Shulamite Green, & Ayelet Ben-Sasson also noted the following: hyper-vigilance, ADD/ADHD, & Autonomic Hyper-Arousal are also found on Autism spectrum dental patients. These patients tend to repeatedly scan their environment in order to detect threatening stimuli. They also have difficulty in regulating negative emotional affectivity-e.g. threat based emotional regulation. They also present with over-activation of affect driven behavior, and can show uncontrollability and overreaction to perceived possible threats such as sensory threats, and this can become habituated thru repeated conditioned responses,

They also have difficulty disengaging from the "provoking " stimuli. Benign images can be misinterpreted as threatening. They over-react to environmental sensory stimuli including stimuli within dental environments. Their emotional regulation tends to be based on perceived threats and on perceived possible threat risks. They tend to over-focus and perseverate and can show over-selective attention, and react intensely to aversive sensory stimuli, they are prone to catastrophic anxiety/floods of anxiety (Levinson, Harold), The Lepicard study (2003) (and the published research of Dr Harold Levinson MD as well) showed that they also tend to exhibit poor balance/postural control/coordination and poor modulation of cerebellar vestibular proprioceptive input.

 They also are known for exhibiting paradoxical reactions to medications- such as anxiolytic medications actually triggering and exacerbating the anxiety. In fact, (Lepicard, 2003) has shown that administering anxiolytic (anti-anxiety) medications to those with anxiety and administering anxiogenic (anxiety triggering) medications) to the normal controls without anxiety-actually reverse the group differences so that the non-anxious control.

the group now had poorer balance/postural control than the anxiety prone patients. Shulamite Green, & Ayelet Ben-Sasson, Ayelet added that : the anxiety prone autism spectrum patients tend to have stronger auditory startle reactions to sound than the control group (non-anxiety prone) and that the autism spectrum patients tend to show preferential attention to aversive unexpected noises and that leads to their over-reactivity-e.g. stimulus + physical reaction = intero-ceptive conditioning common to anxiety disorders ,The autism spectrum patients tend to show avoidance of fearful stimuli and tend to show phobic responses to aversive stimuli, leading to avoidance of feared aversive stimuli, and they tend to exhibit intense over-responsivity and intense over-reaction. Autism spectrum patients tend to be at high risk for fear conditioning and they have difficulty reducing response to threatening feared stimuli, especially if the stimuli are frequent in occurrence.

Dr Marcia Eckerd, Ph.D., in her blog about '" Surviving the Dentist for Adults with Aspergers, noted the following: "Aspies"(those with Aspergers) tend to have sensory hypersensitivity and struggle with the sensory challenges of dental settings, including the feeling of "visual auditory" sensory overload in dental settings, and they tend to feel overwhelmed with sensory overload in dental settings.

 PDTA Post Traumatic Dental Care Anxiety.

Bracha wrote that those with painful dental treatment experiences were 14 times more likely to report a high degree of dental fear & 16 times more likely to be unwilling to return to dental treatment Bracha added that Dental Phobia is really PTDA Post Traumatic Dental Care Anxiety.

DeOliveira Solis noted that traumatized patients tend to have a higher degree of chronic pain ,depression, and various odd physical symptoms and that these traumatized patients have more pain during/after periodontal gum probing than patients without traumatic disorders, and that the traumatic stress these patients experienced from intense emotionally charged events-can increase the odds of orofacial pain, & can affect the biomechanics of mastication(biting/chewing) and ultimately can result in a compromised periodontal condition

Autumn Phelps describes "Spa like Distraction", She mentioned the following: Our job is to figure out how to make someone so comfortable that they can put traumatic past experiences out of their minds (citing Dr Donald Richardson). Allison Thompson describes what she calls the "fear factor" and how dentists "sink their teeth into efforts to end the dread" mentions for example Dr Steve Lindstrom, a dentist in Sheboygan Wisconsin, who burns candles to lessen the dental antiseptic smell.

Chapter 15: Cerebellum & Trigeminal Neuralgia-How they are Connected

I have cerebellar Trigeminal Neuralgia & Experimental full mouth Root Canal Nerve Removal by Dr Schamis stopped very close to all of my pain!

Russo noted the following important findings as follows: There is cerebellar hyperresponsiveness to **Trigeminal** nociception in migraine headaches with aura. There was a significantly greater cerebellar activation observed in patients with Migraine headache-with-aura. There is an abnormal visual pathway response to **Trigeminal** stimulation. There is a functional integration between visual and **Trigeminal** pain networks in the mechanisms underlying migraine headaches-with-aura. There is also an abnormal cerebellar response to **Trigeminal** stimulation. There was also observed a dysfunctional cerebellar inhibitory control on thalamic sensory gating, impinging on the advanced visual processing cortical areas with patients experiencing migraine headaches with aura.

(Rutgers University,10/6/2016) found that the **Trigeminal** nerve is being compressed by the superior Cerebellar artery. Bakhsheshian posits that **Trigeminal Neuralgia** is at least partly due to Cerebellar Compression. Soumya discusses a cerebellar disease patient with a cerebella-**TRIGEMINAL** defect.
(Gomez Lopez Hernandez Syndrome) includes Cerebella-**Trigeminal dysplasia with Trigeminal Nerve Anesthesia.** Eric Alan Moulton (Eric Alan) published his research findings about the **cerebellar processing of Trigeminal Neuralgia pain.** It was based on Functional MRI & Diffusion Tensor Imaging of Cerebellar Responses

to Pain in the **Trigeminal** System. (Clinical Trials at McLean Hospital, for the US Federal Government). I have summarized below the results of his research study: The Cerebellum is involved in processing pain, including **Trigeminal** pain. Pain triggers a Cerebellar Activation, as verified by functional MRI & Diffusion Tensor Imaging. The cerebellum functions during painful events and the cerebellum are believed to modulate neural encoding of noxious pain stimuli.

The cerebellum responds (activates as shown by imaging) to experimental pain. Moulton feels that the cerebellum has been overlooked as a potential pain processor & he feels that more research is needed in this as it could lend invaluable insight into basic physiological circuiting involved with the modulation of pain. (Moulton,2012-2016) adds that the cerebellum serves as an integrator of aversive pain stimuli and related adaptive motor behavior. The cerebellum modulates the emotional/cognitive experience/perception of pain from sensory stimuli. Moulton adds that in terms of human trigeminal modeling of experimental pain -all the pain related circuitry involved can be imaged along with the cerebellum. Moulton suggests that what is needed now is to map cerebellar activations related to sensory coding of noxious pain stimuli. Moulton adds that what is also needed is correlating of functional cerebellar activity to anatomical connections- and- the distinguishing between pain and its anticipation, based on cerebellar responses and anatomical connectivity, in order to determine if physical pain and aversive pain response images engage cerebellar circuitry.

Meier, Snyder Dietrich & Walberg, Patrick & Robinson, Saab, Bukowska, and Holtzman have all found the presence of Direct/Collateral Trigeminal input to Cerebellar structures. **Trigeminal** Brainstem Nuclei Interpolaris, Oralis & Principalis project predominately ipsi lateral to the Cerebellar regions. Cerebellar cortices receive mostly ipsilateral and to a lower extent, bilateral fibers from several **Trigeminal** brainstem nuclei. (see: Dietrichs & Walberg,

Munoz & Santos, Munoz Rojas Castroviejo & Ruggieri, and Choudhary, all did research on Cerebellum-**TRIGEMINAL**-Dermal Dysplasia, including Trigeminal Nerve Anesthesia, Choudhary's research includes cerebellar pons vermi fusion, absence of cerebellar vermis and fusion of cerebellar hemispheres. AJNR, noted the *Trigeminal Nerve* Anesthesia trait coupled with the following cerebellar traits: rare malformation of cerebellum, agenesis/hypo genesis of cerebellar vermis, absence of cerebellar vermis, dorsal fusion of cerebellar hemispheres, cerebellar dental nuclei and superior cerebellar peduncles, cerebellar ataxia, flat cerebellum, parietal alopecia, craniofacial abnormalities, vertebral abnormalities, cardiac/cardiovascular anomalies and abnormalities, and musculoskeletal abnormalities.

Chitre also noted that teeth loss connects also to **TRIGEMINAL** Motor Nucleus volume changes, as well as to **TRIGEMINAL** sensory features including the TRIGEMINAL NERVE and teeth loss is also connected to decreased brain matter volume in the **TRIGEMINAL** MOTOR NUCLEUS and increase in THE   **TRIGEMINAL** SENSORY TRACT NUCLEI & in the **TRIGEMINAL** SPINAL TRACT NUCLEUS. Teeth Loss also affects neurons in the **TRIGEMINAL** BRAINSTEM SENSORY NUCLEI as the teeth loss causes increased somatosensory excitability in those nuclei. Haggard notes that the main sensory nerve innervating the orofacial area is the **TRIGEMINAL** nerve which is a mixed nerve with sensory & motor fibers. These sensory nerve endings innervate teeth, oral mucosa, mastication muscles and facial skin. The periodontal ligament attaches the tooth to the bones of the upper or lower jaw. That ligament is innervated by mechanoreceptors which project to the brainstem via the Trigeminal Ganglion.

 The mechanoreceptors respond to stimuli applied to the tooth that the ligament supports. (AJNR) noted the *Trigeminal Nerve* Anesthesia trait coupled with the following cerebellar traits: rare malformation of cerebellum, agenesis/hypo genesis of cerebellar vermis, absence of cerebellar vermis, dorsal fusion of cerebellar hemispheres, cerebellar dentate nuclei and superior cerebellar peduncles, cerebellar ataxia, flat cerebellum, parietal alopecia, and craniofacial abnormalities. Eric Moulton wrote that the cerebellum responds to noxious pain stimuli and that the cerebellum is involved in pain processing, and that noxious pain input conducts to the cerebellum, and that cerebellar activity occurs during pain & that there are functional roles for the cerebellum relating to pain, including pain connected to motor control/cognition/emotion. (Also see this book's related but separate section on Moulton's cerebellar research into **Trigeminal Neuralgia** pain.)

Baarbe,Julianne & Yielder, Paul et al did research on subclinical recurrent neck pain and its effects on the cerebellum. I have summarized the key points for you as follows: It was to specifically examine how that neck pain impacted on motor skills and motor skill training to see if neural plasticity was shown by the cerebellum. Baarbe & Yielder posited that the cerebellum processes pain inputs and sensory inputs and that the cerebellum interacts with the motor cortex in patients in pain due to a functional connectivity between the cerebellum and the motor cortex.

They additionally stated that cerebellar inhibition may not reduce to the same extent as in those patients without pain, The patients who had mild recurrent neck pain were given a motor skills acquisition test. The pain patients may not show the same cerebellar inhibition as those without pain. Note that the cerebellar inhibition follows the motor acquisition task. They posited further that pain changes cerebellar-motor cortex interaction. Baarbe & Yielder added that Neck pain influences sensorimotor function in older adults. Pain can cause poor sensorimotor performance -and that the motor consequences of pain are partly integrated thru cerebella-thalamocortical loops in the cerebellum. Cerebellar lobules show activation during pain processing.

Patients with cerebellar infarct showed greater sensitivity to experimental pain & poor motor coordination on cerebellar tasks. Painful inputs from the neck result in altered cerebellar integration and altered expression of motor outputs. There is functional connectivity between cerebellum and motor areas. Cerebellar Inhibition "CBI" as shown by magnetic stimulation to affect/involve both cerebellum and motor cortex - the inhibited response =cerebellar inhibition. Neck pain and neck dysfunction alters and impacts both neck & limb sensorimotor function & motor control. Recurrent neck pain alters motor learning and there is tendency of maladaptive motor patterns to be maintained, potentially setting up a cycle of recurrent chronic pain. Perceptual disturbances can result from chronic recurring neck pain. Spinal manipulation may affect cerebellar/cortical interaction and may improve cerebellar inhibition of neck pain. Recurrent neck pain influences cerebellar functional connectivity.

 Neck Pain patients have reduced cerebellar inhibition of pain from motor skill activities. The motor acquisition tasks included typing alphabet sequence patterns quickly on a computer keyboard. This task activates the cerebellum. Spinal manipulation of neck pain increases cerebellar pain inhibition in neck pain patients-as much as a 90% increase in cerebellar pain inhibition after a spinal manipulation vs 50% average normal inhibition rate in patients without neck pain. The cerebellum receives and integrates inputs from the intervertebral regions of the neck. Spinal Manipulation increases the magnitude of cerebellar pain inhibition. Cerebellar lobules 6 & 7b are important for pain related adaptations in motor control.

There are Cerebellar response differences in neck pain patients -The neck pain alters the way their cerebellums function during motor acquisition tasks such as typing alphabet patterns on a keyboard. Spinal Manipulation is a type of cerebellar facilitator, Cerebellar Stimuli affects /interacts with neurons in the motor cortex. Cervical spine manipulation is also very beneficial, not just spinal manipulation, Spinal/Cervical Spine Manipulation has mechanical effects on cerebellar circuits. Lastly, there is heightened cerebellar activity in acute/chronic pain states.

Dyslexia & **Trigeminal Neuralgia**-How they are Connected.

(Jordan, Ian,) noted that Some forms of Visual Dyslexia are produced in association with or by the **Trigeminal** nerve. (Longhurst,Robert) notes that a large number of dyslexics complain of Jaw problems and in some patients the **Trigeminal** nerve may be affected-adding that **Trigeminal** problems may result from DSD Dorsal Stream Dysfunction & that the DSD may be a causative factor in Dyslexia. (DaSilva,) noted that the strongest proprioceptive pathway to treat dyslexia is the **Trigeminal** pathway.

ADHD & **Trigeminal Neuralgia**-How they are connected.

Chadd purports the efficacy of external **Trigeminal** nerve stimulation as a treatment for ADHD. They add that ETNS External **Trigeminal** nerve stimulation treatment yields a statistically significant improvement in ADHD symptoms.

CEREBELLUM **& TRIGEMINAL NEURALGIA**-HOW THEY ARE CONNECTED

Russo noted the following important findings as follows: There is **cerebellar** hyperresponsiveness to **Trigeminal** nociception in migraine headaches with aura. There was a significantly greater **cerebellar** activation observed in patients with Migraine headache-with-aura. There is an abnormal visual pathway response to **Trigeminal** stimulation. There is a functional integration between visual and **Trigeminal** pain networks in the mechanisms underlying migraine headaches-with-aura. There is also an abnormal **cerebellar** response to **Trigeminal** stimulation. There was also observed a dysfunctional **cerebellar** inhibitory control on thalamic sensory gating, impinging on the advanced visual processing cortical areas with patients experiencing migraine headaches with aura. (Rutgers University) found that the **Trigeminal** nerve is being compressed by the superior **Cerebellar** artery. Bakhsheshian, posits that **Trigeminal Neuralgia** is at least partly due to **Cerebellar** Compression

<u>Dysautonomia & **Trigeminal Neuralgia**-How they are connected.</u>

(Mennillo) states that chewing is activated by the largest cranial nerve-the **Trigeminal** nerve that is connected to the parasympathetic nervous system. (Mennillo) further adds that this system is involved in conserving/restoring energy, slowing the heart, lowering blood pressure, promoting digestion, regulating sleep/wake cycles, controlling alertness and attention and calming the body.

<u>Cerebellar Neurology of Dental Pain/Fear -A Brief Summary of the Literature</u>

Michael Meier researched the neural aspects of Painful Dental Stimuli including the "FEAR" factor involved. Here is a summary of his findings that are relevant to this book:

Dentine Hypersensitivity Pain is encoded in the Cortical Pain System. Fear Responses triggered by Dental Pain exhibit significantly stronger activity within the neuronal fear network as compared to equal pain of spinal origin, indicating that enhanced susceptibility to tooth pain connects to fear conditioning. The tooth pain in his research was defined as sharp short pain from stimuli like eating, drinking and brushing teeth. Dental phobics often react badly to remarkably severe dental pain especially if the dental pain is of protracted duration. Dentinal stimulation of teeth can induce short sharp teeth pain. There are supraspinal neuronal responses to tooth pain that trigger fear. Brain regions activated by noxious painful electrical stimuli to dentinal areas include the **<u>CEREBELLUM</u>**. Dental Pain may have a possible connection to the **<u>Cerebellum anterior and posterior lobes.</u>** Teeth pain can trigger brain activation patterns similar to those associated with spinal pain. Cold Air is a natural tooth pain stimulus.

The fear of dental pain triggers the fear network in the body. (Meier, + Peyron, Apkarian & Farrell) all posit that Dental Pain related **Cerebellar** activity has been demonstrated. (Borsook)and Meier conducted research studies of **Cerebellar** activation in acute dental pain. Tooth Brushing Stimuli evoked ipsilateral **Cerebellar** activity, sensorimotor **Cerebellar** activation & Limbic **Cerebellar** activation.

<u>PTSD & **Trigeminal Neuralgia**</u>: A Fascinating Connection

 Dr Andrew Leuchter researched the use of External **Trigeminal** Nerve Electronic Stimulation as a possible treatment for PTSD. It is a 2nd phase study of the effectiveness of External **Trigeminal** Nerve Electrical Stimulation for Military Veterans with PTSD. This is a research study under the direction of Dr Andrew Leuchter at UCLA Semel Institute for NeuroScience & Human Behavior, where Dr Leuchter is a professor of Psychiatry & BioBehavioral Sciences. The Non-invasive electrodes develop small electrical currents to stimulate the **Trigeminal** Nerve-the largest & most complex of the Cranial nerves. This nerve projects to brain structures that relay signals to areas involved with PTSD. Additional studies on this are published in the journal Neuromodulation. The electrodes are placed on foreheads each night over the **Trigeminal** nerve for 8 hrs. A small portable battery powered ETNS Electronic **Trigeminal** Nerve Stimulation Device is used to deliver sequences of electrical pulses to stimulate the **Trigeminal** Nerve for 8 weeks.

(AJNR) noted the ***Trigeminal Nerve*** Anesthesia trait coupled with the following cerebellar traits: rare malformation of cerebellum, agenesis/hypo genesis of cerebellar vermis, absence of cerebellar vermis, dorsal fusion of cerebellar hemispheres, cerebellar dentate nuclei and superior cerebellar peduncles, cerebellar ataxia, flat cerebellum, parietal alopecia, craniofacial abnormalities, vertebral abnormalities, cardiac/cardiovascular anomalies and abnormalities, and musculoskeletal abnormalities.

Chapter 16: Teeth Loss – Neurological Neuropsychiatric Neuropsychological Effects

For ME, the risk of teeth loss has been a 24/7 TERROR! That's why I fled Florida, to save my teeth.

Chitre provides a fascinating analysis of the effects of tooth loss on the brain. That research clearly shows further evidence of why my experimental dental prosthetics are actually "good " for the health of my cerebellar impaired brain.

Chitre, and Velundandi speak of tooth loss and proprioception, and explains how the teeth connect with and are correlated to the other organs in the body, via brain nerves which aid in sensory reception and proprioception, The teeth have a correlation with parts of the brain. Tooth loss impairments can lead to impaired proprioception and even altered emotional function. The teeth provide input to the brain and the teeth are connected to balance and gravity. Chitre and Velundandi notes that a sample survey of adults who had 6 or more teeth removed experienced depression and anxiety, because teeth loss is connected to motor and emotional complications as well as to cognitive impairment and altered emotional function. Tooth loss has cognitive, physical, and emotional impacts.

I have found in the course of my research on teeth loss that teeth loss has long term physical/emotional effects on the brain. For example, molar removal was connected to subsequent undesirable sustained long term neuro-plastic brain changes. Additionally teeth loss can result in diminished oro-facial motor skill and diminished somato-sensory activity as well as decrease in gray brain matter volume of the basal ganglia and decreased nucleus of hypothalamus brain matter, which in turn affects motor control, learning ability and emotional stability, and the decreased brain matter volume can be connected to steep cognitive declines including decreased brain matter volume in the nucleus accumbens (related to motivation and motor learning)which is connected to steep declines in cognitive skill. Additionally, they note that teeth loss resulted in increased fear-based volume in the entorhinal cortex that affects the hippocampus- the enlarged volume due to anxiety/fear triggered by teeth loss.

The teeth loss also resulted in stereognosis defects and proprioception defects. Teeth loss also is linked to decreased volume in somatosensory and premotor cortex areas and can cause decreased jaw motor skill representation and diminished oro-facial motor skill. Teeth loss also resulted in decreased basal ganglia volume-the basal ganglia contribute to motor control, learning ability and emotional reactivity. Teeth loss also connected to decreased hypothalamus function. Teeth loss also is connected to decreased volume of the frontal association cortex involved in motor planning. working memory, and problem-solving skills.

The teeth loss also is connected to increased and enlarged volume in temporal limbic forebrain regions including the amygdala that regulates fear/anxiety. The increased volume in that area/region caused by teeth loss-is associated with excessive fear/anxiety. Teeth loss was also associated with increased gray matter volume in regions controlling fear/anxiety and learning as well as a decrease in gray matter related to motor movement, emotions, working memory and problem solving. Osseo-perception was also negatively affected by teeth loss. Teeth loss also affected brainstem regions.

 (See also Avivi-Arber, who also wrote about excessive fear/anxiety from teeth loss in a study of widespread volumetric brain changes following teeth loss,)They also noted that teeth loss connects also to TRIGEMINAL Motor Nucleus volume changes, as well as to TRIGEMINAL sensory features including the TRIGEMINAL

NERVE and teeth loss is also connected to decreased brain matter volume in the TRIGEMINAL MOTOR NUCLEUS, and increase in THE   TRIGEMINAL SENSORY TRACT NUCLEI & in the TRIGEMINAL SPINAL TRACT NUCLEUS. Teeth Loss also affects neurons in the TRIGEMINAL BRAINSTEM SENSORY NUCLEI as the teeth loss causes increased somato-sensory excitability in those nuclei. Teeth loss is even linked to increased cerebro-vascular risk including silent infarction Those people with silent infarctions had greater number of lost teeth than persons without the silent infarction, 6-10 lost teeth in the silent infarction patients.

 They also noted that Teeth loss also connects to Parkinson's Disease. Parkinson's patients have more missing teeth on average than persons without Parkinson's.
i.e. an average of 13 missing teeth vs the non-Parkinson's sample with an average of 8 missing teeth. And there was a greater incidence of periodontal disease in Parkinson patients with teeth losses than in the non-Parkinson's patients. Teeth Loss/Periodontal Disease is highly correlated with Parkinson's disease.

RJ Shah, made the following discovery regarding Teeth Loss: Difficulty emotionally accepting teeth loss, including feeling unprepared for the unexpected shock, depression, restricted socialization/social activity, a "terrible psychological shock" a "burden'', psychosocial difficulties, a sense of "losing part of oneself", devastating psychological sense of loss, a feeling of wanting to "hide in shame", a loss of self-confidence, shaken self-confidence. restricted food intake, restricted choice of food, avoidance of public places, decreased enjoyment of eating at public food establishments, avoiding speaking, singing, and laughing, avoidance of social interaction, avoidance of close/intimate relationships including impaired sexuality, avoidance of mirrors and reflective devices due to facial changes, upset over facial appearance. avoidance of looking at pictures of oneself, social anxiety/fear/distress.

Shetty,Mody,Kumar (et al) noted that: Extensive teeth loss can represent a "threat" to self and thus trigger anxiety, fear, distress, despair and depression. as well as a sense of hopelessness. as people tend to have an emotional investment in their teeth and appearance. It also triggers feelings of body part loss including shame. For some patients their teeth have become so invested with meaning that the loss of the teeth is perceived as catastrophic. Alterations to one's mouth can trigger bodily change anxiety.

Teeth play a very dominant role in one's life, (Costa,) also noted the psychological and emotional effects of teeth loss. Costa described teeth loss as an intense emotional trauma that can severely affect wellbeing and that can have a dramatic effect on appearance and self-perception. Costa added that one's whole life is lived through one's teeth. Costa also commented that people can be totally unprepared for the shock of teeth loss and have great difficulty accepting the loss. (Friedman, Landesman & Wexler indicated that teeth loss is linked to maladaptive depression, impaired quality of life, emotional despair for a protracted time period, anxiety, fear, insecurity and can even lead to "emotional collapse" over feared loss of teeth.

 Similarly (Cariati) explains that dento-facial deformities from teeth loss create psychosocial distress including insecurity. (Chee & Lee,) noted in dwarf dental patients that the patient's emotional attachment to their own teeth precluded the use of implants requiring teeth extractions.

(Wiener) performed research studies on Comorbid Depression/Anxiety/Behavioral disorders in patients whose teeth were extracted. (Jain, 6/2013) Prosthodontics should be concerned with conservation of what remains rather than meticulous replacement of what has been lost. (Shin) states that lost teeth can cause cognitive impairment and the prosthodontic rehab. of lost teeth is important for the maintenance of cognitive function. Teeth Loss is associated with decreased hippocampus function, decreased acetylcholine levels in the hippocampus, and loss of discriminative learning ability. Makiura et al). Molar teeth loss is associated with a reduced number of hippocampus pyramidal cells that deliver sensory input. (Kondo, & Yamazaki,) indicated that Teeth Loss is also associated with neurodegenerative markers.

Dental Prosthetics reduce cognitive decline. (Kondo,K,) reported that the loss of teeth is a risk factor for Alzheimer's Dementia, The risk of Alzheimer's Dementia increases as the number of remaining teeth decreases.(Kusaga) observed a relationship between chewing and dementia and stated that the number of teeth + molar occlusion chewing may influence the development of Alzheimer's Dementia-& Mastication was viewed as an indicator of brain function in elderly people. David Ricketts and (Science Direct present a FASCINATING opinion on Teeth Loss, one that actually directly applies to my own dental case. I know this information is "spot on target" from my own dental experience. Here is what they wrote: Occlusion refers to the bite relationship of teeth in the same jaw as well as the relationship of teeth in opposing jaws and refers to the way that the maxillary and mandibular teeth come together. They found that a large disruption of occlusal scheme is more likely to give rise to symptoms, a small but significant group of patients will find minor modifications to their occlusal scheme to be highly destructive and disharmonious and lead to symptoms out of proportion to the size of the discrepancy-WHICH EXPLAINS WHY hypersensitive patients like me cannot tolerate having non-wisdom teeth missing. It literally "disrupts my dental-emotional harmony". (Yamazaki, et al) did a research study on the effect of teeth loss on spatial memory. She found that teeth loss accelerates spatial memory impairment, especially extracted molar teeth. 7 weeks after molar extraction, maze performance scores were significantly lower in the teeth loss group than in the non-extraction group. The number of extracted teeth also affect hippocampus cell density. Teeth play an important role in the prevention of spatial memory impairment.

Lin did research on the link between cognitive decline and masticatory dysfunction in the elderly. She found that teeth loss is a risk factor for a decline in cognitive function. Teeth loss also increases dementia/senility. Risk-decreased mastication is associated with diminished cognitive function. There is also a connection between cognitive decline and worsening teeth condition. Additionally the "Nun" study referred to by Lin(1/5/2018) shows that the number of missing teeth is associated with the degree of risk of dementia-the more teeth missing the greater the risk of dementia, Watanabe noted the following : Chewing scores decreased rapidly with the loss of teeth after the onset of mild dementia + there is a relationship between the number of teeth and the number of occlusions, versus the volume of gray matter in the brain.

 In individuals with small amounts of remaining teeth, the volume near the hippocampus was decreased, and the frontal lobe volume was also decreased. Watanabe also noted that the lacunar infarction risk factor for Alzheimer's Dementia increased as the number of surviving teeth decreased. Watanabe cited a study of 218 elderly people in Brazil that showed that toothless people who did not use dental prosthetics scored lower on the mini mental state exam. Results showed that people hospitalized with dementia showed increased risk of dementia as the number of surviving teeth decreased.

Teeth loss was associated with decreased cognitive function. Lexomboom reported that people with multiple tooth loss and difficulty chewing have significantly higher odds of cognitive impairment. The odds of cognitive impairment is higher in those with chewing difficulty. There is a link between reduced masticatory function and dementia. Mastication results in increased metabolic activity which stimulates oral tissues-resulting in increased blood flow to both oral tissues and brain. Cerebral blood flow decreases with aging.

When it decreases-brain atrophy can begin and decreased cerebral blood flow increases risk of dementia. (Watanabe,2/2015) There are also biochemical factors linking periodontal disease and dementia. There is a relationship between periodontal disease and cognitive function, Impaired memory/impaired calculation ability is associated with periodontal disease. There is a statistical relationship between Alzheimer's and bacterial infections. There are also studies of Alzheimer's Dementia and P Gingivalis gingivitis. 90% of Alzheimer's patients have Treponema periodontal bacteria. P gingivalis bacteria can cause periodontal disease.

 Mice with periodontal disease showed lower cognitive function and increased number of senile plaques and increased interleukin/tnf bacteria/tumor necrosis factor. (Watanabe) added that tooth loss from periodontal disease is an internal risk factor for dementia. Thus, proper dental treatment can contribute to prevention of dementia and control its progression.

Hickey & Salter) noted that the loss of teeth can represent a severe handicap that directly impacts on the quality of life ...studies have focused on the clinical/technical aspects of dental prosthetics without considering overall wellbeing-and that wellbeing makes it necessary to restore lost teeth. (BDJ British Dental Journal /Nature.com, noted that occlusal interference tended to increase mental stress + occlusal interference may be reduced or eliminated with the prosthetics.

(Singh, Sandhu & Kaur) discussed teeth loss issues found in a number of their denture patients: Teeth loss is an insurmountable obstacle for many emotionally fragile and emotionally maladaptive patients. Their sense of tooth loss is also their sense of hopelessness, they suffer anxiety and despair from it.

Chapter 16A: Tooth Roots and the Cerebellum

Eckles & Kalkwarf) wrote about impaired tooth root development after treatment of a cerebellar Astrocytoma (brain tumor): After surgical resection of a Grade 3 cerebellar astrocytoma, severe generalized tooth root agenesis was noted. The patient also had decreased growth hormone levels.

Chapter 16B: Temperature Hypersensitivity Dental Pain/ Painful Hyper-Reaction of Dwarf Teeth

Kantaputra. and (Terlemez, noted in a study of Dwarf teeth that there is a loss of dental microtubule integrity and defective microtubules. Kantaputra further hypothesized that this may be possibly caused by a defective PCNT gene that plays a crucial role in tooth development (notably in permanent teeth). Sosa & Burke note the case of a 20 yr. old young dwarf female patient with damaged/defective microtubules, causing pain. (Huneycutt et al,) observed the following: impaired temperature regulation, and sensitivity to temperature changes.

Although not specifically referencing the rare conditions in this book, the following might be useful in better understanding the Hypersensitivity/Pain issue provided above. (Central NJ Prosthodontics, Tooth Sensitivity) explains the situation quite well: Dentin (calcified living issue) sends sensitivity sensations to nerves deep in the inner core of the teeth. The dentin is covered by hard enamel on the visible part of the teeth (the visible part is called the crown of the tooth). The dentin also covers soft cementum on tooth roots below the gum line. Dentin contains many microscopic tubules/canals. If gums are shrinking/recessed, then pain/sensitivity may result. For instance, as the gum shrinks/recesses, root surfaces get exposed, leading to pain/sensitivity.

This becomes even worse if the tooth roots were not totally covered by cementum during development. Tooth decay there causes pain/sensitivity, as decay exposed dentin. The decay can move down to nerves and trigger pain. The pain then begins to increase. Bonding of outer teeth surface may possibly help with reducing discomfort. The damaged dentin/enamel/cementum can end up with cavities, teeth fractures, exposed roots, and gum recession. The enamel layer protects the crowns of the teeth above the gum. Under the gum line, cementum layers protect tooth roots. Under the cementum is dentin. Dentin can lose its protective covering of enamel/cementum then the tubules/canals allow hot and cold temperature to reach the nerve cells in the teeth, triggering pain/sensitivity.

(Dr Jeffrey Chirilio, DMD) wrote about Tooth Sensitivity Pain, generally without referencing the diseases discussed in this book, but I felt the information was important to share here. (Chirilio) cites how a gust of wind can cause some patients to grab their jaws during a change in barometric pressure. He adds the following important material: A periodontal infection can cause mouth pain due to inflammation and swelling. A periodontal gum infection can lead to bone loss extending to the root tips of teeth and its delicate sensitive nerve endings can react in pain. Loose mobile teeth resulting from periodontal bone loss can also cause pain. The movement of loose teeth causes pain. Chirilio notes too that as decayed, diseased pulpal tissue dies there can be decreased sensitivity. It can spread to the periodontal ligament that encases the tooth & attaches it to the jawbone and to the surrounding gum tissue. Periodontal pockets (detachment of gum tissue along tooth surface) and periodontal membrane filled with a rich supply of nerve fibers to relay pain, can also trigger pain/sensitivity. So can endodontic infections as well.

 Chirilio notes that in some cases the bone loss may heal after an infection unless the infection is longstanding. (Yang Z & Li J) researched the influence of temperature on cerebellar metabolite levels and concluded that the cerebellum is extremely sensitive to heat induced injury due to an abundance of Purkinje cells & that cerebellar metabolite levels are influenced by body *temperature*. For further detailed explanatory information on Dentin/Enamel/Cementum defects caused by Ectodermal Dysplasia Dental Disease and Dwarfism Dental Ravage Disease, please refer to the chapter on Dental Abnormalities

Associated with both diseases. In my own personal case involving both dental diseases, the defects were so severe that I was forced to do experimental full mouth Root Canal order to STOP the nearly constant and very severe TEMPERATURE PAIN. Sensitivity toothpastes/creams did NOT stop the pain at all, Luckily & Miraculously, this " last ditch highest risk experimental" full mouth Root Canal procedure invented by and used by Dr Schamis stopped the pain!

Chapter 17: Literature Review of my rare Dental disease

An Astonishing Variety/Combination of Dental-Medical Abnormalities in my Dwarfism Dental Disease / Ectodermal Dysplasia Dental Disease : „a veritable compendium of cerebellar connected symptoms ,.,I am demonstrating the overlap of Dwarfism Dental Disease & Ectodermal Dysplasia Dental Disease Combined with CEREBELLAR-VESTIBULAR DISEASE and showing insights into the Research Literature : Demonstrating the unique complexity :Assembling And Solving both the TEETH SAVING SOLUTION & THE PAIN SOLUTION ...HOWEVER *ONE PATIENT IS WORTH MORE THAN LOADS OF LITERATURE AND BUNDLES OF SYMPTOMS ...I am* Descrambling A Tangled Mess of Contradictions Errors & Conundrums ,Identifying and explaining mistakes fallacies errors and setting forth my HOLISTIC MIND BODY DENTAL MEDICAL MODEL That Demonstrates the Entirety of my disease in a brand new way ....*Please note that I collected and wrote up these research literature findings in summarized explanatory style .*

 (Levinson, Harold) indicated that it is imperative to integrate the works of outstanding scholars into a "new" conceptual framework that answers the questions. I have taken his advice and presented you with research findings of several erudite scholars -and I have incorporated their work into my new conceptual dental-medical holistic framework -This review of the literature also reflects what (Levinson, Harold) described as an attempt to assimilate and integrate multiple insights.

Another reason this literature review was added is related to what Levinson called " diagnostic studies viewed to define the disorder ,And it has helped me to better understand how a primary cerebellar malfunction can be accompanied with a host of secondary manifestations and has helped me to develop a new broader diagnostic methodology and helped to clarify the different roles of various symptoms/factors, & the diverse spectrum of the symptoms & their multiple overlapping factors. I also tried to follow (see Levinson, Harold) the following methods listed there : using different paths of investigation and correlating data into those paths, reconstructing symptoms, correlating symptoms to common cerebellar causation, developing intuitive correlation of symptoms into distinct separate patterns + identifying significant linkages/associations, separating and correlating cerebellar symptoms with specific patterns and factors, 'Bottom line", I felt that I had to present you with a solid explanatory summary of the research literature so that you could have an accurate understanding of the wide breadth of dental symptoms that comprise my rare medically based dental condition.

(Ferrante & Blasi et al,) state that in Hypopituitary Dwarfism there are multiple dental anomalies & that there is the problematic dilemma regarding the use of functional dental prosthetics to treat the abnormal defective dental teeth/jaw/gum anomalies, including the difficulty in using dental prosthetics without surgical intervention. These dwarfism dental anomalies include: a childlike face, thin maxillofacial skin, an abnormally small jaw, deformed/misshapen / malformed/tiny teeth, fused roots, malocclusion periodontitis , overcrowded teeth, tilted/slanted teeth, displaced teeth ,hypodontia, root fusion(fused roots)in mandible arch, i.e. radicular fusion despite separate crowns, impacted teeth, malocclusion, and periapical lesions as well as physical dental abnormalities from tooth eruption that can lead to teeth malformation. (Ferrante & Blasi et al,) also note that the ideal resolution involves fixed permanent dental prosthetics, i.e. zirconium sub-structured dental prosthetics.

They cite as an example the use of a 5-tooth fixed ceramic prosthetic on a 6-fixture zirconia substructure for a mandibular arch. They further explained that "dental tooth stumping" via cutters is often needed in order to fit the prosthetics, as well as chamfer of affected teeth -They close by stating that the validity exists for dwarfism dental prosthetics and that it is possible to succeed in creating dwarfism dental prosthetics. And they agree that the ideal technique of fixing the prosthetics is to fix underlying teeth. They also emphasize the need for continuous monitoring and frequent follow-up. (Ferrante & Blasi et al,) did a sample study of dwarf patients and their key findings are summarized below."

98% of the dwarf patients have the onset of periodontal disease95% have ortho malocclusion.

95% have abnormally small jawbones.

72% have or have had impacted teeth.

55% have no resorption of roots of deciduous teeth at normal time.

55% have development of apical parts of roots of permanent teeth.

35% have tilted permanent teeth.

60% have missing incisors. (Kantaputral, et al,) in a study of extremely tiny size teeth (Microdontia) in Dwarfism, noted the following findings:" Severe and striking dental anomalies" including severe hypoplastic alveolar jawbone loss, severe microdontia (tiny teeth) notably microdontic (tiny) incisors/premolars ,opalescent misshapen teeth, rootless molars, loss of permanent teeth due to severe jawbone loss, loss of dental microtubule integrity and defective microtubules.(Rios & Koushik,) have noted the following regarding dental abnormalities of Dwarfism: severe progressive Incisor enamel defects including anterior incisor surfaces, defects that can progressively deform the entire facial enamel surface of the mandibular /maxillary incisors, hypoplastic incisors, deficient, reduced, translucent incisal surface, mild opacity on incisal surface, reduced incisor width, decreased incisor area, creation of abnormal interproximal space , i.e. incisors show interproximal gaps, worsening enamel defects, highly radiopaque deformed surfaces evident on radiographic x rays, abnormal wear on incisal edges, deformed/clefted enamel surfaces of periostin defect incisors, much thinner enamel layer, irregular pattern of enamel-amorphous irregular prism patterns. much thinner incisors, disorganized pseudostratified epithelial layers related to dentin cover, abnormal enamel epithelium, loss of normal characteristics of enamel/epithelium, early onset periodontal disease/periodontitis weakened periodontal ligaments that exhibit mechanical strain during mastication (chewing/biting), abnormal remodeling of alveolar jawbone including the bone adjacent to incisors, alveolar jawbone destruction, external root resorption, abnormal periodontium, abnormal increased osteoclast activity in periostin periodontium, structural defects in dentin matrix, hyper-mineralization (calcium phosphate) of dentin. obliterated incisor canals, structurally unstable enamel layer, completely distorted epithelium with pseudostratified appearance, decalcification, alveolar jawbone root resorption, molar root resorption, molar mesial roots showing abnormal periodontal inflammatory infiltrate in the periodontal ligament, periodontal inflammatory responses, including inflammatory periodontal granulation tissue-the granulation material representing the body's attempts at self-repair and at periodontal wound healing and can include scar tissue material, inflammatory periodontal responses to traumatic stimuli, increased signaling on surface of periostin molar root/alveolar jawbone surface/roots , rapidly progressive periodontitis, structural instability of gum tissue and jawbone and periodontal ligaments, a failure to establish adequate biological gum/soft tissue barriers between oral cavity and periodontium, lack of sufficient periostin that causes loss of mechanical strength,(i.e. for masticatory chewing/biting) , dramatic vertical height jawbone loss, lack of periostin that affects structural integrity of enamel production- periostin is needed to cushion and mediate mechanical masticatory (chewing biting)forces that affect bone formation/maintenance/remodeling-the mechanical stresses of

mastication (chewing biting)affect attachments of teeth to jaw bone-
the lack of sufficient anchorage of teeth to jawbone making the teeth
more susceptible to mechanical forces of mastication(chewing biting) ,
mandibular jaw hypoplasia abnormal deposition of enamel matrix,
hypoplastic enamel lacking normal prism structure, defects in
structural organization of enamel, lack of enamel organ integrity,
undersized maxillofacial/craniofacial bony skeletal network, decreased
incisor strength for mastication (biting chewing)- mild clefting of
enamel surface-lack of organized membranous layer/epithelial
anchorage. The early onset periodontal disease/periodontitis often
begins as early as 3 months of age in dentally affected dwarfs-this
phenomenon is referred to " early onset periodontal disease like
phenotype."

(Dalkiz & Dalkiz, et al,) have noted the following: micrognathia of
jawbone, protruding prominent thick lips, altered
maxillofacial/craniofacial / oro-dental bone development, including
dento-facial hypoplasia and altered maxillofacial bones, impacted
teeth, maxillary/mandibular jawbone loss, severe risk of jawbone loss
from extraction of teeth, increased thickened jawbone ridge volume in
bucco-lingual directions preventing the fitting of dentures, ankylosed
teeth making extractions too risky, atrophic alveolar
jawbone(mandibular/maxillary), excess occlusal forces on 2nd
molars, short crown length teeth, and diastema spaces between
teeth.(Terlemez, et al,) and (Kantaputra,) observed the following
dental features in dwarf children: severe mandibular molar pain,
rampant tooth decay/caries, rootless molars. short rooted incisors,
opalescent teeth, hypoplastic teeth, micrognathia of jaw bone, enamel
dysplasia, microdontia tiny teeth, periodontal tooth mobility, loose
teeth, very small mouth/oral cavity, increased spaces between
maxillary teeth, small incisors/posterior teeth, rootless molars,
premature exfoliation of incisors, short rooted incisors, hypoplastic
alveolar jaw bone, hypoplastic alveolar jawbone processes,
malformed/misshapen teeth, missing teeth, abnormal predisposition to

tooth decay/caries/cavities, defective microtubules, loss of microtubule integrity, and enamel dysplasia. (Abdel-Salam, et al) and (Ippel,) both noted the following: Microdontia "tiny" teeth, enamel hypo-calcification, tooth decay/caries, teeth loss, micrognathia jawbone, high palate, small teeth, oro-facial -dental anomalies, hypoplastic alveolar jawbone, opalescent teeth, bulbous crowns, short tooth roots, atrophic teeth, enamel hypoplasia, and overcrowded teeth, oligodontia, microdontia. and underdeveloped maxillary bone.

Neville & Chi noted the following dental aspects of Dwarfism: Rootless molars. severely hypoplastic alveolar jawbone, damaged microtubules. Peg shaped teeth. malocclusion, enamel hypoplasia, reduced dental tooth crown height, root anomalies, very short roots combined with coronal tooth enlargement, conical malformed molars. abnormal tooth crown position, apical root resorption, abnormal orthodontic results. difficulty with orthodontic movement of teeth, occlusal interference with the need for selective equilibration, oversized tooth crowns requiring size reduction, damaged cemento-enamel construction, displaced /transposed teeth, abnormal spacing, isolated teeth fit issues requiring tooth size reduction, and localized tooth size discrepancies requiring correction.

(Sosa, Alejandro Dr & Burke Vernon Dr , El Paso Children's Hospital Foundation) discuss the extreme prosthodontic treatment of a 20 yr. old young lady patient a Primordial Dwarf with extremely severe dwarfism dental pathology: Her case includes severe malformation of weak teeth , weak teeth that are crooked and loose, with missing and or weak roots, severe periodontal mobility that makes it severely damaged in terms of the teeth holding in the gums-a simple bite of fruit for example could pull her teeth out.

She struggles with eating, brushing, chewing and biting as her deformed teeth are a very severe risk of shattering, breaking and falling out. Dr Alejando Sosa, A prosthodontist & Dr Vernon Burke, an oral surgeon, are attempting to replace her deformed teeth with implants at El Paso Children's Hospital (Texas). 20 yr. old Giselle has intense pain especially when chewing, and she's at high risk of dental infections. Her dental case is extremely challenging/complex. Typical implants are generally for non-dwarf patients of adult size. She needs dwarf size implants, and her body reacts like a child, due to her dwarf size. They extracted all her teeth and needed to make room in her upper jaw, and they needed to partly fill her sinuses with bone material, and they needed to move a nerve that affects her lower lip and chin. Her extreme case also takes into account that her very small body adds layers of complexity including anesthesia, analgesia, pain management and post-operative care. This is a multi-step process that requires more procedures in order for her to have the custom fit implants.

(Falcon) describes 18 yr. old Hannah, another primordial dwarf, is awaiting a full set of implants to replace her deformed and damaged teeth. Drs Amirali Zandinejad & Likith Reddy at Texas A&M College of Dentistry Dallas TX are working with Hannah. She has had severe primordial dwarfism dental pathology throughout her life. She has temporary prosthetics after preliminary dental surgery. She has typical weak dental structure, dental pain, and difficulty eating. Her dental experts removed all her teeth and created a bone graft from her hip (6-inch incision in the hip) to support implants. These bone grafts are very painful and can cause facial swelling for a month or longer. This treatment can also cause partial oral numbness as well. She has had difficulty speaking without teeth as well as with the temporary prosthetics which are similar to retainers/partials.

This will be followed with screws placed to hold the implants -a 3 + month wait for temporary prosthetics so that the hip bone graft can hold permanent custom fitted porcelain implants. That process can take well over a year to get the implants finally placed. Her case is very complicated & extremely risky due to her small tooth roots, loose teeth, rootless teeth, weak jawbone not strong enough to support implants, and the risk of her teeth falling out- ultimately Hannah had to have all her teeth removed! The jawbone grafts she needs are major and extensive. She will also need temporary starter pediatric size custom dentures, to be used for about 6 months, to allow the grafts to strengthen, followed by custom fitted pediatric size implants. The provisional dentures will be converted to fixed dentures while her final prosthetic is being fabricated.

(Hikita,) identified root length and tooth length abnormalities in growth hormone deficient dwarf dental patients. (Hikita,) also noted a relationship between tooth length and GHR Growth hormone receptors and noted issues with tooth movement forces transmitted including abnormal patterns of tooth movement. These dental abnormalities were also found in Laron Syndrome short stature dwarfism with GH Insensitivity Syndrome, (Mirkovic,) observed the following dental pathology in short stature dwarf dental patients: bilateral painful jaw swelling, gangrenous tooth roots bilaterally, mal-position of teeth, missing teeth, and impacted teeth.(Chee & Lee) observed the following dental pathology in proportionate short stature dwarf patients: The Dental Anomalies included: Hypoplastic Mandibular Jawbone, Missing molars/incisors/premolars, Narrow deformed arches, Gingival inflammation, Gingivitis, Gingival bleeding upon Gum probing, compromised tooth positions, excessive decay, loss of occlusal vertical height dimension, malocclusion, maxillofacial deformity, mixed dentition, and anterior open occlusion. **Often the dentition is inadequate for fixed restoration.** (Dwarfparents.com) suggests that dwarf dental patients have very hard to reach back molars, as well as a very small mouth with average-large size teeth, overcrowding, and tight interproximal spaces. Hallermann-Streiff Syndrome includes Small **Cerebellum**, Ocular abnormalities. Mandibular Jaw Hypoplasia, and Proportionate Dwarfism. (Phillips) discusses a 15 yr old teen primordial dwarf Jessalyn has severe teeth problems caused by her dwarfism. She also has a **Cerebellar** Chiari Malformation that affects her balance & she has learning delays.

(Goyal & Mehta,) mention the following dental abnormalities in Dwarf patients: dysmorphic facial structure, high arched palate/palatal vault, anterior open bite, overjet, oculo-facio-cardio-dental syndrome, underdeveloped maxillary jaw/jawbone, constricted maxilla that needs expansion extreme overbite, root resorption, mandibular hypoplasia, enamel hypoplasia, malocclusion, mal-positioned teeth, missing molars and premolars, transverse discrepancy, arch length defect, mal-position of posterior teeth, short face, insufficient mandibular advancement, mandible with retrognathic face, decreased posterior face height, decreased mandibular length, maxillo-mandibular discrepancy, micrognathia, maxillary growth retardation, faulty eruption of maxillary molars. arch length tooth size discrepancies, occlusal instability, anterior areas needing bone grafts, molar malocclusion, crossbite, misshapen/missing incisors, microdontia, and hypoplastic mandible.

(Atreja et al,) mentions small facial appearance for the age, shedding teeth, small tooth crowns, malocclusion, overcrowding, tilted/tipped teeth. small roots. lack of wisdom teeth, and defective enamel (enamel hypoplasia).

(Kumari & Kumar) list the dental traits: hypodontia of permanent teeth, oligodontia, anodontia, decreased vertical height dimension dento-facially, malformed teeth, loss of occlusal vertical height dimension, underdeveloped alveolar jawbone ridge, narrowed jawbone ridge, poor vertical support, hypoplastic jaws/jawbones, and vertical bite collapse.

(Bansal & Bansal,) and (NFED) list the following dwarfism dental traits : short root anomaly, root dwarfism, facial abnormalities, globe shaped teeth, microdontia, short tooth crown length, anterior overcrowding, misshapen teeth, crossbite, hypoplastic enamel, stained enamel hypoplastic maxillary jaw, deficient pre-maxilla, extremely short roots, missing lamina dura missing periodontal ligaments, microdontia, rotated incisors, taurodontism mandibular molars due to short roots, dentinal dysplasia, dentin dysplasia, arrested root formation, frontal crossbite, deficient premaxillary growth, small mandible, hypodontic features, severely hypoplastic alveolar jaw bone, globe shaped molars(otodental syndrome)and oto-dento-dysplasia meaning abnormal posterior teeth with short root lengths compared to crown height and small premolars, taurodontia of posterior teeth, missing canines, mobility of canines, short conical roots, rootless teeth, abnormal dentin formation, taurodontism caused by dentin defect, varying different root lengths, tricho-onycho-dental syndrome, regional odontodysplasia, ghost teeth, wide open apices with short roots, very wide pulp canals prone to root canal pulp infections,

yellow enamel, chronic periodontitis/ periodontal disease, large quadrangular pulp chambers, abnormal dentine, abscessed teeth, single conical roots. hypoplasia, overcrowded teeth, somatotropin deficient overcrowding, impacted teeth, and misshapen teeth. additionally these teeth are at risk of overstress from chewing pressure, the pressure of impacted teeth, pressure of overcrowded teeth, traumatic occlusion that can cause root resorption, agenesis of permanent teeth(missing),discolored teeth, abnormally thin soft enamel that can cause increased decay/cavities, small pitted indentations in enamel, teeth may be globe shaped and or conical shaped, and may be spike shaped and or pointy narrow sharp stick shaped, pegged teeth(peg shaped), tooth tips may be very sharp and pointy, aka "pointed/pointy" teeth, the roots can be abnormally shaped, the center of the teeth can be larger than normal (thus enlarged) note that the center of the teeth=between crown and the root canal pulp chambers. note that the crowns of teeth are covered in enamel and are what you see when you smile! The roots are embedded in the jaw, anchoring teeth to the bony sockets.

The abnormally shaped roots are called Taurodontia. The teeth position may be abnormal and note that hypodontia means missing teeth and anodontia means complete absence of teeth and edentulous means toothless. The ridge like border of the upper and lower jaws contain the teeth sockets and are known as alveolar ridges- in these disease conditions the alveolar ridges are often underdeveloped, and the alveolar jawbone is abnormally formed, and tooth bud formation is abnormally formed as well. If the tooth buds are missing, the alveolar bone/ alveolar bone teeth will be abnormal. The lack of alveolar bone can cause a narrow-pointed chin that will cause difficulty with chewing, swallowing, and speaking,

(Sherry & Aponte,) noted the following dental traits of dwarf patients: insufficient jawbone maxillary jaw hypoplasia dental malocclusion midfacial hypoplasia, permanent teeth larger than jaw can support and space will allow proneness to gingivitis/periodontitis. tendency to mouth breath, chapped lips, hard palate that is narrow, overbite overjet overcrowding, crossbite, midline shift, bruxism, teeth grinding, teeth clenching. gum inflammations, small jaw structure, impacted teeth, premature tooth shedding, maxillary sinus congested/cloudy on x ray, small maxillary sinus, horizontal jawbone loss, facial deformities, narrow jaws, narrow hard palate, bilateral crossbite, overcrowding, midface hypoplasia, sleep apnea, inflamed gums, occlusal wear from grinding/bruxism, tendency to accumulate plaque. and occlusal interference.

(Bembalgi & Jadhav) note that small dwarf dental arches cannot accommodate all the teeth. Periodontal disease is common, caries or frequent. tooth loss is sometimes due to the periodontal disease, there are often missing teeth, and or impacted teeth, resorbed residual alveolar jawbone ridges, decayed mobile loose molars, difficulty with doing dental impressions due to very small size mouth, and tiny teeth(microdontia).

(JAIN) noted: a retrusive middle 3rd of face, a concave profile, disparity of jaw growth. midfacial hypoplasia, protrusive mandible, malocclusion, posterior open bite, retrusion of maxilla, narrow maxilla, resorbed anterior ridge of mandible. and shallow ridges.

Alves, Ines,) list dwarf dental traits as malocclusion, improper bite, irregular teeth. disproportionate jaw relationships. misalignment of teeth, abnormal fit of upper to lower teeth. dental arch deformities, periodontitis, periodontal disease, midface hypoplasia, lip deformity, diastema gaps between teeth, concave face, gingivitis, crossbite, open bite, anterior reversed jet, abnormal molar relations. overcrowding, decay, mixed dentition, caries, carious lesions, disproportionate jaw relations, misfit of upper to lower, abnormal jaw position, damaged facial skeleton, decreased upper facial height, increased lower facial height, and increased tongue size. (Dovemed) Dwarfism Dental Symptoms can include microdontia (tiny teeth) hypodontia, missing permanent teeth, as well as non-dental symptoms that include **alopecia, sparse thin fine hair, cerebellar** ataxia, **cerebellar** atrophy, awkward gait, and **premature hair loss alopecia**.

(Omo & Ennibulele) describe the Ectodermal Dysplasia Dental Disease as follows: Alopecia, Xerostomia (Dry mouth), anodontia, hypoplastic conical teeth in both jaws, tooth sensitivity, underdeveloped maxillary tuberosities, underdeveloped thin alveolar jawbone ridge of both arches(upper lower), severe abnormal teeth spacing, microdontia, conical incisors/canines, caries, carious lesions on teeth, teeth attrition, impacted teeth, root resorption, periodontal disease, periodontitis, gingivitis, and floating resorbed teeth requiring extraction. (Kornreich & Horev,) performed an intriguing research study on the Craniofacial-Dental & Brain Abnormalities in Laron Syndrome-at the Endocrinology Imaging Dept at Schneider Children's Medical Center of Israel, Petah Tikva, in conjunction with the Sackler Faculty at Tel Aviv Israel.

This study was on adults between 36 and 68 yrs. of age with Laron Syndrome. Here is a summary of the study: Traits included Hypopituitary Human Growth Hormone Insufficiency Dwarfism Short Stature, small paranasal sinuses, underdeveloped facial bone structure/jaw bones, hypoplastic nasal bridge, decreased vertical dimension the face, small jaw/jawbone slow motor development **cerebellar** ataxia, underdeveloped sinuses (frontal maxillary and sphenoid) ,skull abnormalities-with retarded skull maturation, their cerebellum symmetrically small with **cerebellar** atrophy, and small head circumference. (Halder, 1998) in a short stature Dwarfism study, noted the presence of unusual dento-facial appearance, with some patients also showing **alopecia** as well.

Another condition that is similar to mine is Papillon-Lefevre Syndrome (Rostamzadeh, Masoumeh, 2017) This condition includes periodontal gum ravage/destruction, aggressive periodontitis. periodontal bone loss, periodontally damaged teeth, with acute periodontal disease, serious/severe periodontal gum inflammation, periodontal mobility aka loose teeth, gum shrinkage/recession, gum tissue loss, small jaws, overcrowded teeth, and rapid periodontal destruction. (Jeffery, Nathan & Berkovitz, BKB) mention the following very rare dwarfism dental traits: receded chin, thin mineralized roots. and calcification of maxillary canines.

In my own case, as many of my readers already know, I have cerebellar ectodermal hypopituitary human growth hormone insufficiency proportionate dwarfism, with dwarfism alopecia, receded jaw since childhood, short vertical dimension of face, severe jawbone loss, enamel/dentin/microtubule defects, enamel erosion, gum recession, periodontitis, , and delayed motor/coordination/balance/gait. and the small head circumference that requires my wigs to be sewing altered to fit my child size 17-18 inch head circumference, and I have unusual dento-facial/ Maxillofacial-Dental features including tiny mouth. and cerebellar Dwarfism Scoliosis as well as well as cerebellar hypotonic leaky mitral/tricuspid cardiac heart valves and ocular-visual abnormalities.

Abnormalities of tooth development in pituitary dwarfism
J. Kosowicz, M.D. Roentgen studies of the jaws and teeth were performed in forty-eight cases of pituitary dwarfism. Found in all

cases were delayed shedding of the deciduous teeth, marked delay in eruption of the permanent teeth and retention of them in the maxillary and mandibular shafts, development of the apical parts of the roots of retained teeth, obvious underdevelopment of the maxilla and mandible, and complete absence of third molar tooth buds. (Alsayed, Arwa,) described dental traits of Seckel short stature primordial Dwarfism: enamel hypoplasia, hypodontia, microdontia, taurodontic molars/roots, high arched palate, class 2 malocclusion, gingival gum recession. gum ulceration, overcrowding, minimal root development, gingivitis, periodontitis, gingival bleeding, receded chin, damaged roots, missing teeth, tooth malformations, missing incisors, short roots, and class 3 malocclusion. (Dua, Singh & Aghi) described the abnormalities as " Mutilated Dentition". They noted the presence of Severe dentition attrition, loss of vertical dimension of occlusion, depressed facial appearance, unfavorable coordination of stomatognathic system, teeth fractures, increased temperature sensitivity, enamel erosion, and non-resolving periapical infections. (Patel, Jayanti) also described the abnormalities as " Mutilated Dentition". Patel defined it as grossly weakened severely worn badly broken down and added that it includes the fact that the amount of remaining tooth structure is less than the amount of tooth loss, meaning that the teeth lost is greater than the amount of remaining teeth left. They also added the following other traits/symptoms: loss of occlusal vertical dimension aka lost vertical dimension of occlusion, lost teeth structure, uneven teeth wear, uneven plane of occlusion, poor esthetics, reduced chewing ability, centric defects, and abnormal occlusal contact patterns- posts and cores may be needed in order to use full coverage porcelain fused to metal fixed restoration of the entire dentition.

(Kim, Kanghyun et al,) described dental prosthetic care of a patient with Russell-Silver growth hormone deficiency short stature dwarfism: this patient also exhibited micrognathia, hypodontia, decreased lower facial height-short lower anterior facial height-psychomotor impairment, downturned corners of mouth, misshapen teeth, deficient chewing ability, severe caries(cavities), decreased OVD Occlusal vertical dimension due to missing posterior teeth & defective lip support. (Wankhade, Lokade & Rajguru,) described the abnormalities as " Mutilated Dentition": Severely worn dentition, loss of teeth structure, uneven/flattened plane of occlusion, uneven teeth wear. damaged cusps, flattened occlusal teeth surface, loss of vertical dimension of occlusion, loss of anterior guidance, severe attrition, collapsed facial vertical dimension. posterior interferences, excess muscle activity, and excess or inadequate chewing force. (Asulu, Reddy, Gupta & Harilal) noted small dental arches, resorbed alveolar jawbone ridges. and periodontal problem in adult dwarf patients. (Zemes & Holtgrave, described the dental issues found in Johanson-Blizzard Syndrome short stature Dwarfism female patients as follows: scalp **alopecia/hair defects**, tiny "microdontia" teeth, spaces between teeth, conical incisors. missing tooth buds, progressive root resorption, molar taurodontism, broad short incisor roots, mandible deviation, overbite crossbite deep bite, overjet. ectodermal dental defects, misshapen teeth, peg shaped teeth, reduced molar size, missing molar cusps, and oligodontia (missing teeth). (Abduo, Jaafar) noted the following dwarfism dental traits : loss of vertical dimension of occlusion, missing teeth. drifting/tipping teeth, over-eruption of remaining teeth, occlusal interference, overcrowding with insufficient space for prosthetics, occlusal plane abnormality, and insufficient bone/gum support.

CEREBELLAR LINKS TO DENTAL PATHOLOGY

(D. O'Toole & S Swist,) noted the following observations/findings in their veterinary livestock animal **cerebellum** studies but it is applicable to humans in many ways:

dysplastic changes in premolar/molar teeth, dental ankylosis, impacted premolars/molars, misaligned incisors fixed TMJ joints, decalcified teeth-poorly calcified teeth deformed mandible, mineralized connective stroma in tooth chamber periodontal hemorrhaging, caries/cavities malformed roots/crowns malocclusion, overcrowding, misalignment, abnormal pulp spaces reduced enamel, irregular enamel , dysplastic intermingling of dentin, enamel, cementum & bone at the base of the pulp chamber, causing dental ankylosing continuous proliferation of dental tissue in interstices of alveolar bone. leading to dental ankylosing, failure to form eruption pathway in bone overlying teeth, due to defective osteoclasts, absent tooth buds, absent incisors twisted dentinal tubules brachygnathia.

This was noted in livestock that also had: compressed **cerebellar hemispheres, herniation of cerebellar vermis into foramen magnum, and cerebellar lesions.**

(Lida & Kawara) performed research on **Cerebellar** activity before teeth clenching using Magnetoencephalography. They found that the **cerebellum** is involved in intra-cerebral activity immediately before **teeth** clenching and that the **cerebellum** is involved in signal pathways immediately before **teeth** clenching.

The **cerebellum** is activated when **teeth** are clenched (right & left **cerebellar** hemisphere activation) (Soumya et al) discusses a case where the patient has **cerebellar** disease. **dental malocclusion,**

alopecia, learning disabilities. & **dwarfism.** (Ch Kitty) describes a CAT with **cerebellar hypoplasia** (underdevelopment stunted growth) with difficulty walking impaired balance, subtle tremors, who is prone to **CHIPPED TEETH** AND BROKEN NAILS. (Watanabe) says Rhythmic movement of the **jaw** is regulated by **cerebellum** and basal ganglia, (Accogli, Andrea et al,) identified a novel genetic AMDD2 mutation in **pontocerebellar hypoplasia (PCH)** involving **dental dysmorphism and teeth abnormalities.** The traits identified included: **upper lateral incisor agenesis, mottled fragile teeth with cavities(caries), mandibular jaw hypoplasia,** basal ganglia abnormality-small hyperintense basal ganglia, **cerebellar hemispheric atrophy**, and facial dysmorphism. (Aliaghhaei, Abbas,) **Dental pulp stem cell transplantation (DPSC)** ameliorates motor function & prevents **cerebellar atrophy** in rat model of cerebellar ataxia. The transplantation of DPSC's in **cerebellar ataxia** cases ameliorated motor coordination and muscle activity, increased **cerebellar** volumes of molecular/granular layers and white matter, reduced levels of inflammatory cytokines and thwarted degeneration of Purkinje cells against 3AP toxicity.

(Shanmugapriya, Manoharan & Nisha, describe a unique oral manifestation in Dandy Walker Syndrome Case Report -an **odontoma** an **odontoma** is a benign tumor linked **to tooth development.** Specifically, it is a dental hamartoma, meaning that it is composed of normal dental tissue that has grown in an irregular way. It includes both odontogenic hard and soft tissue. This patient in India had a mandible odontoma, **cerebellar hypoplasia**, with retained impacted deciduous teeth, paleo cerebellar malformation, enlarged 4th cerebellar ventricle, cystic dilation that ventricle as well, cerebellar ataxia, nystagmus and heart anomalies. This patient presented with an **aching painful upper maxillary tooth**, reduced visual acuity,14 retained intraoral deciduous teeth,7 missing permanent teeth, overcrowding of anterior teeth of both jaws/arches, high arched palate, and impacted subcutaneous teeth, as well as motor control impairment, enamel hypoplasia, microdontia, and ankyloglossia…

(Warotayanont, Rungnapp et al, 5/17/2016) describes a rare **cerebellar**-dental condition known as Dandy-Walker Malformation- He lists the identifying traits as follows: **Cerebellar** dysfunction, cranial nerve dysfunction, **fractured root canals**, hearing loss, impaired gait, balance impairment, visual impairment. **cerebellar** ataxic gait, delayed motor development, heart-cardiac defects, apnea. headaches, delayed intellectual development, childhood dental damage, concave facial profile, chin deviation, malocclusion, crossbite/overbite with overjet, anterior teeth overcrowding, abnormally short tooth crown length, periodontal mobility requiring splinting, gingival gum damage, & defective incisors.

DENTAL ECTODERMAL DYSPLASIA WITH ECTODERMAL ALOPECIA

Ectodermal Dysplasia is a primary defect in hair, teeth. nails, skin eyelashes & eyebrows and eyes. (NFED ORG BLOG) Hair Skin Nails & Skin are ectodermal derived. Its Dental characteristics can include missing teeth, very small pointy teeth, small narrow jaw, sparse saliva, tooth & nail syndrome (i.e. Witkop syndrome) abnormally small malformed teeth, peg shaped teeth, raised gum tissue areas, irregular position of teeth, defective thin teeth enamel. anodontia, facial asymmetry, pointed chin, thick prominent protuberant lips oligodontia, underdeveloped jawbone/alveolar ridges. hypoplasia of alveolar jawbone, inadequate occlusal vertical jawbone height dimension, insufficient jawbone, maxillary hypoplasia, eversion of lips, conical small teeth, peg like incisors, hypodontia, missing molars/premolars, distorted teeth, insufficient alveolar jawbone that is missing/defective/malformed/undeveloped, insufficient teeth for orthodontic anchorage and in regions where teeth are absent, alveolar jawbone doesn't develop, lack of alveolar jawbone ridge development , reduced vertical height dimension of lower jawbone and of lower face, dry oral mucosa and bone atrophy,. (Note that Alveolar jawbone development is dependent on the presence of teeth. Often there is little or no jawbone ridge upon which to construct-thus restoring function/appearance thru dental prosthetic rehab. is more challenging than usual) even with alveolar jawbone grafting.

(Bain) (Bain) There is also sometimes the presence of perioral wrinkles as well, and very often the alveolar jawbone ridge is too thin, loss of sulcus depth in posterior regions of the maxillary/ mandibular jaw, marked resorption of alveolar jawbone ridges, maxillary retrusion due to sagittally underdeveloped maxilla, forward and upward displacement of chin and mandible, collapsed lower anterior facial height, facial premature aging appearance, wide spaces between teeth, underdeveloped residual ridges, loss/decrease of vertical dimension of occlusion, musculocutaneous alterations/abnormalities, resorption atrophy of alvcolar jawbone ridges which can be severely affected by missing teeth, difficulty maintaining teeth stability, abnormal mandibular posture, reduction in height of lower 1/3 of the face, tendency toward class 3 malocclusion, xerostomia, underdeveloped maxillary tuberosities, underdeveloped alveolar jawbone ridges, short tooth crown heights, hypoplastic malformed teeth, misaligned teeth, unesthetic sagittal/vertical dentofacial appearance, infraocclusion, ankylosed teeth, tipping of teeth, vertical discrepancy between mucosal margin of an implant and the gingival margins of teeth adjacent to the implant, impaired stomatognathic function, see (NFED ORG BLOG) (Rakowska,) (Sciencedirect) (Aldred,)(Bani) (Wilson,)(Aydin Belge. (Vallejo,) (Grover & Mehra, Its Hair symptoms include; **ALOPECIA,** Brittle dry sparse thin hair, slow growing hair, wiry hair, patches of hair loss on scalp-patches of absent scalp hair, abnormal alopecia bald patches on scalp, progressive hair thinning, patchy **alopecia,** scarring alopecia, hair shaft pigmentation defects, light hair pigmentation, scant fine light hair/brows (NFED ORG BLOG (Rakowska,) (Wilson,) (Kumari & Kumar) Its nail symptoms can include: tooth and nail syndrome i.e. Witkop syndrome. round spoon shaped concave nails that grow slowly, and poorly formed/developed nails. onychodysplasia (NFED BLOG) (Wilson,) (Kumari & Kumar)

Chapter 18: Some More Cerebellar-Dental-Dwarfism-Alopecia ''multiple connections''

(Soumya, et al) discussed a rare case of **Cerebellar** fusion where the patient had the following profile-I am sure you will see how my case closely matches that case:

(This patient had Gomez Lopez Hernandez Syndrome-However I do not)

These are the symptoms both I & that patient share in common:

Learning Disabilities, Dento-facial abnormalities, Teeth Malocclusion **Alopecia, Cerebellar** Disease, Dwarfism Short Stature…

Here are the additional details of the patient's record to help clarify a bit further for you: facial dysmorphism, craniofacial defects bilateral parietal / parieto occipital symmetrical temporal **alopecia,** cerebellar vermis defect, cerebello-trigeminal-dermal dysplasia, cerebellar hemisphere defects.(Gomez Lopez Hernandez Syndrome) & (Find zebra of Gomez Lopez Hernandez Syndrome) show Cerebello Trigeminal Dysplasia, Trigeminal Nerve Anesthesia, Cerebellar Malformation, **Scalp Alopecia**, Strabismus, Short Stature Dwarfism, Cerebellar Ataxia, Cerebellar discoordination, Cerebellar dysmetria, cerebellar vermis defects, anxiety ,insomnia, irritability, social/learning disabilities, and midfacial hypoplasia.

(Sukhudyan,) describing Gomez Lopez Hernandez Syndrome it lists underdeveloped jaw bones, **alopecia**, dwarfism, strabismus, learning disabilities, hypotonia, cleft in cerebellar junction, abnormal horizontal orientation of cerebellar folia, horizontal side to side head nodding, & midface hypoplasia.

(Locastro, Adriana et al,) described the neurological/dental aspects of Dwarfism as follows: Teeth defects including Microdontia (tiny teeth), & Micrognathia of the jaw. She also noted **thin sparse hair alopecia,** squeaky high-pitched voice, visual/spatial learning disabilities/ADD, pituitary dysfunction, and hypoplasia of the cerebellar vermis.

I have cerebellar disease, Trigeminal Neuralgia, **Dwarfism Ectodermal Alopecia,** Strabismus, Dwarfism, learning disabilities, anxiety, PTSD ADHD insomnia irritability, & Receded jaw mid-low facial areas.

(Dalkiz & Dalkiz et al) have noted the following: Dwarfism Alopecia, missing/sparse eyebrows, scalp hair loss, hair loss, partial hair loss, coupled with Dwarfism Dental Pathology. (Terlemez, noted the presence of **sparse dry thin hair**. (Abdel-Salam,) noted the presence of **sparse/missing scalp hair. sparse eyebrows**. (Chee & Lee,) noted in proportioned short stature dwarfism dental patients the presence of **Alopecia,** including Ectodermal **Alopecia**. (Soumya,et al) discusses a patient with **alopecia,** dwarfism, teeth malocclusion & cerebellar disease. See also Wikipedia of Gomez Lopez Hernandez Syndrome- that includes short skull, **alopecia.** dwarfism, short stature, midfacial hypoplasia, and Trigeminal Dental Pain.

(Munoz & Santos,) describe Cerebello-Dermal-Dysplasia as follows: cerebellar ataxia, **alopecia (parietal/occipital, /lateral skull)** and **hair hypoplasia**. cerebellar anomaly, midface hypoplasia, Short Stature Dwarfism,and Craniofacial abnormalities,.

(Chan, JK) lists **alopecia,** fused cerebellar hemispheres, and depigmentation areas.

(Al-Semal) does not list the cerebellum but includes **alopecia,** hypotonia, dysarthria, scoliosis, sensorineural hearing loss, extrapyramidal symptoms and basal ganglia decreased signal intensity.

(AJNR,) noted the *Trigeminal Nerve* Anesthesia trait coupled with the following cerebellar traits: rare malformation of cerebellum, agenesis/hypogenesis of the cerebellar vermis, the absence of cerebellar vermis, dorsal fusion of cerebellar hemispheres, cerebellar dentate nuclei and superior cerebellar peduncles, cerebellar ataxia, flat cerebellum, **parietal <u>alopecia</u>**, craniofacial abnormalities, vertebral abnormalities, cardiac/cardiovascular anomalies and musculoskeletal abnormalities.

CONNECTIONS BETWEEN ALOPECIA AND DENTAL PATHOLOGY.

(Dalkiz & Dalkiz et al,) have noted the following: Dwarfism **Alopecia, missing/sparse eyebrows, scalp hair loss, hair loss, partial hair loss**, coupled with Dwarfism Dental Pathology. (Terlemez, noted the presence of **sparse dry thin hair.** (Abdel-Salam,) noted the presence of **sparse/missing scalp hair. sparse eyebrows.** (Chee & Lee,) noted in proportioned short stature dwarfism dental patients the presence of **Alopecia,** including Ectodermal Alopecia.

(Dinkova,) studied a case of **Alopecia Areata** that originated from DENTAL foci: Dinkova stated that the **alopecia areata hair loss** was effectively resolved by eliminating a focalized DENTAL infection via tooth extraction. Dinkova adds that Alopecia patients should receive careful exploration of their oral cavity in search of possible dental infection. She cited that there is an Association between periodontitis and Alopecia Areata/Totalis. Dinkova stated that there was also a finding of decayed teeth roots and periapical dental lesions. After the infected teeth were extracted, the alopecia areata hair loss ceased, and new hair growth was observed.

(Science Daily, + University of Granada-Dept of Stomatology) states that bald alopecia hair loss patches can be caused by a hidden tooth infection. They noted that there is a close relationship between teeth infection and Alopecia Areata hair loss. They advised going to the dentist when/if alopecia areata hair loss occurs, in order to have their oral cavity checked for hidden tooth infections. Research at the University of Granada established a relationship between Alopecia Areata & dental disease. The Alopecia Areata bald patches caused by hidden tooth infection can appear on a line projected from the dental infection and thus can be located on the face at the level of the maxillary teeth, above a line thru the lip angle to the scalp-The Granada researchers also proved how white blood cells attacking the tooth infection migrate to hair follicles.

(Duverger, & Hairlineink) Dr Oliver Duverger at the NIH in Maryland, found that patients with male pattern baldness can be plagued with dental cavities due to defective cellular make-up: in particular, defective keratin proteins. Keratin proteins strengthen tooth enamel and hair shafts are composed of Keratin proteins. Patients with mutated Keratin protein can experience alopecia hair loss, along with weakened teeth vulnerable to disease and cavities.

(Montoya & Soriano,) found that Alopecia Areata is connected to dental tooth infections. The association of Alopecia Areata and infectious dental foci is relatively common and may be explained by the autoimmune nature of the disorder. The Alopecia Areata case was resolved by eliminating a focalized dental infection via endodontic root canal treatment. They found that the presence of common immune mediators in the pathogenesis of both Alopecia Areata and dental infection could account for the dental origin of the hair loss. Patients with Alopecia Areata should have a careful exploration of the oral cavity in search of possible dental infections. (Zivkovic,6/1990) describes Endodontic Root Canal treatment in the treatment of Alopecia Areata. (Balcheva & Abadjiev,) and (Luscious & Maman,) describe cases of Alopecia Areata associated with an infection of dental origin.

(Samuel, & Muthu.) also researched the link between Alopecia Areata & Dental infections: They also found decayed molars. root resorption of molars. & radiolucency of molars. Their treatment included the extraction of molar roots. The hair loss was gone 6 months after dental surgery. Auto-Immune mechanisms explain Alopecia Areata together w/ dental infections. There is a pathogenesis of Alopecia Areata combined with dental infections. They also felt that Alopecia Areata is due to irritation of maxillary jaw origin-located above a line starting at labial commissure and terminating at the occiput. Those of mandibular origin are located below that line. They also noted that decayed maxillary molars are connected to hair loss lesions. The maxillary teeth area hair loss=lip commissures to occiput. Alopecia lesions are connected to maxillary tooth infection. Alopecia Areata is also linked to decay in the mandibular molar area.

Dr Elena Dimitrova from the Belgravia Hair loss treatment center in London UK found that tooth infections are linked to hair loss alopecia. When a tooth gcts infected white blood cells attack/destroy the infection however the white blood cells can migrate to hair follicles. The association/occurrence of Alopccia and tooth infection is often detected close to the affected area. For example, beard areas on crown & lower scalp areas. Dentists are now being trained to look for alopecia hair loss in patients with tooth infections. The alopecia areata is secondary to dental infection and is due to common immune mediators found in both the dental infection and the alopecia areata. **Neurology and Alopecia/Hair Loss** (Potter) mentions that Neurological deficits are sometimes correlated to hair loss phenotypes.

Chapter 19: How 1 dentist helps a special needs terrified adult dental patient very similar to me & my dentist

(Alexandra, Jill) whose dental terror story I shared in the dental terror chapter of this book, had included how her dentist is her friend & ally and I chose to summarize her description here - for illustrative purposes:

,You have to make your dentist an ally in the fight and that takes a lot of strength to even think about trying to do, My dentist, bless his heart, understands my lifetime of horrific experiences and how that caused me to avoid dentists as much as possible...thereby destroying my teeth, he knows all about my panic, my hyperawareness, he knows all the bad experiences. Basically, he knows more than a priest...my death grip of panic serves to make his life harder; I send him long rambling emails. I need to tell him because he's a really good guy who wants to avoid terrifying me with his instruments of torture, I am one of the worst dental patients you could have, he puts his hand on my arm and asks if I am ok, he's extremely patient with me, and with me writing the longest emails he probably ever gets from a patient, Lucky him, I the patient from hell arrives, we've gotten to know each other very well ...he has a gentle knowing smile...a smile that he really gets it ,a smile that says don't worry we've got this, he knows why I am shaking and flinching from panic, he doesn't pass judgment about my teeth or conditions. He doesn't make me feel bad, he doesn't make a big deal that I keep my eyes closed the whole time, he knows how easily I can disappear into my own world, he knows to stop when I hyperventilate, he makes me feel like I don't have to apologize repeatedly, he knows that it's far more than just average dental phobia.

He's become my friend and ally, we're both fighting on the same side now, he helps me battle my terror panic and he knows that my tough as nails act is a superficial and transparent facade hiding my intense fear, he's able to stop my panic attacks quickly and he can spot my traumatic memory recalls, he knows every moment is agonizingly long and knows the worst thing to do is to begin hurrying me ,he truly cares, he's on my side and it means more than he could ever know. He knows my nervous meltdowns, he knows that the mere sight of his office sends me into a tailspin, he allows for extra time for my appointments, allowing me to talk to and confide in him. My dentist helps because he really knows what's wrong and he truly feels my constant struggle, he knows that I still get panicky terrified every time I am about to enter his office, he knows that my breathing gets constricted and my heart pounds and he knows I fight off the urge to flee -he knows all of this -It's so much easier to handle this panic battle with him as my friend and ally ,I'm no longer embarrassed that he knows the reasons my body goes wrong. I am so grateful to have him as my ally since severe anxiety and panic is an enemy you can't do war with alone ...

She's like my twin clone, she understands totally, She's just like me!

Chapter 20: My Cerebellar disease + My PTSD-How they are Connected.

Symptoms of PTSD Post Traumatic Stress Disorder (See also Sorensen, Maria) include:(NCPTSD.VA.GOV)Occupational instability/repeated job losses, memory/cognition/learning/concentration difficulties, mood swings, depression, panic/anxiety attacks, temper outbursts, nightmares, insomnia, hyper startle, hyper arousal, hyper-reactivity, feeling scattered, unable to focus, ADHD, hyperactivity, mania, struggle with waking/sleeping, easily angered, emotional outbursts and emotional numbness, dissociation, memory losses, flashbacks of terror, intense fear, bad memories, obsessive thoughts, racing thoughts, thought flooding, catastrophic overwhelming feelings, social avoidance, cannot handle noise, lights, crowds, traffic, loudness, sirens, flashers, sudden entering of people, persistent horror/panic.

Feelings of detachment/dissociation/numbness, hyper-vigilance. autonomic dysfunction, elevated pulse/blood pressure/heart rate, increased cortisol stress hormone releases caused by the "danger' being sensed, excess response to stimuli. over-sensitization. over-reaction to "cues/triggers/stimuli. (Sorensen, Maria) adds that in PTSD,

Learning/concentration/attention/focus are often impaired, and information processing shows interruptions and interferences. Body memories (memories stored in the body) can and do cause physiological reactions, especially when and if verbalization of the distress is impaired. Many with PTSD show impaired learning & symptoms of ADD/ADHD. They need to be desensitized and need help in refocusing. They need a safe, calm, soothing and predictable environment in order to heal. They often show impaired verbalization of their distress.

Animal/Pet/Music/Hypno Therapies can be very beneficial in treating PTSD. Their information processing is often disrupted and interfered with from their internal distress.

(Rabellino & Densmore,) examined & researched the Cerebellum after Trauma: Focusing on the Resting State Functional Connectivity of the Cerebellum in PTSD, Post Traumatic Stress Disorder as part of their Human Brain Mapping. This is a brief summary of their findings & conclusions: They found decreased functional connectivity of anterior cerebellum, increased functional connectivity of posterior cerebellum and decreased functional connectivity between posterior cerebellum & prefrontal regions. They posit too that the cerebellum is involved in processing traumatic memories & that there are strong connections between the cerebellum and the autonomic nervous system. The cerebellum regulates physiological responses under stressful circumstances and under traumatizing emotional experiences. The cerebellum coordinates traumatic emotions and bodily response to those emotions.

(Levinson, Harold Dr MD) has done many years of publications on the cerebellar cause of anxiety, panic. phobias & PTSD. He was the first expert, medical, research scholar that connected the Cerebellum to these & other related conditions such as ADHD, Autism & Aspergers. see (Davenport,) and (Reynolds,) in articles on the benefits of Ritalin & similar ADD/ADHD psychostimulant medications.

In treating PTSD, he stated that these medications not only improve PTSD symptoms but also improve cognitive symptoms in persons with PTSD. He adds that Dr Harold Levinson MD has found the very same thing-and according to Dr Harold Levinson, this confirms many of his findings reported during his almost 50 years of research. He has found that PTSD, ADD/ADHD Dyslexia Learning Disabilities, Aspergers, Autism, Phobias, Panic, Anxiety & other similar conditions all have common cerebellar vestibular anxiety symptoms that respond positively to Cerebellar-Vestibular "CV" enhancing medications. Dr

Levinson also showed that a diverse group of disorders including PTSD have coexisting Cerebellar-Vestibular "CV" dysfunction and that they respond favorably to CV harmonizing medications. Dr Levinson also connected PTSD to fearful associations linked to traumatic memories. Dr Levinson also cites a " predisposition" to PTSD, from the presence of CV cerebellar vestibular dysfunction.

(Bergland, Christopher) posited that cerebellar injury damage may be at the root of PTSD. He cites that the cerebellum influences emotions-and refers to a 2016 study at VA Puget Sound/University of WA regarding how repetitive blast exposure in combat veterans causes persistent cerebellar dysfunction: The repeated exposure to blasts creates microlesions in the ventral cerebellum, causing in turn a loss of/damage to Purkinje cells in the cerebellum, causing long term cerebellar brain function changes. The cerebellum holds over 50% of total neurons in the brain-The blasts cause chronic changes in neuron activity in the cerebellum. (Psychology Today,) Cerebellar damage may be at the root of PTSD in military combat veterans. Cerebellar Damage from explosive blasts can cause PTSD especially if it creates lesions of the ventral cerebellum-causing Purkinje cell loss in the cerebellum. (Friday Francesca,) shows that the cerebellum is linked to anxiety, depression, and PTSD, & that the cerebellum is involved in processing traumatic memories. (Debellis & Kuchibhatla) found in their study of structural cerebellar volumes in pediatric maltreatment PTSD, the cerebellar structural volume is lower in those abused children with PTSD.

(Priesmeyer, Nicole) wrote about " Cerebellar Hypervigilance in PTSD'': she refers to a cerebellar state of hypervigilance. Above the brainstem is the cerebellum. Here is a very brief "snapshot" summary of her findings, so chronically stressed, they are so focused on survival. it's difficult for them to connect with others, there is overstimulation of the limbic system, hyperactivation, hyperarousal, survival overrides thinking, state of hypervigilance, the experience of chronic stress/fear that can cause thinking in the brain to shut down.

She cites (Lazarus,) with regard to Coping = Ongoing cognitive/behavioral efforts to manage demands that are deemed as taxing or exceeding the resources of a person. Priesmeyer continues on-saying that: Coping Strategy=The level of threat in relation to the resources a person has available- the aim is to reduce the demands placed on the person- one can alter their emotional response to a stressful situation-ie increasing social contact in order to gain support - Emotion based coping -seeking social support for emotional reasons, positive reinterpretation and growth, acceptance, turning to RELIGION -Social support affects how people cope with stressful events,

(Holmes, Sophia,) performed research on the cerebellar and prefrontal cortical alterations in PTSD, including the issue of Chronic Stress & PTSD. Here is a brief summary of her research: A smaller cerebellar volume is found in PTSD patients as compared to persons without PTSD. She also noted that the whole brain functional connectivity in the cerebellum is weaker and slower in those with PTSD vs persons without PTSD. She posited that there is cerebellar involvement in the pathophysiology of PTSD., as well as smaller gray matter volume in the cerebellum of those w/ PTSD, in particular the right cerebellum crus. She also noted hypoactive cerebellar function and stated that the cerebellum affects PTSD Emotional Regulation/SomatoSensory Processing and also affects the distinct patterns of Cerebellar alterations in Dissociative PTSD.

(McDonald,) published research findings on the issue of Pain flashbacks in PTSD. Here is a brief summary of the findings: Intrusive Multi-Sensory memory flashbacks can cause pain to be re-experienced as if it were actually re-occurring again, what McDonald calls a re-experiencing of pain felt at the time of the traumatic past event and feeling the pain again in the present. McDonald adds that the original pain becomes encoded under extreme stress conditions, and pain flashbacks are connected to somatosensory memory where prior past pain is re-experienced in the present time.

Chapter 21: Cerebellum & Short Stature Dwarfism/Hypopituitary Dwarfism

When I was diagnosed with Cerebellar Vestibular disease by brilliant renowned neurologist Dr Harold Levinson MD in Sept. 1984, It "peaked my inquisitive Dyslexic/ADHD/Aspergers Mind to wonder if, how & why My cerebellar disease was connected to my Hypopituitary Proportional Dwarfism and I was "self-compelled & self-driven to pore thru load after load of literature in a quest to better understand my unique status as a "dwarf little person" and its possible connections to my cerebellar condition. Although it was just an intuitive hunch coupled with a leap of faith to embark on this perhaps "quixotic" research venture, my "gamble" more than paid off-it was "mind blowing" to find my inner intuition had been correct, more so than I had ever dreamed of. Being dyslexic dysmetric and dyspraxic as Dr Harold Levinson wrote & taught me allowed me the priceless gift of the freedoms that come with those disorders, the freedom to embark on this self-validating research quest fed by an insatiable dyslexic thirst for solving the mystery-based puzzles that have characterized my intense need to understand how the cerebellum is/was the root cause of my lifelong dyslexic struggles.

The more I studied Dr Levinson's published works the more and more each tiny piece of the grand mystery puzzle began to come together. The crucial tap root is/was the defective cerebellum that caused head to toe lifelong chaos in every bit of my entire life. The Cerebellum was most definitely connected to dwarfism, so what I initially thought of as Hypopituitary Growth Hormone Failure Proportional Dwarfism was and is Cerebellar Hypopituitary Growth Hormone Failure Proportional Dwarfism.

I decided to publish several of my key findings here so that all the readers can better understand how I figured it all out and verified my inner intuitive hunches both combined with and derived from the brilliant groundbreaking research of my world-renowned neurologist Dr Harold Levinson MD. His research sparked an eternal, unquenchable, burning flame of bright light in my freedom filled dyslexic mind, soul, spirit, intellect & thoughts.

Sorry for my prolix introduction to my Cerebellar Dwarfism tale, I now will begin sharing my Cerebellar Dwarfism "tale" with all of you. Listed below are the "rare as hen's teeth & blue moons" "TIDBITS & PEARLS" that clearly show all of you my Cerebellar Dwarfism:

(Orpha.net) wrote about short stature Hypo-Pituitary hormone deficiency Dwarfism and CEREBELLAR defects. (Graf) in his research on CCAS Cerebellar Cognitive Affective Syndrome, found that CCAS was/is characterized by ADD/ADHD (which I have), Learning Disabilities (which I have cerebellar defects (which I have) and Short Stature Dwarfism. Hou described Hallermann Streiff Syndrome that includes Ocular Abnormalities, Mandibular Jaw Hypoplasia, small Cerebellum & Proportionate Dwarfism.

Ferrell mentioned that MOPD Dwarfism includes Cerebellar Vermis Hypoplasia and Hypoplastic Cerebellar Vermis. Miller & Alldinger - Their Veterinary study of Alaskan Huskies described the presence of proportional dwarfism and infancy onset Cerebellar Dysfunction. Chiruvolu, mentions dwarfism & cerebellar cortical dysplasia, Kebapci discusses the case of an 18-year-old young woman with Hypopituitary short stature Dwarfism: cardiopulmonary abnormalities, delayed speaking/walking, facial dysmorphism, human growth hormone insufficiency, and cerebellar atrophy.

ECTODERMAL SHORT STATURE(DWARFISM) SYNDROME + ELLIS VAN CREVELD

(Nethan,) (Naqash,) (Uniprot/RGD) (Hattab & Yassin,) (Cahuana,) (Atasu & Biren,) (Hanemann) all indicated that This Ectodermal ''variant syndrome" has unique DENTAL features coupled with Short Stature Dwarfism) and overlaps greatly with the "regular forms" discussed in this book. So, I thought it was important to give this "variant' its own separate section in this book. Zannoli & Inchingolo, said that There are individuals who do NOT fit neatly into 1 or another recognized category. Cardiac features include congenital heart defects and heart valve defects. Orthopedic features include Skeletal Anomalies. Hair/Nail Defects include Alopecia small dysplastic nails Dental Features include odd, shaped molars, reduced tooth crown size, enamel hypoplasia, dental root fusion, malocclusion, atypical tooth cusps, taurodontism impacted teeth, maxillary gingival margin defects, mucolabial fold defects. lip defects, jagged lower alveolar ridge, labiogingival defects, incisor defects, misshapen malformed teeth, hypodontia, microdontia, crossbite, partial occlusion, alveolar/ mandible/mandibular defects, maxillary labial tissue defects, abnormal labial tissue attachment to alveolar ridge, molar defects, missing teeth, gingival gum defects, periodontitis, excess plaque/calculus, fluoride deficiency, hypoplastic teeth. decayed teeth, caries, gingival soft gum tissue defects, alveolar anterior ridge defects.

Chapter 22: Dwarfism & Extreme short stature Date back to the Bible & Ancient Times: Judaic Aspects

Dahlia Pasik provided intriguing Judaic bible-based information on Dwarfism & Extreme Short Stature. (see also yutorah.org) I have summarized the key information for you to ponder: Bechorot 45b refers to "nannas" which means "dwarf" ,See commentaries of Ibn Esra & Targum Yonatan in Leviticus 21:20 ,the biblical term "dak" refers to "dwarf" & the Gemara also references dwarfism, Gemara Bechorot 45b mentions "nannas;; (dwarfs) Dwarfs were not allowed to serve as a priest because their visible short stature was seen as a defect or blemish making them unfit to serve in Temple(Leviticus 21:20) (Commentaries of Ibn Esra & Targun Yonatan)(see eg biblical training.org) Dwarfs were banned from priestly duties & could not serve as priests.

 Julius Preuss added that dwarfs were not allowed to offer priestly food sacrifices nor were they allowed to even approach the altar of the Holy of Holies in ancient Israel. They were seen as unfit ...the Tanach also references Dwarfism including Pharoah & Nebuchadnezzar: Daniel 4:14 described the dwarfism of Pharaoh -the Pharaoh of Moses' day was 1 amah tall, considered very short and considered a biological dwarf as per Chazral(3) ,Daniel 1:14 Nebuchadnezzar was identified as a dwarf-he was the smallest man to ever be appointed as a ruler over a kingdom,,Midrash in Yalkut reaffirms that Nebuchadnezzar was a dwarf,The Tama D'bei Eliyahu Rabbah(31) states that when Nebuchadnezzar went from province to province ,the people would mock him for his short stature...people were shocked by his great power combined with his extreme short stature dwarfism, God complained of the wicked Nebuchadnezzar" See what this dwarf from

Babylon has done to me" (Pesikta D'rav Kahana 13:42) The Megillah 11a describes Nebuchadnezzar as a haughty short tyrant, Nebuchadnezzar was an evil tyrant that initiated the first exile upon his destruction of the first temple, he was an egotist ,Julius Preuss commented that Nebuchadnezzar was the smallest of all people ever to be appointed as a ruler over a kingdom, and the MIdrash concluded that he was a dwarf. See Yalkut 11:1062 Nebuchadnezzar was as small as a midget dwarf (Babylonian Conqueror)

Zacchaeus (sometimes spelled or Zaccheus, Ancient Greek: Ζακχαῖος, Zakkhaîos; Hebrew: זכי, "pure", "innocent"), was a chief **tax-collector** at Jericho, mentioned only in the Gospel of Luke. A descendant of Abraham, he was an example of Jesus's personal, earthly mission to bring salvation to the lost.

Jesus and the Dwarf | The Man Nobody Knew by Garrett C Whitworth
https://www.amazon.com/Man-Nobody-Knew-Garrett-Whitworth/dp/1512739936

- As it happened, *Zacchaeus* was well known in Jericho, and he was also well hated: He was the chief *tax collector*, not only in the city but also in the surrounding region. He took a portion of all the *taxes* these men collected, making him easily the richest man in Jericho.

As we were about to pass out of Jericho, Jesus suddenly stopped and peered up into a large sycamore tree. It was early spring, but the tree's branches were already fully covered with leaves. I could not see what he saw or understand what he could find of interest in an ordinary tree; we had passed dozens of such trees as we made our way through the city. And then, strangely, he started talking to the tree! "Zacchaeus, come down from there! Today, I must visit your house! "The sun was hot; the crowd had pressed close to Jesus all day; he had eaten nothing since breakfast. Was he all right? I then saw a pair of small legs, followed by an equally small body, emerge from the canopy of the tree. What appeared to be perhaps a five-year-old boy climbed down the trunk of the tree. He landed on his feet, hitting the ground with a slight thud. However, seeing his face, I realized he was not a small boy; he was a man, and an older man at that! He could not have been more than three feet tall—half the height of Peter! I did not know that a grown man could be that small. Utterly confused and astonished, I blinked and glanced at Peter. Peter moved close enough to me to whisper in my ear. "Haven't you ever seen a dwarf before?" he asked. *Dwarf.* I'd never heard the word. "A dwarf is simply a small person," Peter continued in a whisper. "Nobody knows why, but some people never grow to the stature of most other men and women." "When they're born, are they smaller than most babies?" I asked, also in a whisper.

"Maybe a little smaller, but usually not much. Dwarfs are rare; this man is only the second or third one I've ever seen. "The reason Zacchaeus had ascended the tree was simple. In the large crowd that surrounded Jesus, he was too short to even get a glimpse of the Master, so he climbed the tree to see him. He had heard of Jesus and his kingdom message; earlier that day, he had learned of the Master's imminent arrival in Jericho. His curiosity was aroused, and he had to see this man. As it happened, Zacchaeus was well known in Jericho, and he was also well hated: He was the chief tax collector, not only in the city but also in the surrounding region. Dozens of other tax collectors worked under him, collecting levies for the Romans, the temple, and Herod. He took a portion of all the taxes these men collected, making him easily the richest man in Jericho. Jesus had asked if he could visit Zacchaeus's house—rather, he'd told Zacchaeus that he was going to visit his house that day.

Jesus and the Dwarf Part 2 | The Man Nobody Knew

Jesus and the *Dwarf, part 2* An excerpt from the book, The Man Nobody Knew. Zacchaeus was thrilled about entertaining *Jesus*, and the little man eagerly led us to his magnificent home on a hill overlooking Jericho. You will recall that Matthew, a former tax collector and now our colleague, had a large and beautiful home in Capernaum, but it was nothing like this. The grounds and furnishings were exquisite. Zacchaeus had many servants; he needed them for such a large estate. It was evening now, and Zacchaeus ordered his butler to have the kitchen servants prepare a banquet for Jesus and the twelve of us. The dinner was sumptuous, the food and wine excellent.

Afterward, we all withdrew to a large and comfortable sitting room. Zacchaeus had heard some of Jesus's kingdom message secondhand, but he wanted to hear it from the Master's lips. Jesus was happy to oblige him. He spoke for over an hour, telling the same story that he had told to countless thousands during the course of the past two-plus years. I never tired of hearing it; none of us did. Jesus was a marvelous raconteur, whether he was speaking in parables or teaching the gospel message, and it made no difference to him if the audience was small or large. His voice was clear, almost musical, and pleasing to the ear. His quiet passion for the gospel narrative was certain and absolute. What he said manifestly and deeply affected even many of those who could not quite bring themselves to accept the truth of his words. The exceptions were the Pharisees and lawyers; their hearts and minds proved to be impenetrable in most cases.

Zacchaeus—and the rest of us—listened intently to what Jesus had to say, and when the Master finished, the receptive tax collector was clearly overjoyed. "Rabbi, I want to become one of your followers. Wherever you go, I want to go with you. First, I want to make things right with those I have wronged. I'll give half of what I possess to the poor, and if I've defrauded anyone—and I know of several that I have cheated—I will restore to them four times what I've taken wrongly. I understand that you are going to Jerusalem for Passover. I haven't attended Passover for many years, but I will join you and your other followers there. First, however, I will do what I have committed to do." "You, Zacchaeus, are a son of Abraham too. The Son of Man has come to seek and save the lost; this day, salvation has come to your house." (Young, Amos) wrote about Zacchaeus "short and unseen" The Zacchaeus story challenges the normal assumption that disability is a problem needing to be fixed or eliminated, See Luke-Acts Luke 19: 1-10. Zacchaeus was a rich chief tax collector, who was very short of stature (Luke 19:3)

He climbed up a sycamore tree in order to see Jesus. Julius Preuss commented on Zacchaeus: He was exceedingly large in spirit, but had littleness of stature and lack of height, he became a convert to Jesus, & promised to pay 1/2 of his possessions to the poor, and promised to repay fourfold those he had defrauded (Luke 19:8) (his resolutions following his conversion to Jesus) Local judeans despised tax collectors and tax collectors were stigmatized, and viewed as despicable, he collected taxes for the Romans, he was well known for his littleness and little stature....see " helikia mikros" (Luke 19:3) shortness of stature, he had pathological dwarfism ,but was also known to have "largeness of heart"...He hosted Jesus at his home, Luke 19:9 said that salvation came to his house, Levitical(leviticus) prohibitions against dwarfs full participation in the liturgy of ancient Israel was lifted, little people are agents in God's eyes, Jesus accepted Zacchaeus and didn't see him as impaired, damaged, blemished or disabled, nor as needing fixing, in order to fully participate in the renewal/restoration of Israel.

Betty Adelson noted that an important rabbinical invocation that is to be spoken whenever a person sees a dwarf is the prayer that begins "Blessed is God who makes man different" taken to mean that each creation is a miracle of God, including people smaller than the norm.

Blessing on Seeing an Unusual Creature

Jewish law prescribes the recitation of a blessing upon seeing an unusual person or animal, though there is a wide range of opinions over just what kind of animal qualifies. According to Jewish legal codes, this includes an albino, a **dwarf,** an extremely tall person, a monkey, and an elephant. The text of the blessing is: בָּרוּךְ אַתָּה יהוה אֱלֹהֵינוּ מֶלֶךְ הָעוֹלָם משנה הבריות
Blessed are You, LORD, our God, King of the Universe, who makes creatures different.
Baruch ata Adonai, Eloheinu melech ha-olam, m'shaneh habriyot.
myjewishlearning.com/article/8-jewish-prayers-youve-never-heard-of/

Emil Hirsch noted that a dwarf was declared unfit for service-see Hullin 63a, Sifra, Le Bek, Dwarfs are said to have been numerous in the towers of the fortresses of Tyre (Ezekiel 18,10, avii), Caphtorim (Genesis x14) and Cappadocians and Cretes are dwarfs, though be in your eyes a makroelaphos, in our eyes he is a dwarf of the dwarfs (Genesis, R LXV 11 Cant Rii15) Nebuchadnezzar is called dwarf of Babel (Pesik 13, 112a, Pesik R31) (Daniel Chapter 4 V24-V28) the little one ell dwarf (See Daniel Chapter 4 v14-v17) "lowest of men" and Pharoah =Dwarf referred to in Daniel (MK 189)

Dr Chahira Kozma, MD & Renee Twombly wrote about Dwarfs in Ancient Egyptian Society: Dwarfs reached elevated positions within Egyptian Society. Dwarfism existed in the 3000 years leading up to the death of Cleopatra. Dwarfism was a documented condition in Ancient Egypt. There is evidence of Dwarfism in Ancient Egypt in both artistic representations and written forms. In Ancient Egypt, people with large heads relative to their small bodies held positions of seniority and were granted titled positions. Pharaohs wanted dwarfs in their households and Egyptians believed dwarfs were lucky and could protect others from danger. Little People were highly valued -3 Mythological Egyptian figures included dwarfs, Ptah, a master architect, Bes, a goddess musician and Ra a sun spirit. Dr Kozma saw the potential of a depiction of Dwarfism as part of a discourse with health and medical professionals as well as with students in those fields. Dwarfism also held religious significance in Ancient Egypt. There is also a statue of an Egyptian scribe with dwarfism and his wife and two children. Ancient Egypt regarded physical disabilities such as dwarfism as divine attributes granted to humans. See also (Dasen, Veronique regarding Dwarfs in Ancient Egypt/Greece.)

1 Samuel 16:7 The Lord told Samuel: Do not look on his appearance or on the height of his stature -the Lord looks on the heart and not on outward appearance.

Catholic literature (Catholic.org) refers to Saint John the Dwarf,-Feast Day October 17,

Saint John the Dwarf   Born c. 339 Thebes, Egypt[1]   Died c. 405 Mount Colzim, Egypt

Saint John the Dwarf (Greek: Ιωάννης Κολοβός; Arabic: ابو يحنّس القصير (Abū) Yuḥannis al-Qaṣīr c. 339 – c. 405), also called **Saint John Colobus, Saint John Kolobos** or **Abba John the Dwarf**,[2] was an Egyptian Desert Father of the early Christian church.

John the Dwarf was born in the town of Thebes in Egypt[3] to poor Christian parents. At the age of eighteen, he and an elder brother, moved to the desert of Scetes[4] where he became a disciple of Saint Pambo and a good friend of Saint Pishoy. He lived a life of austerity and taught several other monks his way of life, among them was Arsenius the Great. After the departure of Saint Pambo, John was ordained a priest by Pope Theophilus and became abbot of the monastery he founded around the Tree of Obedience. When the Berbers invaded Scetes in 395, John fled the Nitrian Desert and went to live on Mount Colzim, near the present city of Suez, where he died.

In 515, the relics of Saint John the Dwarf were moved to the Nitrian Desert. His feast is celebrated on October 17 in the Roman Catholic Church, on 20 Paopi at the Coptic Orthodox Church and on November 9 in the Eastern Orthodox Church. The Monastery of Saint John the Dwarf in Scetes is now deserted. John the Dwarf is best known for his obedience. The most famous story about his obedience is that one day Saint Pambo gave Abba John a piece of dry wood and ordered him to plant and water it. John obeyed and went on watering it twice a day even though the water was about 12 miles from where they lived. After three years, the piece of wood sprouted and grew into a fruitful tree. Pambo took some of this tree's fruits and went around to all the elder monks, saying "take, eat from the fruit of obedience". Postumian, who was in Egypt in 402, assured that he was shown this tree which grew in the yard of the monastery and which he saw covered with shoots and green leaves. John Cassian tells a similar story of John of Egypt, only he was asked to tend the stick only one year, it did not bloom, and after this test of obedience his superior threw the stick away. According to William Harmless, "Scholars presume that Cassian was closer to the event and may be the more dependable reporter..."**Ababius** was a monk of Scetes and is a saint of the Coptic Church. He is the subject of a long biography attributed in manuscript form to John the Dwarf. The manuscript has yet to be translated into English. See Also Butler, Alban. "St. John the Dwarf, Anchoret of Sceté", *The Lives of the Saints*, Vol.IX, 1866

Chapter 23: Dwarfism & Learning Disabilities

Given my learning disabilities (and ADHD/Aspergers/Dyslexia/Irlen Syndrome) that were diagnosed 9/8/1984 by Dr Harold Levinson MD, I did wonder if there were links between my dwarfism & my learning disabilities (and related conditions listed above). I decided to listen to Dr Levinson's ''advice'' once more regarding the ''freedom to be dyslexic, dysmetric & I allowed it to be my "brain fuel" to try to "add these pieces to my 'puzzle''. In my personal case, my dwarfism is really Cerebellar Hypopituitary Growth Hormone Deficient with Ectodermal Features including the Ectodermal Dental Ravage & the Dwarfism Ectodermal Type Alopecia.

Kelberman & Dattani, stated that variable hypopituitarism is associated with learning disabilities. Larson mentions "multi-systemic syndromes" in which hypopituitarism is a significant component. Interestingly, he cites Machinis regarding how mutations can cause cerebellar defects. Bhatia, Eesh & Shukla, discussed the case of a patient with multiple pituitary hormone deficiencies that also had a rare cerebellar disease " Spino-cerebellar Ataxia and They indicated that Spino-cerebellar Ataxia has a rare association with hypopituitary hypogonadotropic short stature dwarfism with cerebellar ataxia and cerebellar atrophy(latter revealed upon MRI exam.)This patient had unsteady gait, and poor academic performance, along with scoliosis/kyphosis, gaze dependent nystagmus limb ataxia, mild hypotonia, and small amplitude of sensory potentials.

Chapter 24: Dysautonomia & Dysautonomic Abnormalities in Dwarfism Dental Pathology

Huneycutt observed the following Familial Dysautonomia/Dysautonomic abnormalities in Dwarfism Dental Pathology: defective sensory nerves, decreased neurons in sensory/autonomic ganglia, impaired temperature regulation, abnormal neuro-regulation, dysautonomic crisis caused by dental abscesses, lightheadedness, postural hypotension, palpitations, elevated pulse/heart rate, sensitivity to temperature changes, tachycardia, bradycardia, allergic type effects from epinephrine/novocaine, and heart racing/pounding,

Glasner observed the following Familial Dysautonomia abnormalities and stated that dental symptoms are an important issue in treatment: distinctive orofacial characteristics, small jaws, overcrowded teeth, chronic gingivitis, plaque accumulation, history of dental trauma, alveolar jawbone height too low, unsteady gait, malformed teeth, enamel erosion, soft thin weak enamel, worn away enamel, internal resorption of dentin which weakens teeth to the point of risking breakage of teeth, dental resorption which may not stop-requiring endodontic restorations including root canals.

Chapter 25: Dyslexia & Dwarfism

Yourstory.com and Times of India describe the inspiring true story of a Dyslexic Dwarf Apoorva Sharma. Despite being a Dwarf Dyslexic. She has scored 76% in the CBSE Board Exam, even disorders cannot dwarf her achievement. She is a student at the Cambridge School Ghaziabad India & is an inspiration for all those who are thinking of giving up. She dared to write the board exams on her own and scored 76% in class 12 CBSE. Despite childhood trauma and delayed walking/talking, she never gave up.

Abbie Osbourne, Amber Lee Dodd, & Alex Strick are known for " books for dyslexics...including "We are Giants" by Amber Lee Dodd, Their Book Character had to leave her home and everything she had known, living with dwarfism and adapting to major changes and losses that caused her to grieve, she proudly adapted to hardship with love and was proud of who she was and didn't want to be defined by her disability or by her restricted physical growth, Dwarfism Dyslexia & Discovery, the "We are Giants" book was published 4/20/2016,Dodd said she had to do lots of internet research in order to write her book, and that research helped her to really understand, Here is what Amber revealed about the struggles to publish her book "We are Giants" she tried to get help to fine-tune the manuscript, she did not see the book as being that unusual until she started to share the manuscript. She encountered some hesitancy among agents who weren't quite sure they would know how to pitch it, she tried not to get distracted or put off by anyone's doubts -she stuck to her original ideas & was determined to get it right, she strongly identified with "little people" (dwarfs) and really embraced that, she focused on 1 experience regarding dwarfism realizing it would be impossible to write about dwarfism and represent every view as every dwarf is different ,and expresses their identity in different ways, however she wanted the character to be diverse, she decided to use words and ideas that work and make sense to her audience, and said that factoring in language terminology could be something of a mine field. Amber grew up with dyslexia, she's very dyslexic and has dyspraxia as well, she was not diagnosed for a long time, she was always very aware of being the kid who couldn't do things. she felt that she was the last child to manage getting things done, she thinks that her teachers despaired about her. she finally caught up, she devoured everything she could get her hands on, books completely opened up her world, she was really good at writing her own stories, she discovered all sorts of wonderful books, the world started to make better sense, her dyslexic brain works differently, and interprets the world in different ways, and she has excellent language skills.

Chapter 26: Hypnodontics-Hypnotherapy in Dentistry: Hypnoanalgesia+ HypnoAnesthesia

Gilang Yubiliana refers to **Hypnodontics** as the "art of suggestion to control dental anxiety". Dave Berman says that simple language skills are what is needed to create a light state of hypnotic trance, increasing case acceptance hinges on helping patients to feel comfortable saying yes to continued treatment, if a patient needs many visits, it can feel overwhelming to the patient, the dentist can use the "language of ethical influence" -use the patient's own values and the patient's own belief system to guide your choice of words, be verbally flexible, patient focus tends to be on the physical experiences of pain and discomfort, meet what the patient feels is important, meet the patient's criteria/wants/wishes, words matter ,Single language patterns used by hypnotherapists can be learned by dental providers to make patients more comfortable and their dental practices more profitable. Hypnotic words can be embedded into ordinary conversational flow aka conversational hypnosis. Formal trance induction is not needed to influence a patient to experience hypnotic effects, minor adjustment in language produces hypnotic effects. (Acosta, Juan CHT 2014) also refers to the use of hypnotic effects as an ethical influence in dentistry, Acosta uses hypnodontics for scaling/cleaning/root planning.

Helen Skinner speaks of the recognized important role of hypnosis in dentistry. Skinner refers to the 2012 ASCH American Society of Clinical Hypnosis overview: a state of inner absorption, concentration, focused attention with relaxation and suggestibility...the use of suggestibility or "trance talent" to alter perception, cognition, mood and behavior, taken into a deep state of relaxation to stop panic/anxiety- for extremely phobic patients, this may need to be practiced in advance with appointments even before the dental treatment work.

Dr Aaron Moss DDS FSCEH gives a historical description of **Hypnodontics** as follows: credit is due the dentists for initiating a widespread interest in hypnosis, The term **Hypnodontics** dates back to 1948 and signifies use of hypnosis in dentistry but it actually dates back to the 1844 exhibition of hypnosis by GQ Colton a chemist and hypnotist. See 2/2/1891 letter from Colton Dental Association NYC NY regarding ' to facilitate hypnoses. Hypnodontics includes relaxation, relief of tensions, anxieties, panic, pain and fear, improved cooperation/tolerance/acceptance/analgesia/ calmness/comfort, and it can be an effective tool in dealing with dental prosthetics.   It can also modify/stop bad habits such as smoking. It can reduce or eliminate the need for analgesia/anesthesia, and can also be used to create amnesia for unpleasant memories, it can replace pre-medicating with anxiolytics and can be used with or without nitrous oxide, It can minimize gagging, retching, nausea, emesis and can be used to stop bleeding and salivary flow and can minimize post treatment pain/bleeding & it can promote faster healing, It involves controlled suggestion, and it can be used as an adjunctive to chemo-anesthesia such as nitrous oxide.

It can change sensory perceptions/sensory awareness and can change temperature perception, it can induce temporary motor changes, provide emotional healing, emotional calmness, improves provider/patient rapport, enhances trust, improves confidence, changes perceptual processes subliminally, lowers resistance/defensiveness, improves trust, overcomes mistrust, overcomes past negativities, enhances acceptance of recommended treatment, enhances instructions regarding oral hygiene, increases amenability to suggestions, reduces bleeding/saliva/tension/ can be used with medications and numbing agents ,allows patient to be fully aware but peaceful, it is controlled relaxation, reduces pain/insomnia, decreases fearfulness, raises pain tolerance, 20% can go under very deeply, future inductions get faster quickly, takes only minutes to induce trance, can stop bruxism (teeth grinding)and help TMJ, AND it can include iatrosedation psychodental therapy to further extinguish fear/anxiety/ panic and traumatic past memories.

(Moss) explains that the oral cavity carries great psychic/emotional importance due to it being an erotogenic zone, fear/anxiety can be caused by trauma connected to the oral cavity, with proper conditioning a hypnotic state can be reached almost instantly in future appointments, it involves some mindset training, post-hypnotic suggestions, hypno-suggestion testing, it teaches relaxation and deep breathing, and progressive relaxation, and can promote sleep, Hypnodontics can facilitate in adapting to dental prosthetics/dentures, it can condition the patient to wear the devices. Additionally, bleeders tend to be chronic anxiety prone, and anxiety affects coagulation, clotting and fibrinolytic activity. Hypnodontics can help in stopping bleeding, it can also reduce excess salivation and minimize gagging.

Self-Hypnosis, Hypnotherapy & Hypnodontics in Managing Experimental dental pain:

Thomas Gerhard Wolf wrote about the effectiveness of **self-hypnosis in the relief of Experimental Dental Pain.** He described the use of randomized controlled clinical trials in evaluating the effectiveness of self-hypnosis on pain perception & noted that the pain threshold under self-hypnosis was higher than without hypnotic intervention, pain was rated lower with self-hypnosis than without self-hypnosis. He added that self-hypnosis can be used in clinical practice as an adjunct to the gold standard of local anesthesia for dental pain management, as well as an alternative to local anesthetics for some dental patients.

Past life dental hypnotherapy and the Benefits of Songs During Slavery & the Underground Railroad

In many ways, my " desperate fleeing from the deep south Florida to go up north to NY" repeatedly reminded me of Slaves fleeing the plantations by way of the Underground Railroad & reminded me a great deal of Harriet Tubman, the "conductor" of the Underground Railroad. My very frequent and repeated thoughts of this finally led me to ask my Hypnotherapist Hypnodontist dentist Dr Schamis to try what expert Dr Brian Weiss MD calls Past Life Regression Hypnotherapy. It revealed that I had a very dramatic, powerful, and epic past life as a Quaker Church Abolitionist Anti-Slavery Musician, Lawyer, Mansion Owner & Underground Railroad conductor helping slaves escape to the North to reclaim their freedom. My present life strangely mirrored my past life or perhaps my past life eerily permeated my present life and I decided to do some "light" research into historic Music of that time period to gain a more " formal academic" grasp on my unique past life. I am taking my "dyslexic freedom" (actually the Freedom to be Dysmetric Dyslexic & Dyspraxic, as per my neurologist Dr Harold Levinson MD) to do this "slavery music" research and want to share the following source reference with you.

(A Cosmic Field Theory of Mind Author *Dr Harold N. Levinson MD*

In order for science to progress, scientists must be free: free to think and speak, free to daydream and speculate, free to criticize and be criticized, free to be right and wrong, free to be dysmetric, dyslexic, and dyspraxic. This chapter is dedicated to the spirit of scientific freedom. It is the last research chapter in this book, and perhaps the opening chapter in others to follow. Symbolically, it demonstrates the author's belief that knowledge and progress are merely dynamically fluctuating quanta oscillating between any given scientific introduction and summary.) (see Levinson, Harold A Solution to the Riddle Dyslexia, Springer-Verlag, NY 1983)

My other additional ''Historical Musical findings" I also share with you in this book. I hope it will help you better understand the music therapy aspects of my unique experimental dental treatment journey in NY.

Gregory and Hargreaves both indicated that Hymns often accompanied slave labor in the United States during the 1800's. The hymns helped boost the resolve to complete arduous tasks. Spirituals were often sung by slaves during the 1800's to encourage and convey coded information to escaping slaves as they moved along the Underground Railroad routes. Songs communicated messages & directions as well as warnings & cautions. Often escape instructions were encoded into songs.

These songs boosted the morale and spirit of the slaves and improved their sense of hope. The encoded references to the "conductors" were also in the songs. Slave songs carried multiple coded meanings. (See e.g. The Songs of the Underground Railroad), (Chrianity.com-slave-songs 1601-1700) Slaves had to sing, to pour out to God, their deepest prayers, longings, complaints, lifting to heaven their anguish and triumph although Slaves risked being whipped for singing. Some of their lyrics/themes included "keep me from sinking down" & "I'm going to lay down my heavy load".

 Slaves were musical people expressing ideas through song and they turned to songs for solace ...singing on every possible occasion in rhythms that had been long familiar, sang while picking cotton. Shucking corn. sang on chain gangs. sang in prison, sang in church when/if allowed to attend. The Gospel appealed to the poor slaves. The suffering of Jesus Christ and of the ancient Jews drew slaves to Christianity...eg Moses delivering the Israelites from Egyptian Bondage, evoking responses of faith from slave community faith which found utterance in song. Songs transcended sorrow, slave spirituals expressing the deepest religious emotions of souls touched by Jesus Christ. that kindled a flame in their hearts, spirituals gave slaves a sense of identity ...beliefs expressed in broken words, spiritual realities of forgiveness, hope, faith, love, endurance, holiness and eternal life, the slaves took complete refuge in Christianity and the spirituals were forged of sorrow and religious fervor.

They also exhibited a reversion to the simple principles of primitive communal Christianity. Slaves weary after a hard day's work risked the cruel anger of masters in order to sneak into the woods at night and improvise music for hours. The whole group could participate i.e. in repetitive choruses and antiphonal responses between leader and slaves. Many of the songs were filled with the joy of Christ.

Frederick Douglass spoke of buoyant feelings of singing hymns and making joyous exclamations, almost as triumphant in their tone as if we had already reached a land of freedom and safety (Frederick Douglass) Spirituals had rescued faithful Christian slaves from sinking down. Spirituals relieved their burdened hearts and expressed their exultation. Many spirituals found their way into our church hymnals, including "let us break bread together" "go tell it on the mountain" "were you there when they crucified the Lord" " Lord I want to be a Christian" "Balm in Gilead" & "He's got the whole world in his hands" The joy of song gives solace to and emancipates the spirit, oppression was given enriched meaning and depth thru worship music. Spirituals were an outpouring of faith and passion, Paul demolished the foundation of slavery by discrediting all discriminatory human divisions (Galatians, 3:20) & the Book of Philemon established full humanity of & worth of runaway slave Onesimus.

Songs of the Underground Railroad -Harriet-Tubman.org: this music provides repetitive rhythm for repetitive manual labor, as well as inspiration and motivation, and it's a form of expressing inner personal religious and spiritual values and solidarity with each other as well and also as tools to remember and communicate since the majority of slaves were unable to read. Songs were a strategy for slaves to communicate with other slaves in their struggle for freedom. Coded "signal" songs gave directions on how to escape, map songs told where to meet. Secret code language included Canaan for Canada & Chariot for the Underground Railroad. Spirituals are religious folk songs. Slaves sometimes met in praise houses, brush arbor meetings etc. sometimes singing and chanting… slaves were fascinated by bible stories containing parallels to their own lives.

Spirituals told narratives, expressions of faith, & sorrows & hopes, some describe slave struggles and identify with the suffering of Christ. Sometimes they were used as codified protest songs (see African American Spirituals). Gatherings were often banned and done secretively clandestinely. Some of these had improvisation, singers had solid unison refrains. Frederick Douglass wrote in his book " My Bondage & My Freedom" (1855) of singing spirituals during years of bondage. Canaan was code for the North. Spirituals were put in a collection and published in the 1860's then in the 1870's Jubilee Singers (slaves) were formed, then Hampton singers were formed in 1873. Spirituals were sung acapella (No instruments) The Civil Rights movement brought freedom songs adapted from spirituals.

Kenyatta D'Berry described Singing in Slavery: Songs of Survival & Freedom during Slavery...Transition to freedom, singing to communicate, music of hope/inspiration, Spirituals = Spiritual medicine that heals sinners to make the wounded whole (see Balm in Gilead) Harriet Tubman's personal hymn book (1876) was donated in 2010 to the Smithsonian National Museum of African American History & Culture. Lauren Christensen indicated that the hymnals bore witness to the liberating power of the Gospel contained in their pages. Harriet Tubman could sing every word it contained although she was illiterate. Eric Williams. Curator at the Smithsonian's Center for the study of African American Religious Life, said that the hymnal was invested with a spiritual power and was an object of devotion to be valued.

Pamela Crosby wrote that African American Spirituals Still Heal: Oppressed people continue to use them as protest/liberation songs, strong connections to personal experiences -Plantation-Sorrow-Jubilee, expressed yearnings for a better life, underscored a need for a closer walk with God-Emphasized hope for future freedom...themes included love, grace, and mercy, struggle for freedom/survival, expressed hope for life's possibilities, testament to power of the Gospel--hearing of a God who loves cares & provides, invisible church, songs named issues/fears they could not express publicly, worship in woods/arbors., express true feelings to God- offer prayers/requests to God, lay down their burdens & find strength to face another day...timeless messages. soothing spirituals, symbolic messages-singing to notify/warn, make the wounded whole. heal the sick, don't feel discouraged for Jesus is your friend, (See Balm in Gilead).

Helen Gray wrote that Negro Spirituals still resonate. translated biblical verses into song., songs of perseverance and hope, songs without authors...a musical outlet for slaves, songs expressed feelings of oppressive suffering but also reassurance couched in biblical language ,lot of connection to people of Israel whom God delivered from bondage, slaves heard bits of the hymns outside slave owner churches, from little scraps bits & pieces hundreds of new beautiful songs were fashioned and reworked and became musical folk poetry, from 1800-1825 slaves were exposed to religious music of poor whites, Randye Jones wrote that Gospel Truth about Negro Spirituals reshaped Christianity into a deeply personal way of dealing with the oppression of their environment, spirituals arming slaves with courage/faith- Underground Railroad conductors often communicated thru song-Harriet Tubman's success was in part aided by her use of spirituals, songs using secret codes. See Fannette Davis and see ArtsEdge Kennedy Center-secret messages shared thru song.

Helen Gray indicated that groups of slaves used work songs when hauling heavy loads. Om Faigin of JFSMusic.com says that slaves used spirituals to affirm their humanity & to give them hope faith & courage to go on living when life seemed to be nothing but endless physical toil, punishment and deprivation, e.g. Balm in Gilead soothed slaves and gave them hope & assurance Carl G Harris PhD did his doctoral dissertation on Negro Spirituals used on the Underground

Railroad (Hampton University VA). Slaves sang " we're going to lay down our burdens."

Chapter 27: Iatrosedation: Fear Reduction with Iatrosedative Process: (California Dental Assn & USC Dental School)

The late periodontist Dr Nathan Friedman the "father " of Iatrosedation stated that it is basically and simply the relief of patient anxiety via dentist behavior, & it is the building block for other forms of dental sedation. Its origin dates back to 1967 and was created by this now deceased periodontist at that time during his work at USC University of Southern California School of Dentistry. It involves recognition by the dental provider of the patient's anxieties and fears toward dental treatment and it represents a commitment by the dental provider to aid the patient before, during and after the dental treatment. It is an effective communication technique between dental provider and dental patient to aid the patient, and it creates a bond of trust between the dental provider and the dental patient. This helps with relaxation and cooperation and may even help in avoiding or minimizing the use of pharmaco-sedation. It helps remove a patient's fears and anxieties about both the treatment and the treatment provider. In some cases, it decreases anxiety to where the addition of a modest amount of pharmaco-sedation will enable the patient to more easily accept and tolerate dental treatment. The efficiency of most regular pain relief depends on the level of iatrosedation experienced by the dental patient. The key to iatrosedation includes emotional support/trust/bond between dental provider and dental patient, especially in terms of really attentive listening by the dental provider. It also includes elements that resemble hypnotic/posthypnotic suggestion, and often allows reduced use of psychopharmacologic anxiolysis medications for the dental treatment.

Allen Samuelson describes the use of iatrosedation in planning dental treatment and says that it can also be supplemented with hypnodontic dental hypnotherapy and relaxation therapies as well. The sedative effect benefit is obtained via trust/confidence in the dental provider. Often this is all the "sedation" the dental patient needs. The dental patient needs to feel emotionally supported and listened to and the iatrosedation "psychology" helps dental sedatives/anxiolytic drugs to work "better ". The communication techniques create bonds of trust with and confidence in the dental provider.

Stanley Malamed describes combining both Iatrosedation & Hypnodontic dental hypnotherapy to help overcome fears, relieve/reduce anxiety, reduce panic, provide relaxation, improve response to analgesia/numbing anesthetics, improve patient comfort, decrease gagging, even reduce bleeding and salivary flow as well. It can even promote post-op recovery, reduce post-op pain. and may make pre-medication unnecessary. And the post-hypnotic suggestions can facilitate rapid painless and discomfort-free healing.

Dr John Chao DDS MAGD) described how dental phobias can be managed with iatrosedation. USC University of Southern California School of Dentistry-Behavioral Sciences Dept. started using iatrosedation in 1968, and was chaired by periodontist Dr Nathan Friedman, who " invented" dental iatrosedation. This also included having the dental provider teach the dental patient how to unlearn patterns of fear ("fear patterns") and includes interpersonal cognitive reprocessing training of the dental patient by the dental provider and includes repeated calming communications which involves also changing the dental provider's behavior, personality, stance, and voice. The iatrosedation also depends on the dental provider using " repeated conditioning experiences" to help dissolve patient fears and to help extinguish dental phobias. That in turn can be greatly empowering to the dental patient, it can serve as a mark of personal triumph for the patient. and can actually reverberate through the dental patient's personality in astonishing and remarkable ways. 3-5 % of the population is dental phobic. and 40% of the population report having dental fears. 20 million people have dental phobic issues and are terrified of what a dentist might do to them and are terrified of dental pain.

The dental patient can get so panicky that they break out into a sweat and feel physically sick. Even a memory of a non-dental traumatic past experience can be flashbacked into a dental setting. Dental Phobia is a neuro-cognitive pattern, and the fear of dentists and dental treatment is a conditioned response to pain. Dental phobics have a misperception of dentists as a "dangerous controlling authority figure" rather than as a protective authority protecting them from harm. It is crucial to build trust with dental phobic patients. The dental provider needs to determine what the dental provider can/should do to make the dental phobic patient feel safe and protected. The dental provider needs to determine what the dental phobic patient perceives as dentally threatening/dangerous. Fearful dental phobic patients tend to be acutely perceptive/sensitive to dental provider behavior.

Dental phobics tend to have a past dental history of traumatic conditioning from past dental trauma experiences, and they usually have a past history of feeling helpless, out of control, unprotected and powerless and they need to be re-taught so that they can re-learn a better response to dental fear. Non-verbal behaviors that demonstrate empathy to the frightened patient -are crucial. The dental provider needs to show acceptance of the patient's problems, and must show supportiveness, and must show true empathy, a warm facial expression, a gentle calm soothing verbal style, a gentle voice, with sensitive resonance. The dental provider needs to help teach the patient how to unlearn bad neuro-cognitive responses and needs to re-learn the "positiveness" of dentistry, and the patient needs to unlearn fear patterns. The dental provider needs to deal with the sources of the patients' anxiety-Sedation alone is not enough, as it doesn't remove the phobias, sedation does not help in communicating with and bonding with the dental provider.

The dental provider needs to address the underlying causes of the anxiety. The dental provider also needs to show the patient how well cared for teeth provide an incredible sense of wellbeing and a heightened sense of self-regard. (See Friedman, Nathan & McCarthy, FM,1979). (see Friedman, Nathan,1983, & 1968).

The POCKET DENTISTRY GUIDE TO IATROSEDATION -see summary below:

Iatrosedation can be combined with hypnodontic hypnotherapy,acupressure, acupuncture, audio analgesia, biofeedback, EDA electronic dental anesthesia, & Electrosedation. Iatrosedation is the calming relaxation of nervous, fearful, anxious, apprehensive, and phobic patients without inducing loss of consciousness-it relaxes the mind and the body and relieves anxiety. It diminishes fears/anxieties regarding dental treatment. The dental provider can have a profound influence on patients, especially with regard to calming and soothing a patient. Iatrosedation is an integral part of the success of dental procedures and the success of pharmaco-sedation hinges on the use of iatrosedation. It is based on the importance of provider behavior in controlling pain anxiety & fear. It stresses the importance of allaying fears and answering questions.

It also makes the dental provider aware that just because a patient appears drowsy/sleepy does not mean the patient is calm-the patient can still be quite concerned with what is happening and yet appear drowsy & sedated.

A pre-treatment visit can even have an iatrosedation effect by telling the patient about post-treatment visit analgesic pain relievers available to them. Iatrosedation studies have shown that when patients are not informed in advance of possible post-visit pain, the patients required

2x the average dose of analgesics as those patients that were informed ahead of time. Unexpected pain can be worse than expected pain. Anxiety includes fear of pain and fear of something going wrong. Those patients with good pre-treatment visits recovered faster and finished treatment sooner. The fewer days needed to recover; the less drugs needed the less the possible side effects & unpleasant complications. Iatrosedation studies have also shown the power of negative communication with dental patients under nitrous oxide inhalation anesthesia for periodontal procedures (gingival gum curettage root planing) with soft tissue numbing analgesia.

In one case, the dental patient overheard the dentist saying to the dental assistant that he(dentist) had not performed that procedure in 15 years. The dental patient took off the nitrous nose mask-hood, sat up, and said he wanted to go home without having the procedure and refused to be treated further. The dental patient had no confidence in this dentist. The " offhand remark" destroyed the patient's confidence in this dentist. Too often there is a lack of communication between dentist and dental patient. The dentist walks in and starts to proceed without even saying hello. This makes an uncomfortable patient even more apprehensive. The patient is acutely aware of a dentist's lack of concern and caring for him as a patient. After the appointment the patient will likely seek another dentist and not return to an "aloof' dental provider. The patient who had been getting nitrous oxide was premedicated before the procedure and that patient revealed later that he was most acutely aware of the dentist's lack of concern for him as a person because the provider was more concerned about the anesthesia than about him personally. Empathy is extremely crucial in dealing with patients. Impersonal attitudes by providers/staff are a big problem. Great emphasis is placed in dental education on "scientific progress" which leads to isolation and separation from the dental patient. The dental providers lose empathy as they learn scientific detachment and impersonal care and this is exacerbated by the dentist's weariness from overwork, and isolation in their office operatories.

There is a growing problem with dentist impersonalization and patients "get lost in the shuffle" and some dentists refer to their patients as "clients" rather than as patients. (Lile, Samantha 6/28/2018) states that iatrosedation is crucial in calming dental patients -a calm dentist demeanor calms dental patients. (Lile,6/28/2018) adds that the dentist needs to isolate and identify patient fears before diagnosing and treating the patient-The dentist can help the dental patient explore what "dangers" they fear and try to put those fears at ease, Eliminating fear of the unknown is a powerful tool, patients tend to focus on fears and anxieties, anxiety can build up during wait time to levels so high that medication is needed to calm the patient, the patient has waiting time to overfocus on every feared imagined poke and prod, and to worry that something wrong will be found, word choice can help patients calm down ,if a new patient doesn't believe the dentist, they aren't likely to trust the dentist enough to even make/keep future appointments. Taneja speaks of iatrosedation as a holistic tool in the armamentarium of anxiety control: In 1967, Dr Nathan Friedman, a periodontist had identified causes of anxiety/panic/fear/phobia in dental patients and helped patients to overcome these problems, helped the patience to gain confidence, and helped patients to increase their faith in their dental providers.

Dr Frank McCarthy DDS MD described how 20 million people avoid the dentist due to fear, and he said that this fear can be more destructive than cavities or periodontal disease, Fear is a major obstacle and barrier in seeking dental care, avoidance of dentists often results in extensive dental pathology, patients tend to wait until driven by painful emergency dental crises, the dentist cannot get to the teeth until the barrier wall of fear is removed… ignoring fear really= great frustration and stress for both dentist and patient ,causing great fear in the patient, fear is a significant syndrome, fear really = the emergency of fear that the dentist has to deal with, 57% of dentists surveyed say that difficult patients are the most stressful single factor in their dental practice, pharmaco-sedation does NOT eliminate fear and its results are haphazard, it's a temporary solution, it's necessary to treat the fear, and the dentist needs to teach re-learning processes to the patient it's necessary to provide psychological calming to the patient ,that calming involves both verbal and non-verbal communication iatro refers to doctors, sedation refers to calm, psycho sedation refers to making patients calm and relieving their anxiety through the use of psychology.

Sarabjeet Singh, Navreet Sandhu, & Bhupinder Kaur all described Iatrosedation as a solution for emotionally maladaptive complete denture patients. They referred to some of such denture patients as " emotionally fragile patients who become office fixtures who repeatedly visit with "gripes and complaints". They found that denture success was partly connected to denture patient attitudes toward dental providers and dental prosthetics. They also discovered that their dentist becomes a very important figure in their life and they have powerfully strong feelings toward their dentist they have a warm trusting relationship with their dentist, there is goodwill embedded in the dental prosthetic dentures resulting in patient acceptance of both the dentures and the dental provider that warm trusting relationship overrides the mechanical problems experienced with the dentures the caring sensitive and supportive dental provider creates a sense of trust helping to ensure that the patient accepts the dentures physically and emotionally,

The dental provider asks the patient about what kinds of difficulties the patient is experiencing with the dentures, their anxieties about it, and helps the patient explore that anxiety. There is mutual cooperation, communication, and trust the provider understands too that the stress of the unhappiness the patient is feeling with the dentures-can and does affect even the way the gums tolerate the pressure exerted by the dentures and the resulting gum soreness that occurs. The provider talks with the patient about what the provider can do, the provider interacts verbally with the patient, and offers possible solutions, "we will work together, and we can work things out, you will be able to live comfortably with the dentures it will take some time. The provider is willing to spend extra time to make an optimal set of dentures and the patient feels grateful the provider helps the patient to be involved in the fabrication of the dentures this too helps build the trusting relationship often patients seeking technical advice about dentures/prosthetics are seeking emotional solutions. The provider should not view the patient as neurotic,

Armfield indicated that the overwhelming elective avoidance of dentistry is due to powerful fear/anxiety-the underlying reason for dental disease is the powerful fear of pain caused by traumatically painful past dental experiences +fear of the unknown. Part of a dentist's job is to allay anxiety and prevent emotional harm caused by bad dentistry.

The late periodontist Dr Nathan Friedman's an Evaluation of the Iatrosedative process for treating dental fear shows the following: A soothing calm voice filled with compassion, calmness, empathy, kindness, gentleness and patience is crucial. The dental provider needs to invite the patient to discuss their fears, in order to greatly reduce anxiety, the dentist has a responsibility to provide a positive experience there is a failure of dental professionals to address psychological and emotional aspects of dental fear/phobias dentists must.

take it upon themselves to learn the signs of fear/anxiety via observing patient body language ,there needs to be a re-learning process (Friedman, 1967) it's important for the patient to share past pain/fear/anxiety/discomfort with their current dental provider and the patient needs to be given the chance to separate from the past providers/trauma, the dental provider needs to look for both verbal and non-verbal signs of anxiety/fear and needs to respond to those signs the dental provider needs to sit at patient level, instead of only standing over the patient ,the patient needs repeated reassurances, and smiles, the provider needs to interview such patients to learn about their difficulties the dental provider needs to use a "tell show do " strategy what may seem redundant to many will be exactly what a high anxiety patient needs...the dental provider needs to make a commitment to help the patient and needs to help the patient re-learn what good dental care is...the dental provider needs to understand how teeth loss is terrifying....the dental provider needs to help patients acclimate to dental procedures and dental equipment/tools ,it's very important to have pre-treatment non-treatment visits to get to know the patient as a person it has a calming effect on the patient it's the "psychosomatic effect" of just meeting with the dental provider with no treatment that alone can change past perceptions of dentists and dental procedures ,a very calming benefit many patients suffer mental anguish during treatment procedures they are frightened of ...the dental provider needs to understand the patient's deeply seated dental fears/anxieties that have been detrimental to the patient the way a patient has been treated can stay with the patient for years leading to dental avoidance due to the trauma from the past compassion can save teeth, and can even save teeth that were thought of as unsaveable by prior providers by doing extensive restoration work it's crucial to repeatedly reassure/comfort the patient it's crucial to explain even small things like x rays it's crucial to use effective numbing agents i.e. for cleanings, gum probings etc...keep needles out of view go slow, use nitrous oxide patients treated well will become more open and receptive to oral hygiene instructions don't view the patient as a behavioral problem case sedate patients with words and anesthetics stop acting like scientists act socially aware and with compassion, address fears, anxieties and pain reach out to welcome and serve underserved fear/anxiety/panic/phobia patients a population that has been overlooked ,Success is derived from taking the time to help patients by treating anxiety/fear, not just teeth,(Friedman, 2/1983 and 1987-1998)

Chapter 28: Implants-Why are they often a "bad" choice for Dwarf / Ectodermal Dysplasia patients.

Aydinbelge cites briefly the challenge of fitting/designing dental implant prosthetics in ectodermal pediatric patients Grover & Mehra explain why implants are a very risky & quite problematic choice: They opine that implants are not recommended. For instance, there is a problem with cases where the periodontal ligament is absent, where the implants can/will act like ankylosed teeth. They also mention the risk of infraocclusion which disrupts occlusal relationships and can lead to compensatory effects on opposing teeth, including tipping of adjacent teeth. A vertical discrepancy can occur between mucosal margin of implant and the gingival margin of adjacent teeth. If the implants are mixed with natural teeth, placement in mandible may be a problem. The failure of maxillary implants is 30%, implants placed in the anterior maxilla were nearly 3 times more likely to fail than those placed in the anterior mandible. Implant placement in the symphyseal region of the anterior mandible requires caution & bone augmentation may be needed. (Kumari & Kumar) state that insufficient vertical height will make implants impossible in maxilla area, & they add that implant risks would include submergence and movement. Asbjorn Jokstad rhetorically questions by asking "Saving patients by pulling their teeth out but killing them softly afterwards with dental implants?" Please note that Implants are not generally available in dwarf sizes! Custom made custom fitted implants are prohibitively costly & extremely difficult to fit & may be impossible to fit even with bone/gum grafts!

Chapter 29: Why are dentures a poor or even an impossible choice in Dwarfism Dental/ Ectodermal Dental?

Dalkiz & Dalkiz, noted that the presence of increased thickened jawbone alveolar ridge volume in buccolingual directions prevents the fitting of dentures. They also noted the dilemma of leaving 2nd molars off the dentures to reduce excess occlusal force. (Bani) notes that dentures are a poor alternative to healthy dentition.

(Jain) mentions the problems of support/retention/stability of dentures, and little resistance to lateral forces on dentures.

(Suresh & Asopa, did a research study on the use of dentures in teethless patients with neuromuscular disorders. They found that neuromuscular coordination is a necessary prerequisite for successfully wearing dentures. Neuromuscular symptoms included in their study included ataxia, impaired gait, visual blurring, tremors, unsteady walking, nystagmus, head nodding, dysmetria, inability to stop movement at certain points, dysarthria, slow speech, impaired chewing/biting & loss of cheek support. They found that patients with these symptoms were unable to wear dentures. They also noted that patients with degenerative changes in supporting structures were unable to wear dentures. They concluded that impaired neuromuscular balance affects denture stability and could affect prosthetic stability as well,

(Haggard mentioned the following regarding dentures: Denture wearers lack the periodontal ligament receptor ** and Denture wearers show impaired intraoral sensory perception in tasks such as biting force discrimination. Also see Williams regarding bite force discrimination by denture wearers, Agrawal & Bhandari noted the impairment of oral functions in patients with dentures-the dentures reduce the somatosensory afferent information reaching the brain, Enkling, Klineberg, Murray and Trulsson all mentioned r the sensory motor function of human periodontal mechanoreceptors.)

Agrawal stated that patient acceptance of cast metal crowns resembling teeth was greater than patient acceptance of dentures. Agrawal added that the acceptance of a dental prosthetic depends on oral perception and discriminatory skill for external morphology of fixed prosthetics.

Dr Patricia Nihill, DMD mentions the following: The difficulty in obtaining a good border seal when severe bony undercuts are present...the need for the use of a resilient soft denture liner to enhance retention needing to reshape stock teeth, The need to extract periodontally mobile loose decayed teeth,

 Singh, Sandhu & Kaur, provided the following additional insight into the problems that have occurred in some of their denture patients: Gums can have great difficulty in tolerating the pressure exerted by dentures and it often results in gum soreness.

In my & countless other cases, SEVERE GAGGING prevents the use of dentures.

Chapter 30A: Psychosocial Factors of Past Dental Trauma in Planning Current Holistic Dental Treatment

Helen Rodd, and Fiona Noble discussed the negative psychosocial impacts of past dental injury trauma & they state that it needs to be addressed as part of a current holistic dental treatment plan. I have summarized the key points of their discussion for you as follows: Traumatic Childhood dental injury to teeth(dentition) is linked to future oral health problems that affect quality of life after the injury. Psychosocial impacts of past dental trauma influences patient resiliency during current dental treatment and affects their ultimate recovery. Dentistry today needs to recognize the need to address psychosocial aspects of dental patients as part of a more holistic approach to dental care. Past dental trauma is connected to self-perception, social interaction, psychosocial wellbeing & affects everyday life.

Those with unaddressed past dental trauma were 20 times more likely to report negatively on their current present daily life. The past trauma can even include repeated past failures of large dental restorations and the upset caused by it. For example, uncorrected dental restoration failure and poorly corrected dental restoration failure can cause lifelong personal difficulties. Social judgments connect to dentofacial appearance and can have profound lifelong consequences including even career prospects and social relationships. Negative social judgments can be caused by visible unesthetic dental damage. Compromised dentofacial appearance is connected to receiving unkind comments from others, i.e. teeth that look messy & unattractive to others. This can even cause a ''social anxiety/phobia/panic'' others may make comments or display behaviors which are hurtful to the dental patient psychological conditions may be encountered in the maxillofacial prosthetics patient.

Chapter 30B: Psychosocial Considerations in Dental Prosthetic/ Prosthodontic Treatment.

Alan Hickey & Margery Salter wrote about the psychological/psychosocial aspects of Dental Prosthetics/ Prosthodontic treatment & included ectodermal dental disorders in this article. I have summarized below the key items from this article for you:

Providing maxillofacial dental prosthetics (and prosthodontic dental appliances) should not only address physical & functional deficiencies but also should evaluate the possible psychological effects of dental deformities/defects. This portion of the treatment evaluation is often overlooked or ignored although it should be integrated into the overall dental/prosthodontic treatment plan. Both physical and psychological factors should be considered when treating these patients. The treatment presents psychosocial as well as technical challenges. Unusual dentofacial features exacerbate social challenges and social isolation may result from looking different and can lead to impaired social interactions and there still exist stereotypes that correlate decreased intelligence with dentofacial abnormalities. Sometimes some of these patients may also have learning disorders and some develop coping mechanisms to reduce social interaction to avoid scrutiny and to avoid negative social contacts/responses. Some may feel anxiety/fear including social anxiety, psychological conditions may be encountered in the maxillofacial dental prosthetics patient.

Dr Kim Daxon, Kim DDS Prosthodontist at the PerioImplant Advisor said that it's crucial to preserve the patient's physical and psychosocial wellbeing. Harold Preiskel indicated that the provider must consider all the needs of the patient.

Chapter 31: Frequent Dental Care in Dwarfism & Ectodermal Dental patients is a MUST!

Terlemez, notes that the thorough maintenance of oral health in dwarf patients is of the utmost importance in order to prevent dental problems, especially due to the abnormal tooth development which predisposes these patients to tooth decay and fragile teeth. (Bani) states that there is an ongoing need for frequent follow-up visits at least every 3 months. The Follow-up can include modification/repair/revision & replacement and monitoring. Ferrante & Blasi, state that frequent follow-up is necessary and essential, as the fixation to teeth must be checked often and that periapical lesions and fused roots must continually be checked and monitored for. Robazza, stated that prosthetic patients need frequent regular chronic monitoring for apical periodontitis. (Britto,2011) cautions that adult growth hormone deficient dwarfs are at high risk for periodontal disease and need to be monitored. Falcon,2018 indicated that 17-year-old primordial dwarf Hannah has to get dentally treated several times each month.

Koob states that the treatment is a protracted course into adulthood. Omo & Ennibulele greatly emphasize that there is a need for continuous recall visits. Jokstad, says there's a strong need for follow-up care and the importance of patient compliance with regular dental maintenance appointments.

HIckey & Salter noted that each improvement can give the patient resolve to continue on with additional treatment, i.e. a long-term complicated treatment plan, involving multiple procedures.

Dr Kim Daxon, DDS prosthodontist at the Perio Implant Advisory, notes that treatment can last several years- and includes long term follow-ups that may include modification/replacement/repair of the dental prosthetic and long-term dental rehab.

Jaafar Abduo indicated that his prosthetics patient was reviewed weekly. This patient had porcelain fused to metal prosthetics.

Chapter 32: Inspiration from Another Cerebellar Patient

Inspiring Encouragement from another Cerebellar disease patient book Author Deborah Levi, a cerebellar ataxia patient for over 30 years, published "Finding Level Ground-My journey with Cerebellar Ataxia'. Her book teaches that life need not be lived as a victim and teaches how to accept and cope with life with a cerebellar disease. She emphasizes self-loving & self-accepting, and she tells her story with courage, and heart.

Chapter 33 Importance and Benefits of having a Multi-Disciplinary Team.

 Levinson, Harold mentions the importance of having a meaningful multi-disciplinary approach.

VanDorsten notes the importance of having a multi-faceted team that provides a collaboration of multi-disciplinary providers. VanDorsten also notes that Pain is a multi-faceted biopsychosocial phenomenon not readily managed by any single professional provider of a single discipline. Adding that interdisciplinary assessments are invaluable in planning treatment, and that multidisciplinary treatment is more effective than single provider single discipline approaches, especially in terms of yielding positive outcomes and a positive quality of life, especially in treatment over a course of years. A combined approach often results in decreased anxiety/pain and less need for pain medication. A treatment team of contributing members can better focus on and address personal daily lifestyle factors that affect recovery and pain management.

VanDorsten adds that team meetings with patients several times can best assess things such as mood /behavioral changes and social relationship issues. VanDorsten also adds that the team members should familiarize themselves with the treatment processes/procedures, including possibly observing the treatment itself to see it from a patient's perspective on the experience-what he terms " immersion" in order to truly offer specialized insights into the treatment processes/procedures. He adds that the team can also help teach the patient of learning coping strategies in order to improve patient capacity to self-manage discomfort and anxiety. He also noted that anxiety/pain are interconnected, and that pretreatment anticipatory anxiety can affect post- treatment appointment pain and he added that the team can also help patients to identify recreational activities that they can consider engaging in in order to improve quality of life. He also noted that the team can address minor psychosocial stressors that can lead to increased frequency & quantity of office visits (of the treatment providers) & suggests that the team can address ways of helping patients to self-monitor comfort/mood changes and changes in ability to cope further such as providing resources for improving coping skills, learning new coping skills and even to consider new recreational activities.

(Bani) states that Oral Dental Prosthetic rehabilitation of Dental Ectodermal Dysplasia is often difficult, often necessitating multi-disciplinary teams including prosthodontists. Aydinbelge mentions that treatment by a multidisciplinary team is needed. Grover & Mehra, state that a multi-disciplinary dental-medical team is most appropriate. (Naqash recommends a multi-disciplinary treatment planning approach. (NFED) indicates that the dental symptoms can be very complex, requiring a team of treatment specialists.

(Omo & Ennibulele) state that overall management of Ectodermal Dysplasia dental patients requires a multi-disciplinary medical-dental approach. (Linuma & Honnlee,12/11/2018) state that it is crucial to work with providers in a variety of disciplines in order to provide the best care for patients. (Jokstad, 10/26/2018) encourages shared treatment decision making.

(Glasner, 2011-2012) noted that when treating dysautonomic dental patients one must consider the whole person made up of interrelated challenges that cannot be treated in isolation. Dental treatment may be the vehicle for improving their overall health and wellbeing. (Hickey & Salter, 2006) noted that dental prosthetics in conjunction with other dental/medical treatment may be necessary and that treatment teams need to provide both medical and psychological/psychosocial support to these patients & the team needs to evaluate the patient's level of distress and to make referrals to other professionals that may be helpful .ie in terms of social self-confidence for example...connecting the physical deformities with a multispecialty treatment team is critical.

(Giddon, Dr Donald PHD,4/1980) states that there is a need to evaluate the biosocial aspects of the patient, even including musical skills dependent on the oral cavity.

(Daxon, Kim DDS, & Perio Implant Advisory,12/13/2017) stated that what is desperately needed is the expertise of a multi-disciplinary specialist team -due to the challenge of treatment planning for a multi-faceted case, where treatment may last several years. (Meyers, Arlen MD + Burgess, Jeff DDS,11/9/2015) advises dental patients with neuro. diseases require special management in terms of dental treatment planning. (Kao, 2004) It is crucial for team members to monitor the patient for signs and symptoms of Relocation Stress Syndrome.

(Hanlin, SM 4/2012) discussed the rehab. of mutilated debilitated dentition- & stated that an interdisciplinary treatment plan/team is often required to allow restoration of function and aesthetics-planning and treatment highlights interdisciplinary patient care based on a prosthodontic perspective. (Bilodeau, JE 4/2009) also discussed the rehab. of mutilated debilitated dentition and noted that the dentition could not be restored with prosthetics alone and that a multidisciplinary treatment team was needed. (Abduo, Jaafar 3/2011) also wrote about mutilated dentition & prosthodontic devices. He stated that a well-coordinated treatment team is needed that involves liaisons with different disciplines an innovative combination he described it also in terms of a coordinated team due to the extreme and rare case features,

(Miettunen, Kate 8/2011) Many adults present with mutilated dentition that often require multi-disciplinary approaches for optimal treatment outcomes. Teamwork is essential for multi-disciplinary treatment.

Complex adult cases require a multi-disciplinary approach for optimal treatment outcomes-treatment goals among all providers must be aligned to reach ultimate treatment goals. (Miettunen, Kate 8/2011)

Gatto Luigi (10/16/2018) interviewed top tennis player Novak Djokovic 'and Novak said " I'm fortunate because I have a great team of people around me that's where there's a big source of positive energy for me."

(Levinson, Harold 1982 pg. 316) Only an integrated religious scientific multi-disciplinary approach will enable God's servants to properly treat God's children,

Chapter 34: Intersection of Cerebellum, Religious/Spiritual Faith & Religious Philosophy

Paul Brown describes the following ideas/thoughts regarding the **Intersection of Cerebellum, Religious/Spiritual Faith & Religious Philosophy :** A "moral **spiritual** revolution " in **cerebellar** studies, the **cerebellum** is the primary origin of Volition and handles perceptual control, a **cerebellar** lobe executive, AND volition subtends motor, cognitive and moral/**spiritual** function, there are moral/**spiritual** aspects of volition that are constitutive to **religion and philosophy**, Dr Andrew Newberg MD believes that **God changes the Brain**, & Introduces the concept of <u>**Jewish**</u> **NeuroTheology which involves A relationship between Brain and Judaism.** *Neurotheology is a Multidisciplinary* field of study that seeks to understand the relationship between brain theology and mind and religion. It is a 2-way street in which science and religion can mutually inform each other and it can provide a new perspective to old questions. It provides different perspectives that integrate the best of what science can offer with what religion and spirituality offer. This integrated approach shows that science and religion need not be at odds with each other. It can be an important intersection for science and religion. They are compatible and there's evidence regarding the impact of religion on the brain and Neurotheology can even provide new perspectives on Jewish thought/liturgy.

Religious/Spiritual beliefs and practices reduce anxiety and depression and help with better coping during stressful life events and can even lead to improved relationships. Brains are affected by spiritual beliefs/practices. Religious/Spiritual activity can lower blood pressure and heart rate. and improve the immune system. Meditation & Prayer can also help with concentration, attention, and focus. He says that God won't go away & that belief is both Brain & Science based. He adds that it is important for clinicians to understand the sum-total of their patients including their psychological, social, and spiritual aspects. Patients can use those beliefs in the context of their healthcare. We can learn something about how those beliefs/practices help some patients. If a particularly religious patient is going to have surgery, it may be appropriate to help those patients stay in touch with that side of themselves and to remind them that staying connected to their religious communities may be very valuable. Prayer can help reduce anxiety levels. Perhaps providers can help patients select practices that may be beneficial, Patients might be able to be encouraged to try different practices- help patients engage their psychological, spiritual, and biologic parts of themselves in an integrated way.

Chapter 35: ASPIES(Aspergers) & Healing *benefits* of Church"

Brant Hansen wrote 2 intriguing pieces about Aspergers, "Aspies & Church: "Blessed are the Misfits "(2017) & "Mr. Spock goes to church" (2013) (***NOTE: "Aspie"-Aspergers=High Function Autism).*** He describes his Aspergers effects, and his relationship to Christian Culture & God & he is a Christian Radio Host. I have selected bits and pieces from those 2 pieces to include here in this book to give you a "sampling" of his comment's opinions and ideas. He states that his writings are intended for spiritual strugglers, the misfits, oddballs and introverts and says he's an introverted "aspie" ,he describes his Aspie effects/symptoms & his relationship with Christian Culture & God, he has a sense of isolation on some island of misfit Christians ,he describes his walk of faith with his fellow misfits and their deep spiritual needs reaching out to fellow misfits who might be tempted to give up on Christian fellowship & corporate worship misfit believers need to be with each other in a Christ like community body of believers ,a Safe place Christian community to teach one another...to be with other Christ followers to help build up the church body, as a family called to unity. persevering in Christian community building ,In his piece on "Mr. Spock"(see above) he describes how he copes as a Christian with Aspergers he says " it gets even trickier for aspies of faith" and how they "feel like an alien" at church-feeling out of place he says to imagine Mr. Spock at an evangelical tent revival as a cold observer ,God loves Aspies although Aspies often feel alienated from parts of Christian culture. Jesus offers what no one else does- "come to me, all of you who are weary and burdened, and I will give you rest" (Matthew 11:28-30 NIV) Aspies don't fit in & wonder if God loves them, they feel like aliens in the Christian subcultures...

James Bradford Pate says that the various religious beliefs of Aspies
are rooted in who they are as people Aspies like structure and
predictability and regular rituals such as attending services.

Chapter 36: Religious Clergy as a Vital Part of the Inter-Disciplinary Treatment Team

In my personal Experimental Dental Prosthetics Treatment Journey, 3 Pastors & a Rabbi are crucial members of the Interdisciplinary Team I created to be my "Rocks of Gibraltar" my " lighthouse beacons of light " and my " bridges over troubled waters". No man is an Island. It takes this extraordinary multi-disciplinary team to help me, an extraordinary experimental dental prosthetics patient, to succeed against "severe and herculean " long shot odds stacked against me. I could never ever succeed without my team "players" they are my "guns & ammo" against my rare diseases. Even the strongest fighter needs a military force unit backing them! Before going into specifics about how they are my loyal "army" I felt it was necessary to first give you an academic "scholarly" background corroborating my need for this "army" to include my " spiritual religious faith clergy warriors" helping me battle fiercely to save my teeth and life.

 Easton & Andrews published a study on the role of a Pastor as part of an interdisciplinary rehab team and I have summarized their findings for you: The onset of a long-term illness requires the patient to rethink values and to develop new coping strategies in order to adapt to a life changing illness event. At such times, people may draw on sources of spiritual support, finding comfort from a pastor or other clergy. Patients have reported using faith and prayer as effective coping strategies. Religious faith can have a positive influence on emotions and may result in improved functional ability. The discipline of faith may promote mental health. It is important to consider a wide range of spiritual representatives.

Stacy Weiner explained how hospitals integrate spiritual care- I have chosen to summarize her thoughts and ideas on this as follows: Physical & Spiritual wellbeing are connected; physicians & chaplains are connecting with each other in order to best help patients' chaplains are viewed as those that "bridge gaps". God is powerful enough to heal importance of comfort measures patients have a right to religious/spiritual care holistic collaboration among disciplines, clergy are spiritual care professionals, patients too often feel a "lack of spiritual connection " and clergy/chaplains can provide that spiritual connection they can deal with more than strictly spiritual/religious issues-they can address existential issues and provide support.

The chaplain/clergy person is really a team member in an interdisciplinary team approach., patients have spiritual concerns that should be addressed by everyone on the team with the chaplain/clergy person being expert in spiritual care, each team member brings a different perspective, and when combined-can provide a richer understanding of the patient ...chaplains/clergy can also unearth essential health related information such as abusive situations, deepest fears. and deeply personal issues. The interdisciplinary team addresses spiritual needs of patients in order to provide the highest possible quality of life, which is the goal of the team, the team develops personalized solutions, and a wide range of supports, encouraging faith and reinforcing spiritual foundations and religious traditions. It's crucial for everyone to get to know an interdisciplinary team (Hospice of Dayton.org blog). The Connecticut Hospice compares its team to a finely woven tapestry with many different threads an interplay of skills spanning many different professions… that assists with a myriad of challenges surrounding incurable illness it contains pastoral caregivers for spiritual support including community clergy,

David Lichter discussed the role of chaplains in interdisciplinary teams: they provide supportive spiritual care and promote deeper spiritual engagement with patients they integrate spirituality into patient care and sometimes several different clergies are involved with the same patient that promotes interpersonal relational skills via interdisciplinary spiritual care chaplains/clergy have made progress in being members of the team.

(Cedars-Sinai Hospital) uses spiritual care multi-disciplinary teams in order to heal the whole person, mind body and soul part of the healing process is addressing spiritual/religious needs,

(HCCN 2017-2018) describes the "new world of Spiritual care" at HCCN Chaplaincy Network: The integration of spiritual care in Healthcare helping patients find comfort spiritual support plays an important role in physical healing patients can feel disconnected from religion...spiritual help with difficult decisions/challenges-it is the heart of patient centered care chaplains/clergy can provide 1 on 1 spiritual care that is mindful of all aspects of a patient's experience working together to provide care for the body, mind and spirit addressing spiritual, existential, and emotional challenges arising during illness, opportunity for growth and wholeness.

Pastor N Ashok Kumar wrote about the benefits and importance of pastoral clergy visits to those battling illnesses - I have summarized his thoughts on this for you: Visiting people who have become discouraged because of crises in their lives, e.g. many of whom may have not been in church in weeks or longer-after visiting them, both pastor and "parishioner" will often feel encouraged-the blessing of a pastoral visit reaches past those whom the pastor visits it also became a blessing to the pastor ...Jesus went from house to house, healing the sick, comforting the sick, soothing the afflicted and speaking peace to them,

By the faith of a believer. pastors are strengthened by the trust that members have in the pastor when pastors visit, they receive a spiritual blessing, a divine intervention-that assists pastors in understanding certain things in a better way ...a pastor can feel amazed about a person's faith in spite of their sicknesses a sick person's faith can encourage a pastor to look beyond the pastor's own problems and can help pastors who have begun losing enthusiasm they can understand their members better ,hospitality can yield encouragement and even lead to rejoicing the person may have felt as though he or she was being treated as a stranger ,pastors can also receive blessings from new believers (see Acts 16:33-34),Know the needs of the members i.e. their psychosocial needs uplift their spirit and restore them by pastoral visits… their needs may be different from others that the pastors visit...pastors can direct people to God who has the capability to meet the person's needs...the pastor needs to show an interest in the needs of these members ...have a good relationship with these members pastoral visits may not solve a problem but can help pastors to better understand the causes of the problems that their members face great gifts are received from pastoral visitation...the gift of faith strengthening by listening to members' spiritual journeys, their faith building experiences, their approach to life and the gift of the opportunity to listen to their needs thru visits, we have opportunities to help spiritually, physically, mentally and socially...mutual interactions evoke a desire to know each other better and a better knowledge of God and themselves,

Relationships are vital in ministry a pastor's sincere caring is crucial. giving pastors insights into the lives of members which enables preaching with a particular focused relevance coming close to people is essential in nurturing them, attaining nurture thru shepherding is crucial including healing, sustaining, and guiding ...many clergy are poor in comprehending weaknesses and needs of their own inner being...they can rediscover themselves by visiting people,

Kate Jackson, Tracey Greene-Mintz, Kim Warchol, & Tach Branch-Dogan's, CRTS all indicated that a multi-disciplinary clergy/medical team should help those traumatized by a sudden and unexpected forced relocation, for example, spending time learning the patient's life story, and have a process to facilitate with that, and the team can create routines/schedules etc. the more others learn about the new person, the better the "link ups" i.e. new strong friendships/relationships, help the person find new activities, give them a foundation to help build new friends/relations, help build sense of purpose/comfort/build them a sense of welcome and "wanted-ness", be responsive to the person, let them know that their presence is valued and beneficial, gain their trust, build their confidence, encourage them, alleviate their loneliness and isolation, help them with getting to know people, assist them in forming friendships. invite them, include them, make them feel wanted and appreciated…help them to feel as if they have gained instead of lost. help plan to minimize their distress/fears provide supportive assistance with adaptation and help minimize their depression and regret. Stan Friedman explains the importance of having chaplain/clergy helping in times of personal trauma: people are known to say "I wish I had someone there in that moment" ,they often need to talk to a pastor/chaplain after a tragic situation occurs in their lives critical incidents can cause a disruption to the soul ,These events can negatively change the way people think of themselves and how they view the world the brain can become so overwhelmed that it freezes up and reacts with fight or flight panic it becomes hard to process information impaired cognitive functioning sets in hard to think straight ,memory impaired from the stress...and they begin to ask the same questions repeatedly because their brain is trying to make sense of their circumstances ,heart racing/pounding ,sweating nausea as the body tries to release stress induced "toxin". It is crucial to validate/reassure/comfort/acknowledge/understand/accept/respect their overwhelmed senses, confusion, and disorganization / and it can always be a part of that patient's life.

(Operation We Are Here Clergy Resources, US Army chaplains, 9/2008) explains the need for clergy to minister to military personnel affected by deployment.

Chapter 37: Religion Religious Faith Religiosity

Dr Cheryl Lantz wrote how Religion can offer guidance and direction those older adult cancer patients that have a high level of intrinsic religiosity tend to have higher hopes and greater wellbeing RJ Fehring indicated that Elderly cancer patients tend to have spiritual wellbeing, religiosity, and hope. Religiosity links to wellbeing and happiness (Dr Lantz, and Linz) and religious faith bolsters wellbeing...Dr Lantz defines religion in terms of an organized belief system + works rituals events practices dogma doctrines rules & observances & she adds that religion helps older adults to cope with aging, and can bolster their sense of hope and wellbeing ,Religion is the supporting segment to the total picture of a person's spirituality -religion is the tool used to develop spirituality, Dr Lantz & Coyle indicated that Religion includes a strong sense of religious commitment & practices associated with churches, faith communities & religious networks Also see Field's Religiosity & Spirituality at End of Life. And see Ai & Mackenzie regarding Spiritual wellbeing.

Dr Harold Levinson citing John Eccles's Facing Reality, described how Eccles turned to religion & God for answers to Mind's functioning religious explanations for scientific events religious conceptualization of Mind and mental events come closest to explaining scientifically its site/action demonstrating that the gulf between scientific and religious conviction and explanation is one more than pseudo-scientific illusion. Religious theorists term this invisible and indescribable electromagnetic computer system "God" religious conceptualization of God comes closest to solving the mind-body problem......If one equates God and his powerful functional description with both man and mind and if one equates God's location in heaven Eccles also mentioned religious philosophy and special creation of God.

Dr Harold Levinson, citing Thorpe says that Thorpe sees science as a religious activity but clearly incomplete in itself there's a necessity for belief in a spiritual world that transcends what we see in the material world ...creative and sustaining spirit of God may be everywhere present and active,

Dr Harold Levinson also wrote that about the attempt to integrate science and religion: God is a cosmic mind. Man's religious convictions, both religious and non-religious theories and convictions are of equal scientific validity and thus worthy of exploration. For real science and understanding to progress meaningfully, both religious science and hard science must be integrated and harmonized with one another, and the sibling-like rivalry and competition between the two must be analyzed and resolved. Their neurotically determined conflict is and has been neither truly religious nor truly scientific. Only an integrated religious scientific multi-disciplinary approach will enable God's servants to properly treat God's children.

Chapter 38: Spirituality – Research Studies Found

Dr Cheryl Lantz indicated that the mortality (death/dying) studies did not address spiritual implications/adjustments during relocation & prior to death. No studies existed in 2009 regarding how the spirituality of older adults is affected by relocation, nor regarding the spiritual responses of older adults during relocation. Please note that the definition of relocation in her doctoral dissertation was the physical movement of living arrangement from one locale to another locale & the spirituality definition was a person's relationship with God + the supreme experience of relationship with God thru beliefs, values, lifestyles, and interaction with others (e.g. in a faith community). (see Stoll, RL regarding Guidelines for Spiritual Assessment) (also see Saunders J regarding spirituality in nursing). J Saunders defines Spirituality as the center of people's being & a life force that gives rise to their sense of wholeness, faith, hope, trust, giving and receiving of love & forgiveness, reconciliation, meaning in life, the fundamental characteristics of spirituality which are considered the basic determinants of the totality of human beings.

Mo Amerita studied Spiritual concerns within Nursing Care of the Terminally Ill, & spirituality there included God within self the part that communes with the transcendent - it is the part of each human being that longs for ultimate awareness, meaning, value, purpose, beauty, dignity. relatedness & integrity. J Walton examined Spiritual Relationships as part of Holistic Nursing. -Spiritual relationships are connections to self or soul, to a higher power or to nature.

 Narayanasamy looked at Spirituality as applied to Nursing & described the need to expand the holistic understanding of spirituality- mind body and soul- to include its biological root. Current beliefs did not attend to the need for Spirituality as a biological survival mechanism. The Spirit is needed for the physical body to survive the thread of relationships being present with a higher power and relationships that promote connectedness with others.

Elizabeth Mckinlay looked at the spiritual dimension of aging in terms of wellbeing spirituality lies at the core of each human "being" ,an essential dimension which brings meaning to life., it's not just religious practices but also as a relationship with God/Higher Power as perceived by a person ,self thus is a spirit being spirituality helps transcend losses and helps one to find intimacy with God & hope as well. The spirituality models address end of life issues and the dying process but don't address the role of spirituality during relocation (see also Dr Lantz's doctoral dissertation.)

(Young & Koopsen) & (Tornstam) each noted that spirituality may possibly increase as one ages. Young & Koopsen looked at Spirituality. Health & Healing, while Tornstam looked at "GeroTranscendence" **Gerotranscendence** is a natural and individual process towards maturity and wisdom, normally accompanied by more life satisfaction. It may be described as a transformation, characterized by new ways of understanding life, activity, and oneself. Spiritual awakenings/development during aging=growth opportunities and the ability to release beliefs we no longer find relevant (also see Leeton regarding wellness spirituality in older adults). Spirituality is a journey and time for growth as per Young & Coopsen.

Dr Lantz indicated that the AHNA American Holistic Nursing Assn. (2007) uses philosophies including the right to care that honors mind/body/spirit and that disease/distress allows for opportunities to increase awareness of the inter-connections of mind, body, and spirit. Human beings have a holistic nature that includes emotion and spirit. Cynthia Kociszewski noted that Spirituality should be in the forefront of holistic healthcare/nursing professions. Elizabeth McKinlay examined the Spiritual Aspects of Aging- Spirituality lies at the core of a person's being, an essential dimension bringing meaning to life it is not just religious practices but more importantly a relationship with God. Spiritual practices=actions and activities that express and strengthen one' s faith. Good care needs to include needed spiritual support, including listening, prayer, reading and rituals. Dr Lantz indicated that Holistic health includes the role of the spirit and she also indicated that Religion is the supporting segment to the total picture of a person's spirituality -religion is the tool used to develop spirituality.

Congruence is present when humans buffer tensions in their lives and balance them with spirituality, according to Friedemann, Mouch & Racey and according to Narayanasamy. Energy is strengthened from a strong sense of spirituality within their being. (Stoll) wrote that Spirit=Source of hope/strength + religious practices + Spiritual beliefs regarding healing-There is a relationship between spiritual beliefs & health. Kirkland & McIlveen, mention " Spiritual Therapy" as a way to facilitate healing and as a way to feel joyous and whole and enriched by the sacred.

Dr Lantz stated that There had been no studies of the processes used by older adults regarding their spirituality during relocation-there has been a dearth of studies on the uses of spirituality to cope with stressors when a person moves from their home...Research has not been carried out to determine to what extent spirituality is used or if it has been used at all, to buffer or alleviate life's stressors. More research is needed on adults suffering from Relocation Stress Syndrome. Dr Lantz also indicated that patients drew upon their spirituality to assist them with their relocation adjustment. Their spirituality flourished after the relocation. Closeness and desire for God grew within their holistic being… spiritual influences altered their religious/spiritual feelings.

Dr Lantz also indicated that Spirituality=intrapersonal relationship with God. One can grow spiritually during relocation-there are blessings in spiritual lives during relocation increased desire/time for spirituality a new sense of time to focus on their spiritual life after they relocated. The relocated person continues to search for spiritual guidance there are blessings in spiritual lives during relocation. Their health status becomes a spiritual opportunity a new sense of time to focus on spiritual life more time to study bible and to attend services and more time for spiritual practices. See bibliography for citations/references.

Chapter 39: Secondary Language - Therapeutic Uses/Benefits

Despite my dyslexia, I always enjoyed studying/using the Spanish language & struggled my way thru barely to a BA in Spanish from Hofstra University Spring 1983, over a year before I was diagnosed Dyslexic (9/8/84). Once I was successfully on the Dyslexia inner ear medication from Dr Harold Levinson MD & wearing the Irlen color tint dyslexia eyeglasses he referred me to, I had a "gnawing yen" for trying to "start fresh & new… a clean slate with both my Music (BA Hofstra University Spring 1984) and my Spanish. Especially with the Spanish Music I loved to play. Unfortunately, opportunities for me slowly petered out to none in Florida. This left me despairing, & almost out of hope. However, once I was back to LI NY as of 4/2016, I slowly began to find opportunities & resources, ESPECIALLY church based. for my Music & Spanish & Spanish Music.

Since it was so long long ago (1983) that I had last used my Spanish intensively, I was very "rusty" at it & had become weak in it from almost no use. However, I never stopped craving my return to Spanish. God must have finally heard my impassioned pleas & got me active in (2) Spanish churches in Hicksville NY, where my "starved" brain could finally have the very best intensive Spanish immersion/remediation free of charge several times a week! New Generation Church (Pastor Juan Reyes) & Ministerio Emanuel (Pastor Fredy Sermeno) Despite my multiple disabilities & past struggles in Spanish, they embraced me & "adopted me spiritually" & my Spanish began to scrub off its layers of thick rust & I could finally have that intensive Spanish immersion my brain desperately craved for years. Once very happily immersed 4X/week in Spanish thanks to the 2 churches & the pastors & their wives & other church members, an idea "popped into my dyslexic dwarf head- I began wondering if it was merely my imagination that my body and mind were craving "Spanish language immersion". I put on my "thinking cap" & began to research especially as I didn't know anybody else with my disabilities with a "Spanish language immersion craving' like mine.

The more I began rebuilding my Spanish skills, I literally began to feel a lot better even physically. This could not be imaginary nor "snake oil placebo" type effect-I was convinced that I was "onto something". I began "scouring internet research sources" to see if anyone had found similar therapeutic effects from Spanish language immersion. It did not take me long to confirm my inner intuitive hunch about this therapeutic effect.

Dr Dana Goren PhD, in 6/2014, wrote about "Therapy in a 2nd Language" in a blog in an issue of Psychology Today Magazine. Here is my summary of her material" :She cited the "challenge" of "reorganizing one's identity" and mentioned the "nomadic experience" -each piece of a person has significance each piece is what she called "an essential aspect of the individual" and "part of the therapeutic encounter", She also mentioned the "therapeutic" aspects of a "shared language" ,and she added that it's like "weaving together of all different kinds of fabrics " -she also mentioned the "emotional gap" between words and the feeling with which it's associated when speaking in a 2nd language. She also mentioned the 'grief about being lost in translation" and the "opportunity to discover other experiences of being known and recognized and mentioned its " transformative " benefit. She also mentioned the "frantic inward search for words" to convey emotions and feelings. She also mentioned how a person can show others their innermost emotions and deep feelings thru what she calls "linguistic collapse"...She also referred to "sharing an affinity a comforting familiarity that can quickly cut thru layers of emotions and feelings and she added that it feels good for sure to see someone who shares cultural references and the social landscape of one's childhood/teenage years...she added comments about "creating a cultural island ,thinking in terms of 'us' & mentioned what psychoanalyst Salman Akhtar calls "nostalgic collusion".

She also mentions living away from one's home and she mentions the importance of creating a "home" within, a place of security and warmth, an emotional home through relationships with others geographically.
Dr Marianna Pogosyan PhD also had a blog in a different issue of Psychology Today Magazine (08/2017) about the psychology of learning another language. She mentions "metacognitive" effects of learning and practicing a foreign language. She writes about how you can watch and listen to the native speakers, enthralled by their ease and fluency wondering how it would feel to be able to talk like them, as months go by...you will devotedly memorize new words and dissect complex syntax structures you will observe, absorb. study and repeat ,until one day you will realize that strings of syllables are no longer indecipherable ,somehow ,you have permeated through the curtain of foreign sound, they ring familiar to your ears now,, you can comprehend sentences and recognize grammar rules, and you can now begin to guess the meanings of unknown words by using your existing knowledge you can make inferences and verify their accuracy you no longer feel the urge to translate long winding conversations word for word. You replace your anxiety with confidence and learn to focus even harder,

In short, you begin to use your "seventh sense" of learning (Nisbet & Shucksmith, 1986) your metacognitive abilities such as the ability to become aware & conscious of your mental processes. It thus facilitates knowledge of self and the world. and helps with the desires and plans for accomplishments it enhances learning by increasing awareness of one's learning processes such as learning and memorizing words and phrases and your listening skills are enhanced, and your comprehension improves as well...learning is made more

effective and one learns strategies...you're improving motivating you to learn more...
(Pogosyan 08/2017) also mentions developing a "mentally active attitude" and the facilitating of strategies to learn and cope and the ability to ask questions for clarification is enhanced (also see Charnot, 2005:pg115). (Pogosyan. 08/2017) also mentions how a person learns how to reflect on the process of language learning. i.e. strategic thinking and the teacher can guide the person to become more aware of the person's thinking processes. Thus, self-evaluation is facilitated. She adds that increased familiarity will speed understanding including entire passages of speech in a foreign language and when you like what you hear. It makes the "learning game" more enjoyable. Each language has its own music (see Limacher-Riebold) You will develop a feel for the language's music such as rhythm & intonation of the foreign language ,seeing a foreign language in printed form helps one to learn word structures and helps to imprint the structures in one's mind (see Limacher-Riebold) .Dr Ute Limacher-Riebold, author of 4 tips to learn a new language for adults notes the importance of talking in a foreign language and it can help in making new friends. It also helps with "being prepared to make mistakes " and teaches the person how to welcome corrections. You start enjoying your new language long before your sentences are faultless & before your pronunciation sounds "near-native".
Please note that in my own case my life has to include constant learning so the "total Spanish immersion" at the 2 churches and 1 messianic synagogue, is a crucial part of my need for 24/7 learning. and ultimately coping through that learning.

Chapter 40: What Churches Temples & Synagogues need to understand/know/do to help

The United Church of Christ ("UCC" & "UCCDM' published a Guide Manual on what religious congregations need to understand, know & do to help special needs adults like ME. The theme of their Guide Manual is " **Any Body Every Body Christ's Body-Becoming Accessible to All.** This was written under the direction of their **Disabilities Ministries** ("DM") division, along with their board of directors. I have copied their resources list within the bibliography of this book. Since this Guide Manual is quite detailed and lengthy, I chose to summarize condense and excerpt it here in a simplified form for you and I have tried to maintain their order in this abridged version composed by me:

Social attitudes are a large barrier for inclusion, and we need to break down those barriers to inclusion...We also need to recognize and address the barriers to inclusion, and we need to follow the call to wholeness ...They initially reference the late Harold Wilke and his "Signs of Liberation & Access". Yet for many people today with disabilities, the barriers still remain the stone is still in place… the waters are not parted the way did not open the words cannot be heard the flame of the Spirit's tongues cannot be seen the message not understood,

Proclaiming the message to all includes braille, sign language, audio enhancement, and colorful large print, inter alia,(not just wheelchair ramps & building alterations/accommodations).The congregations need to be more accessible to those with silent invisible conditions such as cognitive impairments mental illnesses drug/alcohol addiction recovery, Autism ADHD Dyslexia Learning Disabilities Irlen Syndrome & Aspergers (high function Autism aka "on the spectrum" and anxiety/panic disorders including PTSD. (Wilke, Harold) said that the stone needs to be rolled away, let the glorious message be proclaimed everywhere to everyone, so that all may "hear, see, and understand". One in 5 persons lives with a disability and one in 4 persons experience a mental health concern. John 13:34 (NRSV)-*Jesus declared ' I give you a new commandment, that you love one another just as I have loved you, you should also love one another.',*

We can find new ways of loving one another when we expand our hearts, minds and actions to encompass the "Any Body Every Body Christ's body" theme "church of extravagant Welcome/Hospitality" ,we have an obligation to ensure that each person can share a full experience of worship and fellowship ,A crucial and important part of Social Justice is Accessibility and it includes attitudes of leaders and laity. Create opportunities for everyone to fully participate in all aspects of life in a faith community it is important to communicate readiness to provide whatever support is needed it's important to maintain a posture of hospitality find out what people need and provide what is necessary recognize that some individuals are hypersensitive to sound/noise/bright lights, i.e. those with Autism/ Aspergers/ Irlen syndrome etcetera. Be Aware of & Sensitive to Neurodevelopmental disabilities such as ADD ADHD ASD (etc.) and learning/attention/concentration disorders and also to PTSD Post Traumatic Stress.

Ask special needs adults what would make their participation more fulfilling. Special needs adults want to be able to fully participate in the life of a religious congregation. Provide learning/tutorial/study/fellowshipping assistance including meetings, classes & materials and remember that sensitivity is key. Also be aware of Chronic Fatigue, Lyme disease, cancer, Traumatic Brain Injury, Stroke & head injury & MS/Parkinsons disease etc.-ask all these people what they need in order to fully participate in the life of a faith community also be aware of and sensitive to Dementia/Alzheimers /Memory Impaired people and offer them extended support thru outreach and pastoral assistance. Mental health conditions are often invisible and silent it is incumbent on congregations to provide welcoming inclusive supportive and engaging programs and activities for those with special needs see for example, United Church of Christ UCC Mental Health Network process for congregations to become WISE congregations for Mental Health (see mhn-ucc.blogspot.com) Congregations need to address mental health issues. Understand the importance of Leadership Accessible to All...the United Church of Christ Disabilities Ministries Board involves both pastoral and lay leadership-leadership that supports inclusion of people with disabilities in all aspects of congregational life ministry. Recognize special gifts/talents/skills that the special needs members have to contribute to the whole congregation. Leadership "accessible to all" must recognize wholeness of the Body of Christ,

It is important to provide/have training in disability awareness especially regarding invisible silent disabilities and attitudinal awareness/sensitivity is paramount there needs to be attitudinal accessibility training in disability awareness training including training in psychosocial aspects of disability inclusion in religious faith communities,

There needs to be awareness of disability related social justice issues and awareness of disability theology, both in terms of pastoral leaders and lay leaders Nurture the leadership skills of people with disabilities -invite and encourage their participation and mentor them as well it's so important that those with disabilities feel wanted, included and appreciated include them in volunteer roles and the congregation needs to provide advocacy for disability rights never forget the importance of "so that all may worship" -every worshiping community needs to have an honest sense of welcome to all of God's children and these things don't have to be expensive at all people with special needs need to be included in the active life of the church…

Welcome the disabled into the active life of the church. Remember that it is most often an unwelcoming and un-accepting attitude that leads visitors with disabilities to not return and not join as members. A 2010 Harris Interactive Survey of people with disabilities noted that people with disabilities are 35% more likely to never attend worship services, stating it is not due to physical barriers, but attitudinal barriers that make them less likely to feel comfortable and welcome in houses of worship. Remember too that a large variety of impairments can lead to a person becoming disabled.

NAMI, The National Alliance on Mental Illness says that 1 in 4 adults will experience mental illness in a given year.

Attitudes/Actions can ensure that potential members with disabilities feel welcome and included in the life of a congregation. Impairments are only 1 aspect of a person's humanity and people are more than their disabilities. They are whole people with many interests. Don't expect them to speak only of their disability. Don't try to "repair" the disabled. Mainstream the Alienated and respond to this new ministry. Form an inclusion team that includes people with disabilities form church learning groups to discuss the challenges felt by the disabled. We need to welcome all people regardless of their conditions.

Nancy Eisland said that we need to "encounter the Disabled God"...Harold Wilke said we need to mainstream the alienated and we need to respond to new minorities. We must address all dimensions of faith including ministering to those with disabilities. Gaventa said that We need to have a " that all may worship-interfaith welcome to those with disabilities (AAPD.COM), Jennie Weiss-Block, calls it "copious hosting-a theology of disability", Fritzon & Kabue speak of a church of all for all.

David Pailin speaks of a Gentle touch-theology of Human Being. Thomas Reynolds speaks about "vulnerable communion", Erik Carter and Brett Webb-Mitchell, said to include the disabled in faith communities, + Also see the Thornburgh Guide for Community Faith Congregations.

Lastly, see Appendix 5 UCC Resolution to Become Accessible to All-Called to Wholeness in Christ: Becoming a Church Accessible to All. It speaks of a biblical vision of Great Messianic Banquet-all gathered at table with bounty for all -any barrier that limits the wholeness of all diminishes all… all UCC members will be touched by a disability in some way at some time in their lives. People with disabilities want to worship and serve the Church needs to take measures in its ministries to implement equality and accommodation for the disabled the Church needs to embody the philosophy of inclusion… accessibility for all, the Church needs to remove barriers to welcoming and including all people in church the Church needs to consider a progression of ministry concern, not only to/for people with disabilities, but also ministry with/by people with disabilities. The Church needs to be open, affirming, and accessible to all inclusion planning is key. There is a group called the Accessible Congregations Campaign of the National Organization on Disability. There is a need to establish local church inclusion committees to evaluate/modify practices and procedures nothing about us without us… invite disabled persons to participate in and lead worship.

Chapter 41: When is a bathrobe not merely a bathrobe?

Dedicated to Peggy Alba, wife of Pastor Phil Alba,

for the WONDERFUL BATHROBE SHE GIFTED ME WITH as

a ***SPECIAL THANK YOU TO HER FOR THE "HEALING***

BATHROBE'

I am providing some biblical verses/phrases taken from 38 BIBLE

VERSES ABOUT ROBES:

- Exodus 28:4 holy garment to be made- robe and sash for Aaron & his sons.
- Exodus 29:5 put on Aaron the robe of the ephod.
- Exodus 28:31-34 make the robe of the ephod.
- Exodus 39:22-26 robe of the ephod.
- Leviticus 8:7 clothed with the robe.
- 1 Samuel 2: 19 and his mother would make him a little robe and bring it to him.
- 1 Samuel 18:4 Jonathan took off his robe & gave it to David.
- 2 Samuel 13:18 She had on a long-sleeved garment robe.
- 1 Chronicles 15:27 David was clothed with a robe of fine linen.
- 1 Kings 22:30 King of Israel told Jehoshaphat to put on robes in order to disguise himself for the battle.
- Matthew 27:28 Stripped him & put a scarlet robe on him.
- Isaiah 22:21 I will clothe him with your tunic and tie your sash securely about him.
- Isaiah 6:1-10 he has wrapped me with a robe of righteousness.
- Luke 15:22 Quickly bring out the best robe and put it on him.

My BLANKET MIRACLE

At one low point in my Experimental Dental Journey, The Winter Weather was bone chilling & I was very low on finances & hesitated on spending money on an extra flannel blanket & an extra quilted comforter. One frigid night I was walking the mile from the railroad station to my rented room & became tearful about my need for the purchase vs my low funds- money was very tight-and praying to God as I walked. Suddenly in the middle of the roadway was a big white trash bag standing tall despite the winds blowing. Out of unexplainable curiosity, I stopped to take a peek. I was overcome-choked with emotion-the bag contained a flannel blanket & a quilted comforter. WOW. God is so good & so amazing-He answered my prayers.

Chapter 42: The Therapeutic & Healing Benefits of Playing Tambourines

Thank You to Pastor Fredy Sermeno, of Ministerio Emanuel (& his wife "pastora" Dorka) for introducing me to the Therapeutic & Healing Benefits of playing Tambourines at their church. I had never played Tambourines in Church until joining their church. It was & is amazing to play Tambourines in Church there. It literally makes me feel joyous & full of praise & helps keep me away from the racing distraction of my ADHD. It also led me to want to search online academic/theological materials to see what researchers have to say about this. It was euphoric to find materials corroborating my intuitive feelings & anecdotal self-reporting about this & decided it needed to have its very own chapter in my book (this book). After reading my findings I hope that you too are similarly amazed by the results of a brief summary review of the online literature.

Jean Wise wrote about the Spiritual Practice of Taking Your Tambourine. Here is a 'summary of her paper: Miriam the prophet, Aaron & Moses' sister, took a tambourine & led all the women as they played their tambourines & danced.(Exodus 15:20) ,Miriam, Moses & Aaron & all the Hebrews were leaving Egypt they packed in a hurry, taking only a few precious possessions that they could carry amid the chaos of a sudden escape from Egypt being chased by the Egyptian Army. They headed towards the Promised Land. Dusty Bedlam unknown future and fear also pursued them. God interceded and the waters crushed Pharaoh's horses and chariots the Israelites were safe on the other side of the sea and leaving the past behind as they began their journey into a new future. That is when Miriam & the women brought out their tambourines before they left, before they knew what would happen before they even took the first step toward their destiny. They had packed their Tambourines & knew that they would dance again. They knew someday somewhere they would have reason to celebrate. They wanted to be ready when the invitation came to rejoice. They trusted the God of the Dance to provide music once again. They didn't forget their tambourines… tambourines gave them hope. This simple instrument symbolizes that God is with you. And You should pack your tambourine. So be ready like Miriam for when the time is right. Tambourines are shaped like prayer-I pour into its open shell shattered unfulfilled dreams… my leftover anger & disappointments… my delights & dreams & lift them up to God. I turn the Tambourine over & empty all the joy & junk from last year into God's hands. Then I dance for God, with God, and we will keep dancing together in gratitude that no matter what happened before, God was & is with me. No matter what will happen God will be with me. And that is reason to celebrate. Raise your tambourines moving to the beat of God's love (Timbrelpraise.org) "Tambourine in the Bible": The tambourine is an instrument of praise, worship & warfare it was also used for joy, gladness, rejoicing, triumph, singing, victory, celebration, welcoming, and it was even used to lead armies into battle. For example, (Genesis 31:27) ' why didn't you tell me, so I could send you away with joy and singing to the music of tambourines and harps?' Tambourine was even played on the Battlefield. Some say that the priests in the temple took the tambourine and used it at the temple. Psalms 68:25 maidens playing timbrels with the singers and instrumental musicians Exodus 15:20 Then Miriam the Prophetess, Aaron & Moses' sister, took a tambourine(timbrel) in her hand, and all the women followed her, with tambourines(timbrels) and dancing,

So, it is so noteworthy, that in my faith based experimental dental treatment journey here in NY, my self-healing therapies include playing tambourines at Ministerio Emanuel. I am overjoyed to see a prolific quantity of additional online articles verifying the healing therapeutic aspects of playing Tambourine. Thus, it was & is clear that

God's amazing plan for me includes this fantastic opportunity for me
to play Tambourine 4x/week at Ministerio Emanuel.

Chapter 43: Therapeutic Use of Music dates back to the Bible

Nicole Moskowitz talks about the Davidic Harp & about the existence of musical instruments throughout the Tanakh: the existence of musical instruments throughout Tanakh is quite remarkable. Be it in the context of mourning, celebration, or ritual, the use of advanced forms of mechanics is quite striking. A most renowned example is the harp (kinor) of King David, which, central to the musicality of Tehillim And to the book of Shmuel I, is often employed as a cure for King Saul's evil spirit and as a means of giving praise to God. While the music of this instrument most commonly results from the plucking of its strings, there exists evidence of an additional, rather unique performance of this harp, one by the powerful northern wind. The topic of this property of David's harp comes from the Talmud in Berakhot which discusses a statement of Moshe's from the book of Shemot: "About midnight I will go out into the midst of Egypt." The Talmud contrasts Moshe's statement with a statement of David's in which David says that at exactly midnight he rises to give thanks to God. If Moshe did not know the exact time of midnight, as suggested by the term "about," how did King David? The answer, in the name of Rav Shimon Chasida, is that David had a device to awaken him: a harp hanging above his bed which would be played when the northern wind of midnight would blow upon it. The fact that King David had his own alarm clock is incredible. In fact, regarding the above statement from Shemot, the Ibn Ezra comments: "It is known that a scientist can calculate the moment of midday with great effort and huge copper instruments, but calculating the middle of the night is far more difficult" In that case, what exactly was the mechanism of this harp; what properties did it hold enabling David to awaken at precisely midnight when it was met by the force of the northern wind? In essence, David was awakened by an Aeolian harp which, by definition, is played by the wind. In such a phenomenon, the energy of wind is transformed into harmonious sound by the laws of fluid dynamics. A harp most commonly sounds when its strings are plucked and begin to vibrate, causing the air around them to move and creating a sound which is amplified by the soundboard, a component of the instrument which improves the coupling of the vibrating string with the air. However, when it is the wind that plays the harp another concept – that of vortex induced vibrations – is featured, which allows the wind energy to be converted into musical tones. The idea of vortex-induced vibrations is inherent to any situation of fluid flow in which a constant fluid stream encounters a bluff body causing it to change course and produce a very phenomenal pattern in its wake.

In the case of the harp, as the wind passes at a high velocity perpendicular to the thin cylindrical strings and vortices form on either side of the string, then close in behind the string in an alternating, counter-rotating fashion, leaving behind what is known as a von Kármán vortex trail. As these alternating vortices break away from the strings with a certain frequency, they slightly lift the strings, causing them to oscillate from side to side at the same frequency. When the frequency of these oscillations matches any harmonic of the string (any integer multiple of the natural frequency which is heard when the strings are plucked), resonance takes place, producing an audible tone which is then amplified by the harp's soundboard. The frequency of these Aeolian vibrations has been studied rigorously, initially by Vincenc Strouhal in 1878, and was discovered to be proportional to the wind's velocity divided by the string's diameter (with a proportionality constant of approximately 0.2 for most velocities) From this relationship, it becomes obvious that at higher wind velocities, vortices will form more frequently, while at larger string diameters, vortices will form less frequently. For very low wind velocities, in fact, air will simply flow in streamlines over the harp's strings, never forming vortices, and thus not causing the strings to vibrate. For the case of David's harp, the wind prompting these AeoT. What exactly was the mechanism of this harp; what properties did it hold enabling David to awaken at precisely midnight when it was met by the force of the northern wind? derech haTeva 47 lian vibrations was the northern wind. As explained by Rashi, four winds blow each day, with the northern wind blowing at midnight. Elsewhere, the Talmud states that four winds blow each day, and the northern wind blows with all of them. In both cases, the velocity of the northern wind became noticeably increased at precisely midnight, and thus produced an air flow capable of shedding vortices about the harp's strings at a precise frequency to elicit a melodic sound. In studying these unique mechanics of David's harp, it is important to have a feel for the general design and the material composition and to visualize the instrument which was played by the northern wind. While the precise design of the harp is not known, there exists strong evidence for its form in the coins minted by Bar Kochba during his revolt against the Romans. David's harp is among the various emotional objects which were featured on these coins to prompt the Jewish people to attack the Romans.

Bar Kochba coins feature David's kinor with a floating bridge, a soundboard, strings, and tuning pegs, much like the images of Biblical harps seen today. Evidence of the material used to make the harp strings stems from the Talmud, which discusses the ram, an animal which contributes parts of its anatomy to various musical instruments. The ram's intestines in particular are commonly used for the strings on a harp.

 Further, the number of strings on David's harp is also known and stems from Rabbi Yehudah's understanding of the phrase in Tehillim, "in thy presence is fullness (soba) of joy" Rather than "fullness," the word "soba" can be interpreted as "seven," from the word of the same root, "sheva," because the Davidic harp and that of the Beit HaMikdash had seven strings. Together, these details paint an effective picture of the mechanism which allowed David to awaken, faithfully, at midnight.

Finally, returning to the original question in the Talmud – why could Moses Not have such a device to pinpoint the precise moment of midnight? The answer lies not in the mechanism of the harp but in the wind that played it. Yonatan ben Uziel explains that when the Jews were about to leave Egypt, the Ananei HaKavod lifted them to the place where the Beit HaMikdashwould be in order for them to offer the Korban Pesakh. If the northern wind had blown on this night (and throughout the forty years in the desert) the clouds of glory would have scattered! Therefore, God prevented the northern wind from blowing, making David's harp inapplicable as an alarm clock for Moshe. As a mechanism, David's harp of the tenth century BC was undoubtedly sophisticated. The application of vortex-induced vibrations to harness the force of midnight's northern wind is incredible. Moreover, the fact that David utilized fluid dynamics to ensure that he would awaken to praise God at precisely midnight is very fascinating and a lesson in the importance of taking advantage of the laws of nature to go beyond the letter of the law in *our service of God*.

Chapter 44A: Music Therapy for PTSD Posttraumatic Stress Disorder

Maria Sorenson wrote about the **<u>Neurology of Music for PTSD treatment</u>**: She was researching neural implications of music and trauma and the brain. Music can be used as a tool to neurologically aid in the treatment of PTSD. Music can harness neuroplasticity to recondition the brain back to healthy functioning. The Music therapy can also help build rapport and help "ground" a PTSD patient in reprocessing trauma. Music therapy can also provide positive distraction for those in crisis who have a hard time self-regulating. It helps the PTSD patient to express their narrative non-verbally, and it reduces stress cortisol and releases dopamine. Music therapy can balance neurological pathways to normal function, and it helps traumatic memory to be reprocessed and integrated. It enhances an alternative positive thought "I am now in control" and can help even those with prolonged multiple traumas.

Music evokes emotion and impacts the brain, and the music can be incorporated as part of PTSD treatments. Music therapy dates back to 1789 as "music physically considered" in Columbian Magazine but actually originates in the Bible. It allows the person to be in a safe calm predictable environment to help desensitize the person. Music helps them focus on the "here and now" instead of on past traumas. It helps refocus the mind aka "intentional refocus" and helps with impaired concentration/attention common to PTSD. The music is also soothing and calming, predictable and paced. It has a positive distraction effect on crises.

Here is some additional information on Music Therapy:

Music has the power to transport the performer, the patient, and the student. Beautiful harmony transcends words and connects people's faith and arts ... It enriches the mind soul spirit & emotions & can actually increase intelligence.   It can improve thinking, focus concentration & attention & decrease anxiety/panic/hyperactivity/hyperarousal & hyper-reactivity it can calm, soothe & quiet both mind & body it can help with the expression of emotions/feelings/fears/anxieties & helps release trauma. It can help manage debilitating side effects and distressing symptoms it recommends one to love it's part of an overall treatment plan there is a connection between music therapy and treating symptoms ,It combines motor/cognitive skills with creativity, attention focus ,social interaction, multi-sensory processing, coordination balance and dexterity ,it provides "musical/clinical" moments, where arts and science come together to create beautiful awareness accomplishments & breakthroughs.

Edo Banach says that all other ground is sinking sand regarding the important role that music therapy can play in an interdisciplinary team. Instruments & Voices are spiritual/emotional & are deeply connected tools that can be extremely meaningful to those in need of healing peacefulness,

Sharon Graham wrote that the music of our lives remains long after our bodies pass away, the love continued therein is eternal & will last beyond our pain.

Tamera Norris wrote that Music is an opportunity for emotional contact with mental focus music even facilitates learning of life skills helps build human relationships and social skills and helps with self-expression. Jefri Franks wrote that Music throughout a fight with disease helps one get thru harrowing treatment journeys.

 Dr Richard Fratianne MD wrote that by working out on the piano as part of his therapy all his other therapies started to become more effective, I could think better. There are psychoacoustic properties of that which a person is trying to express a neuroplasticity response where the brain re-teaches itself how to regain normal function. Music helps people cope with the effects of illness. pain, loneliness and fear,

Florence Cohen wrote that creating a comfortable space in which trusting bonds of friendship would quickly form bringing encouragement adding purpose to one's life and resuscitates one's spirit in a most gentle way it generates power of positive thoughts and connects to kind words. smiles. compassion, happiness and enjoyment ...self-expression thru music. Dr Mary DiCamillo wrote that Music enhances relaxation and eases emotional expression it decreases pain, it assists with cued rhythmic breathing helps with focus concentration/attention diverts mind away from physical pain establishes rapport. It can be individualized and enhances verbalization.

Dr Ann Lipe wrote that singing yields emotional expression...improves moods, decreases nervousness/anxiety. it comforts, reassures and is calming and is a great leisure time activity. Theme based music groups improve cognitive skill, encourages social interaction communication and self-expression, and assists with nurturing meaningful human contact. It draws a person out of a world of isolation and into a world of comfort and connection. It restores a sense of personhood; it makes things easier… music offers a way to communicate that does not depend on spoken language. Music experience makes "testing" situations more enjoyable.

<u>MUSIC & THE CEREBELLAR-VESTIBULAR "CV" SYSTEM</u>

 (Reynolds) & (Levinson) each briefly mentioned the case of a gifted musician/conductor with Dyslexia & ADD, who began reading music books with enhanced concentration and greater perfect pitch after starting the cerebellar vestibular inner ear harmonizing medications.

Chapter 44B: Cerebellum & Music

Dan Ferber examined the sounds of music in the cerebellum and the effects of music on the cerebellum. The cerebellum helps interpret rhythmic timing-rhythmic changes alter blood flow to the cerebellum. The cerebellum responds to musical training and the cerebellums of musicians are 5% larger than those of non-musicians. Years of precise finger movements can stimulate extra nerve growth.

Siobhan Hutchinson examined the cerebellar volume of musicians, particularly of professionally classically trained keyboard players...and she found a significantly greater cerebellar volume in those musicians. A lifelong intensity of musical practice correlated to relative cerebellar volume. Females have larger relative cerebellar volume the intensity is defined as the average number of hours practiced per day. A significantly larger cerebellar volume in male musicians' correlates to lifelong intensity of practice and the intensity is defined as the average number of hours practiced per day. There is an important connection between the cerebellum and musical skill and music playing -the cerebellum is activated during music playing females reach adult cerebellar volume maturity earlier in childhood.

 Callan, Parsons, Kawato & Turner examined the role of the cerebellum in speech and song- and determined that there is cerebellar activity during singing (production of song): for example, 6th lobule of the posterior cerebellum that relates to lips and tongue. and the left cerebellar hemisphere for processing of singing-6th lobule + crossed pattern of cerebellar cortical anatomical connectivity, and left cerebellum processes melodic properties.

 Lega & Vecchi, et al) examined cerebellar roles in discrimination of pitch/timbre discrimination-there was a causal role of the cerebellum in sound processing and that the cerebellum plays a critical role in timing. There is also cerebellar activation during passive music listening. Cerebellar activation was also connected to pitch/melody discrimination, sound intensity and sound duration. Cerebellar activity increases significantly during auditory pitch discrimination. The cerebellum responds more when the difficulty of the discrimination is increased. Cerebellar disorder signs can include deficits in melody recognition, and discrimination deficits in dealing with small differences in sound/pitch duration discrimination. The cerebellum contributes to auditory perception and sound processing the cerebellum is also involved in timbre-the property of sound which allows people to distinguish musical instruments when pitch loudness and duration are the same...there is significant cerebellar responses to sound timbre this study used the following format: timbre sound files=musical instrument samples-digitized samples of real instruments from wind and string families. Paul Brown mentions the neuro-imaging of the cerebellum that includes musical task performance.

Linda Maguire indicates that the frequency/intensity of music practice (Piano and Violin) increases cerebellar volume. She identified the following music related functions of the cerebellum: motor intent into action, motor memory storage acquisition of motor memory, determines quality of a

performance. unconscious proprioception, tool use skills, dance skills, sharpens precise rhythmic timing, smooth control of rapid motor responses. analyzes movements, receives sensory inputs, loops to other systems, brain plasticity (ie omega sign) self-discipline, planning, imprinting. identifies musical resonances, stimulates brain thru resonance, internalizes musical rhythm, affects vocal music respiration, controls automaticity, music memory, jazz improvisation.

 Tillman, Justus & Bigand, posited that cerebellar disease patients demonstrate implicit knowledge of association strengths in musical sequences. Daniel Levitin indicates that the cerebellum receives songs then synchronizes itself to the rhythm of the music.

Chapter 45: Vocal/Choral Singing & Dwarfism

<u>Despite my dwarfism dental nightmare, I love to sing in 2 local choral groups.</u>

Jeffery & Berkovitz mentioned that some rare dwarfism forms exhibit a reduced angle of the craniocervical skull at the cranial base...that can influence the proportions of the vocal tract, which may cause vocal impairment.

<u>Vocal/Choral Singing & the Cerebellum</u>

Linda Maguire indicated that the cerebellum affects vocal respiration. Daniel Levitin indicated that the cerebellum receives songs then synchronizes itself to the rhythm of the music.

Pidoux & LeBlanc performed a study in Paris, France on a subcortical circuit linking the cerebellum to the basal ganglia engaged in vocal learning. They stated the following: Vocal learning involves both basal ganglia and the cerebellum. The cerebellum provides strong input to the song related basal ganglia nucleus in zebra finches. The cerebellar contribution to avian song learning remains unknown. Cerebellar signals are transmitted to the basal ganglia via a disynaptic connection thru the thalamus and then conveyed to their cortical target and to the premotor nucleus controlling song production. Cerebellar lesions impair juvenile song learning. There is a need to investigate further the subcortical interactions between the cerebellum and basal ganglia in terms of their contribution to sensorimotor learning.

Songbirds are used as a model for how the brain drives vocal learning -whether of speech or song. Juvenile songbirds go through a process similar to human infants, in terms of learning to sing and they learn to produce their own songs. The basal ganglia help with learning fine motor skills. Vocal learning in infants involves the cerebellum, so does planning and performing movement. Anatomical studies of songbirds suggest a connection between the cerebellum and song related circuits. Stimulating the cerebellum in anesthetized zebra finches activates basal ganglia neurons involved in song learning. This activation spreads through a song related circuit to neurons controlling the vocal cords. Disrupting the cerebellum makes it harder for juvenile birds to imitate adult songs. The cerebellum plays a role in the acquisition of bird song. We can use songbirds to study the cerebellum and its interaction with basal ganglia. Abnormal cerebellar-basal ganglia interaction is observed in humans with Parkinson's disease. Brooks et al & Izawa et al & Gomez & Lewis & Maler all indicate that the cerebello-thalamo-cortical loop is crucial for vocal learning in humans. Doupe & Kuhl indicated that Avian song learning is very similar to human speech learning in infants.

Pidoux & LeBlanc indicate that cerebello-thalamo-cortical circuits are part of sensorimotor learning in primates. (See also Brooks, Gomez. and Lewis Maler)

Pidoux & LeBlanc add that the cerebellum also drives correction of movement -building on the sensory error prediction aka error based supervised learning error prediction denoting mismatch between sensory prediction and actual sensory feedback. (See also Tseng), The Cerebellum also controls time duration of movement and its prediction-during sensorimotor learning. (see also Day, Flament & Hove & Izawa). There is a pathway from the cerebellum to song related basal ganglia, see Person, Vates & Nicholson). Cerebellar Circuits may be involved with avian song learning-cerebellar signals may reach basal ganglia to drive error correction and reinforcement learning. Cerebellar inputs are conveyed to basal ganglia in songbirds thru the thalamus. Cerebellar signals contribute to juvenile song learning and to the timing of song elements. Cerebellar inputs drive activity in the cortical target of basal ganglia. Cerebellar signals are sent to song related basal ganglia circuits. The cerebellum participates in song learning. Deep cerebellar nuclei send projection to thalamic areas which then project to the song related basal ganglia nucleus area x and its cortical targets. The neural pathway is also involved with pharmacological manipulations. There is a disynaptic connection between the cerebellum and song related basal ganglia Area X. (see Person) Deep cerebellar stimulation elicits strong excitation in pallidal cells. Cerebellar responses are conveyed through the basal ganglia loop. There are Disynaptic cerebellum-thalamus-basal ganglia pathways in songbirds. The cerebellum contributes to song learning during development and contributes to avian song learning. There is cerebellar activation during human speech. Cerebellar damage/defects cause speech impairment. The cerebellum interacts with song-specific circuits in the basal ganglia of songbirds and contributes to the acquisition of song during development in juvenile birds. The cerebellum modulates basal ganglia activity and manages sensorimotor timing processes.

Chapter 46: Tennis Therapy/Therapeutic Healing Aspects of Tennis

I was blessed to find a tennis teacher and his tennis lessons with me have been a very important part of my mind/body healing, &I decided to add this as the final chapter of this book. I decided to show all of you a brief summary review of the literature regarding the healing therapeutic benefits of Tennis.

Dr Robert London MD wrote a sports psychology article about the Tennis Racquet & The Mind, and I have extracted the salient information for you to review. He said that Tennis improves concentration, relieves anxiety, decreases performance nervousness, reduces insecurities, alleviates fear of failure and helps to overcome a negative review of oneself as a "loser" - the tennis game helps one to focus on the moment-to-moment action of the game. It resembles a learned spiritual process. One's fears and worries are displaced through the process of concentration on the racquet, the ball, and the net. It starts the patient on the path of a newer and better way to focus his/her mind and concentration and helps build achievement and self-confidence.

The keys to its success include the integrating the racquet/balls as an ongoing mental process of connected movement, rather than as separate singular entities that get distracted by intruding thoughts of anxiety/failure that distract one's mind away from hitting the tennis ball-Tennis teaches a Zen like calming relaxation philosophy. Some people have anxiety before playing and are filled with recurring thoughts of losing the game, and they can be helped to see anxieties without experiencing them via training. A planned reciprocal inhibition method allows pleasant experiences to relieve projected anxieties-it allows for a better game & a more relaxed game. The person can be taught how to sense/feel the arm, hand, and racquet as 1 entity, learning to make contact with the ball, seeing oneself placing the ball where it needed to land on an opponent's side of the tennis court. The racquet/ball would become an extension of the person. The person would be taught how to conceptualize, and the person would truly feel that he/she was onto something exciting, new and different as the person, the racquet and the ball become "one". Cognitive "fragmentation disappears" as does the anxiety as well, along with the thought patterns that were distracting the person, by learning how to be at one with the game. It really improves the quality of life.

The Martin Effect website Tennis Psychologist describes the following: choking when faced with pressure filled situations-nervous and anxious- feeling self-doubt and one's confidence decreases, tension builds feelings of getting defeated, and of losing, YET-there is a confident tennis player desperate to break thru -beneath the feelings of uncertainty, Tennis Psychologist can teach you how to get back your confidence unexpected downturns can lead to fragile confidence. Confidence becomes brittle after losses-the person's self is being undermined by self-doubt, and losing confidence in one's ability-you can overcome doubts and become mentally strong thru tennis psychology. A person can have a mental game that needs fixing--such as losing concentration at key moments. You can learn to develop simple effective strategies to "get your game back on track.

Dr Robert Heller describes Tennis Sport Psycholeffectively, and Therapy sport psychology that allows one to perform at their best to go from good to great one can overcome mental blocks that interfere with performing at one's best a mentally tough player will have a winning edge i.e. mental toughness training to provide life skills to better manage people, situations and circumstances-learn to relax-how to handle defeat, manage mistakes and manage stress more effectively and reduce distractions, identify and maximize mental and emotional strengths.

Tennis as a therapeutic tool for Autism

Pugliese, Lisa explains that Tennis as a therapeutic tool for children with Autism- Repetitive learning opportunities that transfer into daily living skills- enhanced social skills via tennis court training self-expression on the tennis court- tennis social story thru routines ,social engagement thru tennis + Reasons to play Tennis for individuals with Autism include Increased motor skills, improved social skills, increased focus/attention/concentration, decreased distractibility/hyperactivity, improved brain power… improved cognitive processing skills, improved problem solving skills, decreased stress/anxiety/panic, enhanced life skills, improved hand/eye coordination, improved cardiac heart function, better muscle condition, and better bone strength and improved sustaining of energy, and increased auditory/visual processing and communication skills. Repetition helps enhance skill building. Tennis also provides familiarity/consistency of routines, and tennis drills enhance spontaneous thinking function both on and off the court, and it helps the brain with predictive planning as it is challenging to figure out where the opponent is returning the next tennis ball.

(Pugliese adds that it teaches about flexibility, and self-control of frustration. It improves tactical planning skills, it's a social sport, as you play vs an opponent, or as part of a team, or in doubles) Rallying is an enjoyable social engagement that can help lower anxiety. It enhances language communication skills, it helps develop self-discipline, and reduces stress, it enhances the ability to physically plan /prepare, which decreases anxiety, and sharpens self-regulation. and the new skills can be generalized into non-tennis environments.

Jan Spencer described how Tennis was therapeutic for a grieving father: Tennis has ties to the darkest times in life a phenomenal support system of people who hold you up encouragement thru tennis instruction. I need tennis now more than ever.

Ahmet Yazici described how Tennis enhances well-being in university students. Depression & Anxiety significantly decreased and there was a definite anxiolytic benefit. It helps regulate serotonin and dopamine and noradrenaline levels in the brain and controls oxidative stress and it increases the brain's neurotrophic factor-its BDNF level in the striatum. It is recommended as a complementary treatment choice in depression and anxiety disorders. It also improves cardiovascular health and bone health as well-and improves agility and coordination. It builds aerobic and anaerobic conditioning and builds muscle strength/memory/endurance. It improves a sense of vigor/optimism/self-esteem/confidence, it decreases anger, anxiety, tension & confusion, and it has positive effects on personality. Tennis has a healing effect on psychological distress. Anxiety/Depression scores significantly decrease after tennis training started. Psychopathology test scores also decreased after tennis was started. Additional benefits noted with Tennis include decreased somatization, reduced obsessive-compulsive behaviors, decreased hostility, decreased psychoticism, decreased phobic responses, decreased paranoia, decreased insomnia, relief of anorexia, and even decreased neurotic guilt.

It increased endorphin levels in the brain, and reduced cortisol stress hormone levels & restored impaired limbic function related to depression. Tennis can lead to an integrated recovery in mental health and should improve sleep dysfunction disorders. These benefits were observed/measured with 90 minutes per week of tennis instruction for 13 weeks. Shafali Jeste, Shafali, also wrote about the therapeutic benefits of Tennis in kids with autism. It teaches reciprocity & mutuality. Especially so with Rally between opponents which is like a physical dialogue. It involves reading one's opponent and predicting the opponent's behavior. It improves eye contact, and the tennis lesson curriculum parallels the learning progression from basic motor skills to advanced strategic forecasting skill. It improves hand grip skills and swinging skills, Excess sensory overstimulation can be minimized by using smaller nets. It teaches visual cueing such as where to stand. It also helps with walking, running and jumping motor skills for instance gripping racquets improves muscle tone. It improves self-regulation and decreases distractions.

Scott Shapiro described how Tennis helps with ADHD. Tennis can be like physical therapy for the ADHD brain. It can help decrease over-thinking and improves clear focus and decreases negative self-critical thoughts. (Li, Jian Jose, 2010) said that Tennis is a good sport for ADHD. It teaches how to mentally "converge" and how to plan/strategize.

<u>Intersection of Tennis & Religious Faith</u>

Cerith Gardiner wrote about Four tennis players who say that their faith helped make them tennis champions. They say that their most important service is their Christian Faith & their faith in God. '

Blair Henley wrote "On a swing & a prayer: Faith's place in Tennis" and says that Faith & Spirituality are often relevant aspects of an athlete's preparation & perspective Religion is a compelling layer of the on-court personality praying during tennis matches spiritual protection from the negative side of success publicly thanking God after victories giving Glory to God on the tennis court and prayer as a calming force in life.

Dr Ralph Wilson, notes that "Tennis mirrors Christian Life": Tennis matches mirror life as per the Pastor at Joyful Heart Renewal Ministries.

Mark Oppenheimer wrote that "Bring Christ to the tennis court" as per Sam Owen, a tennis enthusiast and Episcopal seminarian at Berkeley Divinity School at Yale University. He often brings these religion & tennis together & he says that Tennis is a microcosm of life what he calls "Between inner Jesus & inner McInroe". He also sees Tennis as something like a "sports ballet dance" that honors the tennis player who hits a good shot. He cites Comron Yazdgerdi head tennis coach at Hastings College in Nebraska, member of FCA Fellowship of Christian Athletes. God can tell you how to pick up a tennis racquet his way and how to play his way. Lord, show me how to pick up this tennis racquet and play it for you". Pursue Tennis in God's Way-use your Tennis playing to make God Smile....

Juan Martin Del Potro talks about Serves & Rallys -The Art & Psychology of Tennis: He says to give thanks & praise for victories & successes even to give thanks & praise when you lose! Juan Martin Del Potro, despite the adversities he has faced with his bilateral wrist injuries that required numerous wrist surgeries and several lengthy recovery periods that tempted him to quit...he persevered and continued to give praise to God,;;;testament of his faith that got him to the Olympics at Rio Summer 2016,an internal source of inner strength attributable to one's religious faith/beliefs, his injuries could have ended his career. His faith was brutally tested…wrist injuries that could have derailed his tennis career, but they didn't end his tennis career he's a man of faith and believes strongly that God gets him through.

 His faith allowed him to fight for and win silver in 2016 summer Rio Olympics and his faith saw him lead his team to the Davis Cup Title in 2016 as well he was haunted by memories of never beating his opponent in 6 prior attempts-yet he won the set by fighting off break point "shrugging off the losses" ,digging deep, relying on his strengths to get him back in a match even after tripping and falling on his left wrist and was in painful distress ,he opted to continue playing and he won the match one's inward spiritual state affects one's game. Calmness comes from one's religious faith/beliefs. Without calmness you cannot get thru and win. Spiritual beliefs affect state of mind-the beliefs/faith help one to find solutions on the tennis court and off it as well even when the odds are stacked against you. You can win.

Asher & Ellis, describe how Novak Djokovic, a Serbian Christian, survived bombings and became a top tennis player: To win, a tennis player needs composure ...tennis teaches you how to maintain poise under pressure he had started out living in fear, but something changed in him he decided to stop being afraid he stopped hiding he decided to make fun of how ridiculous his situation was ,(see his memoir "Serve to Win"),if you can play tennis while dodging bullets and standing in long lines for bread and milk, then nothing can unnerve you after facing the hardships of war, the psychological games on a tennis court seem tame by comparison inner resolve results in victories ,a highly trained concentration level to screen out distractions. Djokovic even recovered from a breakdown in the 5th set and beat his opponent in the Australian Open 2013. Djokovic wins a lot of matches he should lose, as per a sports reporter Djokovic, jubilant over a triumph-tore off his shirt to celebrate the wooden cross around his neck bore visible testament to his faith he brings out his best when the heat is on, and he frequently gestures thanks to God on the tennis court.

Luigi Gatto wrote how Religious Faith plays an important role in Djokovic's life & his tennis. He feels grateful for all the good things that happened to him along the way. Djokovic describes religious faith as something that he always kept, always had to be present for him regardless of what situation and condition he was in. Even when he was struggling mentally/emotionally and even when he didn't know if he could make it or if he could get it. He had faith in himself and fought his way through and maintained the balance that a tennis player needs to have he embraces whatever life brings him including a lot of challenges. He added that he's fortunate because he has a great team of people around him, that's where there's a big source of positive energy for him.

Lastly Peter Lundell described a spiritual/philosophical view on "devotion to tennis as follows: "What's your Tennis Ball" he asks rhetorically Drew Houston, founder of DropBox said "it's not about pushing yourself. It's about finding your tennis balls, the thing that pulls you, he compares it to a dog chasing a tennis ball, plowing through whatever gets in their way Your tennis ball might be a promise that attracts you...a moral wrong that makes you indignant enough to take action or what you perceive as your destiny" difference between bondage and freedom ,a dog will passionately pursue a tennis ball ,wouldn't you rather chase a ball than roll a boulder? What is your tennis ball? Ask yourself what in your life needs you to go after it what pulls you, Lundell defines tennis ball#1 as what has God called you to do on earth? & he defines tennis ball#2 as spiritual life-pursue your highest calling of who God made you to be. Lundell refers to the Apostle Paul "training toward what is ahead"..." I press on toward the goal to win the prize for which God has called me heavenward, *Chapter 3: v12-v14-Letter to the Philippian Church* that was Paul's tennis ball.

Bibliography | References | Footnotes | Citations

Ferrante,Franco & Blasi, Sergio et al . Dental Abnormalities in Pituitary Dwarfism. (3/28/2017) DOI 10.1155/2017/5849173. Researchgate.net publications 316000973.Dept of Prosthodontic Dentistry Genoa Italy. ID 5849173. Volume 2017. www.hindawi.com/journals/crid/2017/5849173/University of Genoa Italy. Franco_Ferrante@yahoo.it copyright 2017 by Franco Ferrante.

Cohen, M Michael DMD. (8/1948) Dental Development in Pituitary Dwarfism. Journals. Sagepub.com/doi/abs/10.1177/0022034548027004201.

O'Toole, O & Swist, S et al (2012) Neuropathology and Craniofacial Lesions of Osteopetrotic Red Angus Calves. Veterinary Pathology, V4#5:745-754. DOI .10.1177/030098581141262 Journals.Sagepub.com

DICK, HM & W Simpson (1972): Dental Changes in Osteopetrosis - Oral Surgery Oral Med. Oral Pathology, V34#3:408-416

Chitre, Swati & Velundandi, S (9/30/2017) The Effects of Tooth Loss on the Brain, Insight Medical Publishing imed pub,com/articles, Journal of Oral Medicine V1#1:5 Chitresd@udmercy.edu

Kantaputra, Piranit.et al (5/2011-6/2011) Clinical Report: The Smallest Teeth in the world are caused by mutations in the PCNT gene. Doi .org/10.1002/ajmg.a.33984 American Journal of Medical Genetics Part A 155A:1398-1403 155A (6) Division of Pediatric Dentistry Craniofacial Genetics Lab -Faculty of Dentistry. Chiang Mai University Thailand email dentaland17@gmail.com

Kantaputra, Piranit et al (2002) Apparently new osteodysplastic and primordial short stature with severe microdontia, opalescent teeth and rootless molars. American Journal of Medical Genetics Volume 111 #4: pg 420-428

 Kantaputra, Piranit (2004) MOPD Dwarfism with severe microdontia, American Journal of Medical Genetics Part A 130A: 181-190,

Rios, Hector & Koushik, Shrinagesh. (12/2005) Periostin Null Mice Exhibit Dwarfism, Incisor enamel defects and an early onset periodontal disease like phenotype. Molecular Cell Biology. V25#4 pg 11131-11144. PMCID=PMC1316984 PMID=16314533. DOI 10.1128/MCB 25.24.11131-11144.2005.

Dalkiz, Mehmet & Dalkiz, Ahmed et al, (1/24/2019). Prosthetic Rehabilitation & Cephalometric Evaluation of GAPO Syndrome-- Growth Retardation. EC Dental Science Research www.ecronicon.com/ecde/pdf.ECDE-18-00912.pdf, pages 252-269. Volume 18 #2. Brussels Belgium Prosthodontics Research.

Terlemez, Arslan et al MOPD TYPE 2: Clinical Findings & Dental Management of a Dwarf Child patient age 5. Journal Istanbul University Faculty of Dentistry. (2015) V49#1: 41-46.DX.DOI.ORG/10.17096/jiufd.73283. Case Report. Email arslanterlemez@gmail.com Dept of Endodontics / Prosthodontics Faculty of Dentistry Necmettin Erbakan University Konya Turkey, Oral Presentation: 18th BASS Congress 4/23/2013-4/27/2013. Skopje Macedonia

Abdel-Salam, Ghada et al, A Homozygous mutation in RNU4ATAC as a cause of MOPD Type 1 Primordial Dwarfism. American Journal of Medical Genetics (8/17/2011) Part A 155: 2885-2896. Cairo Egypt Email: Ghada.AbdelSalam@yahoo.com Copyright 2011 Wiley Periodicals.

Thompson & Pembrey. Seckel Syndrome. Journal of Medical Genetics.V22(1985);192-201

Shah, RJ. A Study of the Emotional effects of Tooth Loss NCBI.NLM,NIH.GOV/PMC/ARTICLES/PMC 4762342 (2015) Journal of Indian Prosthodontic Society (July-Sept 2015)V15#3:237-243.

Shetty, B Moody P Kumar G et al Psychological Aspects of Dental Treatment in Geriatric Patients. International Journal of Geriatrics & Gerontology (2010) V6#2.

Costa, Dr Samedayme.com/2015/06/28/the psychological and emotional effects of tooth loss. 6/28/2015.

Cariati, Paolo. Psychosocial Impact of Orthognathic Surgery. Journal of Clinical Exp Dental, Medicina Oral.com/medora/free01/aop/s3007.pdf (2016)

Friedman, Nathan et al, The Influences of Fear, Anxiety & Depression on the patient's adaptive responses to complete dentures. www. thejpd.org/article/0022-3913 (87)90419-7/full text. doi.org/10.1016/0022-3913(87)90419.7

Moon, Won & Kim, June. Psychological Considerations in Orthognathic Surgery & Orthodontics. Seminars in Orthodontics. 10/2015 V22#1

Chandrashekar, S et al Mental Attitude & Psychological Adaptive Response in Complete Edentulous Patients. (10/2013)

Chamberlain, Barbara & Kenneth Depression: A Psychological Consideration in Complete Denture Prosthodontics. Journal of Prosthetic Dentistry. (6/1985) Volume 53#5 :673-675.

VanDorsten, Brent Ph.D. Psychological Considerations in Preparing patients for implantation procedures. Pain Medicine (5/2006) Volume 7#1: 547-557.

Neville, Brad & Chi, Angela, DMD's. ScienceDirect.com/topics/medicine-and-dentistry-microdontics Color Atlas of Oral & Maxillofacial Diseases (2019)

Sosa, Alejandro & Burke,Vernon, + El Paso Children's Hospital Foundation, El Paso TX.(2018-2019) Patient with Dwarfism receives special procedure at El Paso Children's Hospital -. ElPasoChildrensFoundation.Org/News/-43.

Falcon, Julia- 18 yr. old on track to get a full new set of teeth. Dentonrc.com Denton Record & Chronicle (4/23/2018) +

Zandinejad, Amirali & Reddy, Likith. Texas A&M College of Dentistry Dallas TX. (See Falcon,4/23/2018). vital record. tamhsc.edu/the-gift-of-a-smile also see reprint in today.tamu.edu/2018/02/27/the-gift-of-a-smile

Hikita, Yu et al. Growth Hormone receptor gene is related to root length and tooth length in human teeth. International Journal of Orthodontics & Dentofacial Orthopedics, (9/2018) Volume 88 #5. www.angle.org/doi/full/10.2319/092917-659.1 Corresponding Author=Dr Tetsutaro Yamaguchi.

Mirkovic, Sinisa. Oral Changes in Congenital Syndromes. (9/2005) researchgate.net/publication/256708345. Dept of Oral Surgery Dentistry Clinic at University of Novi Sad-Vojvodina

Russo, Antonio. Advanced Visual Network and Cerebellar HyperResponsiveness to Trigeminal Nociception in Migraine(headache) with Aura. Journal of Headache and Pain, The Journal of Headache pain.biomedcentral.com/articles/10.1186/s10194.019-1002-3. Volume 20 #46: (5/3/2019) doi.org/10.1186/s10194-019-1002-3.

Rutgers University. Easing Excruciating Facial Nerve Pain. www.medicalexpress.com(10/6/2016)

(Jordan, Ian) Books.google.com/books?id=bFZwDAAQB. Circle of Achievement:pg85

Chadd.org/ADHD-in-the-news/external-Trigeminal-Nerve-Stimulation-Effective-for-pediatric-ADHD (11/1/2017) presented at the American Academy of Child & Adolescent Psychiatry Annual Meeting)

Longhurst, Robert J, Is there a common etiology for Dyslexia, Visual stress, and Pattern Glare OVPjournal.org/uploads/2/3/8/9/238982651/ovp5-2_article_longhurst_web.pdf

DaSilva, Alves MD. A new treatment for Dyslexia & other proprioceptive dysfunctions. Posturmed.com/2008/06 (6/12/2008)

Mennillo, Michelle. Chewing through the facts. Occupational/therapy children.com.au

Chana, H, Briggs P & Moss,R. Degradation of a silver endodontic point associated with Endodontic infection. International Endodontics Journal (3/1998) Volume 31#2:141-146.

Pidlisny, Roman Dr. Multimedia.3m.com/mws/media/1548030/fenestra-15-for-gulf-region-in-english.pdf. Aesthetic Periodontal Splinting. LVIV State Medical University LVIV Ukraine. meduniv.lviv.ua.

Strassler, Howard DMD FADM. Ribbond.com/Periodontal-Splint.php. Seattle WA Ribbond@ribbond.com Strassler, Howard DMD FADM. Oralhealthgroup.com/features/tooth-stabilization -of-the-periodontally-compromised-dentition-with-fiber-reinforced-adhesive-composite-resin (10/1/2009)

DentistryToday.com/Periodontics/1603-sp-640967890. (9/1/2003)
Periodontal Splinting

Ruddle, Clifford J. DDS,Dr.Microendontic Non-Surgical Retreatment
& Silver Point Removal,(1997)
endoruddle.com/tc2pdfs/52/SilverPoints/_Feb1997.pdf.

Langley Endodontics.ca/silver-point-endodontic_retreatment.

Gulati, Shikha, Et al, Retreatment of Silver Point
Obturation,10.5005/jp-journals-10031-1023.
pdfs.semanticscholar.org/077b.952.ca263895.

Ase.org/Specialty/wp-content/uploads/sites/2/2017/06.Silver Point
Statement. pdf. AAE Position Statement, reaffirmed 10/2017. AAE
Clinical Practice Committee.

Seltzer, S Green, DB et al. A Scanning electron microscope exam of
silver cones removed from endodontically treated teeth. Oral Surgery
Oral Med Oral Pathology (1972) Volume 33: 589-605.

Brady, JM & Delrio, CE. Corrosion of Endodontic Silver Cones

Endodontics (1975) Volume 1: 205-210.

Tarnow,DP & Fletcher,P. Splinting of periodontally involved teeth,
NY State Dental Journal(1986) Volume 52 : pg. 24-25.

Waerhaug,J. Justification for Splinting in Periodontal Therapy. Journal
of Prosthetic Dentistry. (1969) Volume 22: 201-208.

Bhaskar, SW & Orban, B, Experimental Occlusal Trauma. Journal
Periodontal (1955) Volume 26: 270-284.

Kegel,W Selipsky H & Phillips C. The Effect of Splinting on Tooth
Mobility. Journal of Clinical Periodontal (1979) Volume 6: 45-58.

Galler, C Selipsky, H & Phillips C. The Effect of Splinting on Tooth Mobility, Journal of Clinical Periodontology (1979) Volume 6: 317-333.

Li, Jian DDS, Jiang, Ting DDS PHD, Lu, Ping DDS PHD. 4 Yr Clinical Evaluation of Periodontal Splints to Replace lost anterior teeth. Journal of Prosthodontics (2016) Volume 29:522-527. pdfs.semanticscholar.org/07fb/05ocf9ee23ce

Rajaram, Sujeetha Vijayalakshmi & Mahendra, Jaideep. Stabilizing Teeth with Non-Surgical treatment: (2) Splinting cases. Researchgate.net/publication/32693042. International Journal of Recent Scientific Research (6/28/2018) Volume 9#6F: 27616-27618. Dept of Periodontology Faculty of Dentistry. Meenakshi Ammal Dental College Hospital Maduravoyal Chennai.

Chee, Winston DDS & Lee, Wonsup DMD. Hallermann-Streiff Syndrome Patient Treated with Removable Prosthetics. A Clinical Report. University of Southern California Los Angeles Prosthodontics Dept. Journal of Prosthetic Dentistry (2011) Volume 106:74-77.

Sclaroff, A & Eppley, BI. Evaluation & Surgical Correction of the Facial Skeletal Deformity in Hallermann-Streiff Syndrome. Journal Oral Maxillofacial Surgery (1987) Vol 16: 738-744.

Lida,Takashi & Kawara,Misao, Cerebellar Activity Before Teeth Clenching using MagnetoEncephalography. Journal of Prosthodontic Research. (10/2009) researchgate.net/publication/38018215. DOI=10.1016/j.jpor.2009.09.003 www.semanticscholar.org/cerebellar

Bakhsheshian, Joshua Trigeminal Neuralgia and Cerebellar Compression. (2017) N.Neurology.org/content/89/24/e290.full.pdf + American Academy of Neurology (12/11/2017) Volume 89: pg. 290

Rabellino, D & Densmore, M.Et.Al. The Cerebellum after Trauma: Resting State Functional Connectivity of the Cerebellum in PTSD.

Human Brain Mapping (8/2018) Volume 39#8 :3354-3374. DOI=10.1002/hbm.24081 Epub2018April17

Thomas, Ben & Leuchter, Andrew, Trigeminal Nerve Stimulation offers hope for PTSD sufferers, (3/3/2016) Discover Magazine.com/crux/2016/02/03/nerve-stimulation-offers-hope-for-PTSD-sufferers/ #XRAY nYc-R6A "The Crux" UCLA Semel Institute for NeuroScience & Human Behavior-Dept of Psychiatry & BioBehavioral Sciences. Also see studies published in Neuromodulation.

Bracha, HS (2006) Post-Traumatic Dental Care Anxiety-PTDA. ncbi.nlm.nih.gov/pubmed/17152624.

Davenport, Liam. Ritalin & other medications improve Dyslexic & ADHD related Symptoms in PTSD & TBI. Medscape Medical News (11/13/2015, posted 11/16/2015) see also medscape.com/viewarticle/854472. Neuropsychopharmacology Online Publishing Abstract (10/28/2015).

Reynolds, Jennifer Lea (10/20/2017) (2/4/2010) A Medical Solution & Dramatic Treatment for Adult Dyslexia. HealthNewsDigest.com Healthnewsdigest.com/news/Guest_Columnist_710/A_Medical_Soluti on_And_Dramatic_Treatment_For_Adult_Dyslexia_Printer_html. And "A Predisposition to PTSD from Dyslexia & Learning Disabilities/ADD/ADHD/Occupational Disorder Syndrome. + Health.usnews.com/health-care-is-there-a-connection-between-ADHD-and-Dyslexia. (10/20/2017)

DeOliveira Solis, AC. (9/2017) Impact of PTSD on oral health. Journal of Affective Disorders. pg.126-132. DOI=10.1016/j.jad 2017.05.033 Epub 2017 May 20,

Wiener, R & M. (2015) Comorbid Depression/Anxiety & Teeth Removal. Behavioral Risk Factor Surveillance System 2010, Community Dentistry & Oral Epidemiology. Volume 43:433-443.

Bergland, Christopher. Cerebellar Damage may be at the root of PTSD. Psychology Today. (1/15/2016) www. psychologytoday.com/us/blog/the-athletes way-201601/cerebellum-damage-may-be-the-root-of-PTSD. VA Puget Sound Healthcare System/University of Washington. (1/2016) study: Repetitive Blast Exposure in Mice and Combat Vets causes persistent cerebellar dysfunction. Journal of Science Translational Medicine.

Friday, Francesca. (10/30/2017) New Study links cerebellum to Anxiety/Depression/PTSD Observer.com/2017/10 referencing Journal of Cancer Survivorship Cerebellar study on processing of traumatic memories.

Debellis, Michael & Kuchibhatla, Maragutha. (10/1/2006) Cerebellar Volumes in Pediatric Maltreatment Related PTSD. doi.org/10.1016/j.biopsych.2006.4.035 Volume 60#7: 697-703.

Avivi-Arber L. (2016) Widespread Volumetric Brain Changes following Teeth Loss. Frontiers in Neuro Anatomy Volume 10:pg 121.

Buck, David. BalanceEpigeneticOrthodontics.com/services/special-needs-children.html and dwarfparents.com/dental-care.

Quinn, Gwendolyn. Et Al. (2007) The Guinea Pig Syndrome: Improving Clinical Trial Participation. Journal Thoracic Oncology. Volume 2 #3: 191-196.

Paige's Story. CrohnsColitisFoundation.org/personal-stories/Paige-enrolls-in-a-uc (ulcerative colitis) -trial.

Forster, Victoria (2/19/2019) Why do only 8% of cancer patients in the United States participate in clinical trials? Forbes Magazine.

Hambridge, Karen. (3/14/2007) Taking Terror out of the dentist's chair. Coventry Live. Coventry Telegraph News, CoventryTelegraph.net/news/local-news/

Hansen, Jenny. (3/29/2012) Why going to the dentist makes me neurotic. jennyhansenauthor.wordpress.com/2012/03/29/why-going-to-the-dentist-makes-me-neurotic: Cowbell Blog

Dinkova, Atanaska, et al. Case of Alopecia Areata originating from Dental Foci (Oct-Dec 2014) Volume 20 # issue 5:669-673. dx.doi.org/10.5272/jimab.2014205.669. Medical University Plovdiv Bulgaria. Journal of IMAB, www.journal-imab-bg.org/issue-2014 ISSN 1312-773X Dept of Oral Surgery, Faculty of Dental Medicine.

Science Daily. Developing a bald patch? It could be a hidden tooth infection (11/28/2007) Science Daily.com/releases/2007/11-07112708349.htm. University of Granada-Dept of Stomatology

Duverger, Oliver Dr. NIH Maryland. www.express.co.uk,/news/uk/563922/hair-loss-bald-brush-teeth-stop-going-bald-male-pattern-baldness. cited in hairlineink.com/dental-health (9/21/2017)

Montoya, Gil & Soriano, Antonio Cutando et al (2002) Alopecia Areata of Dental Origin ncbi.nim.nih.gov/pubmed/12134132.MJA GIL, Med. Oral 2002 (July-October) Volume 7#4:303-308

Zivkovic,S. (6/1990) Endodontic treatment in the therapy of Alopecia Areata. Stomatol Glas Srb Volume 37 #3: 299-305.

Balcheva, M & Abadjiev, M. (2009) A Case of Alopecia Areata associated with a foci of dental origin. Journal of IMAB,Volume 15 #2:73-74.

Lescious, P & Maman, I. (9/1997) An unusual case of Alopecia Areata of Dental Origin, Oral Surgery Oral Medicine Oral Pathology Oral Radiology/Endodontics.Volume 84#3 :290-292.

Samuel,Victor & Muthu,MS,(2/19/2013) Alopecia Areata & Dental Foci. ijdr.in/article.asp?issn-0970-9290-year 2012 Volume 23 issue 51 pg 665-669.Pedodontists in Tamil Nadu India Journal of Dental Research 2012:

Dimitrova, Elena Dr. Belgraviacentre.com/blog/tooth-infection-linked-to-hair-loss 025/ Belgravia hair loss treatment center. London, UK.

NFED. NFED.ORG/BLOG/Top-10-most-common-ectodermal dysplasias/dental anomalies

Rakowska, Adriana. MD Ph.D (2015) Trichoscopic Hair Evaluation in patients with Ectodermal Dysplasia. Journal of Pediatrics jpeds.com/article/50022-3476(15)00360

Aldred. Michael J. & Widmer, Richard P. (2013) Handbook of Pediatric Dentistry,4th edition.

Sciencedirect.com/topics/medicine-and-dentistry/ectodermal-dysplasia.

Bani, Mehmet Dr et al Ectodermal Dysplasia with Anondontia. Ankara, Turkey. Gazi University Dental Faculty. pdfs.semanticscholar.org/8013/6ee33dfce19a485336ccef7706514129b99e.pdf

Wilson, WG et al (1989) Ectodermal Dysplasia with distinctive facial appearance. American Journal Medical Genetics Volume 34:227-229.

Rockman, Roy DDS & Hall, K Brad Dr DMD & Fiebiger, Mark. (05/2007) Magnetic Retention of Dental Prostheses in a child with Ectodermal Dysplasia. Journal American Dental Assn, Volume 138: 610-615.

Jada.ada.org/article/s0002-8177(14) 62361. doi.org/10.14219/jada-archive.2007.0231 Assistant Professor Dept Pediatric Dentistry School of Dentistry Medical College of Georgia Augusta Ga.+ Prosthetic Lab, Medical College of Ga, Augusta Ga.

Vallejo, Pipa.et al (2/1/2008) Treatment with removable prostheses in Ectodermal Dysplasia: Clinical Case: Medical Oral Pathology Oral Cir Bucal Volume 13#2:119-123

Aydin Belge, M et al (Sept-Oct 2013) Implants in Children with Ectodermal Dysplasia, Volume 35#5:441-446.

Grover, Rashu & Mehra, Manjul DDS'S MD's (10/10/2015) ISSN 2161-1122. www. ornicsoline.org/open-access/prosthodontic-management-of-children-with Ectodermal Dysplasia: A Review of the Literature -2161-1122-1000340 mehramanjul@yahoo.co.in Dentistry 5:340 doi:10.4172/2161-1122.1000340. copyright 2015 by Rashu Grover,

Pigno, MA et al. (1996) Prosthodontic Management of Ectodermal Dysplasia. A review of the literature. Prosthetic Dentistry Volume 76:541-545.

Vieira, KA et al (2007) Prosthodontic treatment of Ectodermal Dysplasia. Case Report. Quintessence Intl Volume 38:75-80.

Yenisey, et al (2004) Orthodontic & Prosthodontic Treatment of Ectodermal Dysplasia. Case Report: British Dental Journal. Volume 196:677-679

Nabadalung, DP (1999) Prosthodontic Rehab, of an Ectodermal Dysplasia patient. A Clinical Report. Journal of Prosthetic Dentistry; Volume 81: 499-502.

Lomuzio, L et al (2005) Prosthetic Rehab. of a child affected by Ectodermal Dysplasia. Case Report. Contemporary Dental Practice. Volume 6: 120-126.

Hickey, AJ & Vergo, TJ Jr. (2001) Prosthetic treatment for patients with Ectodermal Dysplasia. Journal Prosthetic Dentistry. Volume 86: 364-368.

Suri, S et al (2004) Simultaneous Functional and Fixed Appliance Therapy for Dental Alignment prior to prosthetic habilitation in Ectodermal Dysplasia. Clinical Report" Journal Prosthetic Dentistry Volume 92: 428-433.

Tanner, BA (1988) Psychological Aspects of Ectodermal Dysplasia, Birth Defects Original Article Series 24: 263-275.

Kaul & Reddy (2008) Prosthodontic Rehab. of an adolescent with Ectodermal Dysplasia with partial anodontia. Case Report. Indian Soc Pedod Prev Dental Volume 27:177-181.

Strubelt, Suster & Maas, Uwe. (3/2015) IbogaineAlliance.org/wp-content/uploads/2015/03/Mass-The-Near-Death-Experience.pdf. The Near Death Experience: A Cerebellar Method to protect body & soul, Originally published in Alternative Therapies (2008) Volume14#1: 30-34. See also Global Ibogaine Therapeutic Alliance, Montreal Canada.

Schulter, DJ et al (2006) A case of illusory own body perceptions after transcranial magnetic stimulation of the Cerebellum. Cerebellum Volume 5#3: 238-240.

Graf, Heiko Dr (2013) Cerebellar Cognitive Affective Syndrome. neuro.psychiatryonline.org/doi/full/10.1176/appi.neuropsych.1.2070179 heiko.graf@uni.ulm.de GERMANY.

Orpha.net/consor/cgi-bin/OC_exp. Short Stature Pituitary & Cerebellar Defects.

Pereyra, Aubree. Trichotillomania. Statpearls.com/kb/viewarticle/30593

Soumya, Juvaina et al A rare case of cerebellar fusion: Gomez-Lopez-Hernandez Syndrome.Case 13156. Eurorad.org/case/13156

Psychiatryonline.org/doi/full/10.1176 ajp.2007.164.4.568 Lifting the veil on Trichotillomania.

Swedo, SE et al Archives of General Psychiatry (1991) Volume 48:828-833.

Keuthen, Nancy. et al. (2/2007) Evidence for reduced cerebellar volumes in Trichotillomania. Biological Psychiatry. Volume 61#3: 374-381.

Cardona, Dodanid MD & Franklin, Martin E Ph.D (12/2004) Help children and teens stop impulsive hair pulling. MD Edge,com/Psychiatry/article/662071 anxiety-disorders/help-children-and-teens-stop-compulsive-hair-pulling#bib11. Current Psychiatry,Volume 3#12:68-76.

Wikipedia.org/wiki/Gomez-Lopez-Hernandez_Syndrome.

Pesic, Danilo et al. (3/11/2014) Cerebellar Cognitive Affective Syndrome. Hindawi.com/journals/crim/2014/894263/ Volume 2014 id#894263 dx.doi.org/10.1155/2014/894263.

Potter, Gregory B et al (2001) The hairless gene mutated in Congenital hair loss disorders encodes a novel nuclear receptor corepressor. Genesdev.cshlp.org/content/15/20/2687.full Genes & Development Volume 15:2687-2701.

Hou, JW (July 2003) Hallermann-Streiff Syndrome Associated with a Small Cerebellum, ACTA PAEDIATRA Volume 92#7 :869-871. ncbi.nlm.nih.gov/pubmed/12892173.

Ferrell, Steven et al (2016) MOPD TYPE 1 Dwarfism: Volume 2016. Case Reports.bmj.com/content/2016/bcr-2016-215502-full.pdf and case reports. bmj.com/content/12/5/e224197. re Majewski Dwarfism Type 2.

Miller,G & Alldinger, S et al (5/2001) GM1-Gangliosidosis in Alaskan Huskies: Clinical/Pathological Findings. Veterinary Pathology Volume 38#3: 281-290. ncbi.nlm.nhi.gov/pubmed/11355658. doi:10.1354/vp.38-3.281.

Findzebra,com/rare disease?q=ed&f=oxycephaly Source Gard Genetic & Rare Diseases re Gomez Lopez Hernandez Syndrome and Cerebellotrigeminal dermal dysplasia.

Eckles, Terry & Kalkwarf,Kenneth. (10/1989) Impaired Tooth Root Development after treatment of a cerebellar astrocytoma: Case Report. Volume 68#4:414-418.

Phillips, Samantha (2/17/2019) Liberty Teen has a rare condition of only 100 in the USA. Vindy Sports Live. www.Vindy.com/news/2019/Feb/17.

Goodwin, John Jr. Small but Not Different. Vindy.com/news/2012/March/18. Rising -to-the-Challenge/(3/18/2012) jgoodwind@vindy.com

Jauhari, Prashant. (2014) SIL1 Negative Marinesco Sjogren Syndrome. Pediatric Neurosciences.com/article.asp?issn=1817-1745, Volume 9 Issue 3.pg 291-292,

Bhatia, Eesh & Shukla, R. (9/1993) Multiple Pituitary Hormone deficiencies in a patient with spinocerebellar ataxia.: MRI & Hormonal Studies. Vol 16 #8: 639-642.

Malacards.org/card/cerebellar_ataxia_mental_retardation_and_Dysequ ilibrium _ syndrome.

Machinis, Kalotina et al, (11/2001) Syndromic Short Stature in Patients w/ a germline mutation, europepmc.org/articles/pmc1274372, American Journal of Human Genetics Volume 69#1: 961-968.

rgd.mcw.edu/rgdweb/ontology/view.html? acc_rd=DOID: 9008992

Monarch Initiative.Org/Disease/0M1m 262700. Short Stature Pituitary Growth Hormone Deficiency.

Mendelian.co/symptoms/short-stature-and-nystagmus.

Goyal, Ishan & Mehta, Veneet. et al, Orthodontic Management of Syndromic Patients (8/31/2018) ActaScientific.com/ASDS/pdf/ASDS-02-0314.pdf ACTA Scientific Dental Science (9/2018) Volume 2#9 ISSN 2581-4893.

Atreja, Gaurav et al (5/2012) Oral Manifestations in Growth Hormone Disorders. Researchgate.net/publication/225061170_

Kumari, Nirmala & Kumar,G Vinay. et al Ectodermal Dysplasia: Prosthodontic Considerations, www.ijohnmr.com/upload/Ectodermal%20Dysplasia %20 Prosthodontic & %20 Considerations.pdf Dept of Prosthodontics College Dental Sciences Davangere IJohnmr.com

Hickey,AJ Prosthetic Treatment for Patients with Ectodermal Dysplasia, (2001) Journal Prosthodontic Dentistry Volume 86: 364-368

Bansal, Sumidha,Bansal Pankaj,Rustagi, Sudha, (2015) indjos.com/article.asp?issn=09766944, Volume 6 Issue 3: 88-92.DOI 10.4103/0976-6944,171071, and Generalized Severe Short Root Anomaly: Indian Journal Oral Science (2015) Volume 6 Issue 3: 88-92. College of Dental Sciences, Faridabad, Haryana, India, Periodontics Dept.

Kosowicz, & Rzymski, (1999) Pituitary Dwarfism Pediatric Dentistry, Volume 21: 213-215.

Sewell,Josalyn RDH OMT. (8/26/2015) The World of Autism-Treating Patients with Autism Can Be Very Rewarding for the Dental Hygienist. RDH Magazine.com/career-profession-students-article-160405421

CRC Robazza (2013) Chronic Apical Periodontitis. Journal of Contemporary Dental Practice Volume 14#3: 556-559.

Britto, Impa. et al (2011) Periodontal disease in Adults with untreated congenital growth hormone deficiency. Journal of Clinical Periodontology. Volume 38#6: 525-531.

Sherry, Jennifer & Aponte, Sophia. RDH'S (8/26/2015) Achondroplasia-Oral Health Concerns Associated with Genetic Disorder Commonly Referred to As Dwarfism www.RDHMAG.com/career-profession/students/article/16405429/

Bembalgi, Mahantesh & Jadhav, Prashant. (09/2010) 2009848/www.academia.edu. Small Denture A case report. Dept of Prosthodontics & Oral Implantology Tatyasaheb Kore Dental College, New Paragon Kolhapur Maharashtra JIDA Volume 4#9

Pigno, Mark & Blackman, Ronald, (1996) Prosthodontic Management of Ectodermal Dysplasia. Journal of Prosthodontic Dentistry Volume 76: 541-545

Jain, Sumeet. Reporter. (6/2013) Researchgate.net/publication/256684825_ Prosthodontic Rehabilitation of Achondroplastic patients. Dept Prosthodontics. Clinical Dentistry Volume 7 #6 .

Terlemez, Arslan. (1/1/2015) MOPD2 Dwarfism: Dental Management of a Child Patient .worldwidescience.org/topicpages/dwarfism .html.

Ippel, PF. (11/1/1992) Wiley online library, American Journal of Medical Genetics Volume 44#4, doi.org/10.1002/ajmg.1320440428

Khoo, Isabelle, Gaten Matarazzo of Stranger Things talks about his genetic disorder. Huffington Post Canada (9/28/2016) updated 11/6/2017.

DeFraia, E et al (3/10/2003) admin. ejpd.eu/download.pdf, Orofacial characteristics of Hallermann Streiff Syndrome. Dept of Orthodontics University of Florence Italy,

Moulton, Eric Alan et al (10/2010) The Cerebellum and Pain. Brain Research Review Volume 65#1: 14-27. doi.org/10.1016/Journal of Brain Research Review.2010.05. 005

Moulton, Eric Alan et al (11/30/2012, updated 9/15/2016) Functional MRI & Diffusion Tensor Imaging of Cerebellar Responses to Pain in the Human Trigeminal System. Clinicaltrials.gov/Ct2/show/NCT017381,36, McLean Hospital.

Baarbe, Julianne & Yielder, Paul et al (2/28/2018) Subclinical Recurrent Neck Pain and its treatment impacts on motor training induced plasticity of the Cerebellum. Journals.plos,org/plosone/article?id=10.1371/ journal.pone.0193413.

Baarbe, Julianne & Yielder, Paul et al (2/15/2014) A Novel protocol to investigate motor training induced neural plasticity & sensorimotor integration in the cerebellum & motor cortex. doi.org/10.1152/jn,00661.2013. www.physiology.org

Shamir, Merav, Goelman, & Chai, Orit. (2004) Post-Anesthesia Cerebellar Dysfunction in Cats. Journal Veterinary Internal Medicine Volume 18:368-369. onlinelibrary.wiley.com/doi/10.1111/j.1939-1676.2004.tb02562x/pdf Study at Koret School Veterinary Medicine Teaching Hospital. Hebrew University. Jerusalem Israel.

Shamir, HM et al (1999) Late Onset of cerebellar abiotrophy in a Siamese Cat. Journal Small Animal Practice. Volume 40: 343-345.

Kelberman, D & Dattani, MT (2007) Hypopituitarism Oddities: Congenital Causes. Variable Hypopituitarism Associated with Learning Disabilities. HORMONE RESEARCH, Volume 68 Suppl.5:138-144.

Larson, Austin et al (3/21/2015) Genetic Causes of Pituitary Hormone Deficiencies DiscoveryMedicine.com Endocrinology Pediatric-University of Colorado. Denver Children's Hospital Aurora CO.

Bhatia, Eesh, & Shukla, R. (9/1993) Multiple Pituitary Hormone Deficiencies in a Patient with Spinocerebellar Ataxia. Journal of Endocrinological Investigation. Vol 16#8: 639-642. Post-Graduate Institute Lucknow UP India.

Ectodermal Dysplasia-Short Stature Syndrome. www.uniprot.org/diseases/DI-04239. RGD.MCW.EDU/RGDWEB/ONTOLOGY/VIEW.HTML

Nethan, Suzanne et al (9/2017) Ellis Van Creveld with an unusual dental anomaly; A Cse Report, Iranian Journal of Medical Sciences, acc_id=DOID.9008992. Article 12 Volume 42#5: 501-504. ijms.sums_ac.ir/index,php.IJMS/article/view/3055/0

Naqash, Talib Amin, & Al Shahrani, Ibrahim. (1/23/2018) Ellis Van Creveld Syndrome: A rare clinical report of Oral Rehab. by Interdisciplinary approach. Case Reports in Dentistry Volume 2018, article ID8631602, doi.org/10.1155/2018/8631602. www. hindawi.com/journals/crid/2018/8f Dept of Prosthetic Dentistry King Khalid University College of Dentistry. Abha Saudi Arabia, Dept of Pediatric Dentistry & Orthodontic Science. go4talib@yahoo.com

Hattab, FN & Yassin, OM, (1998) Oral Manifestations of Ellis-Van-Creveld Syndrome. Journal of Clinical Pediatric Dentistry. Volume 22:159-165.

Cahuana, A & Palma C, et al (2004) Oral Manifestations in Ellis -Van-Creveld Syndrome

Pediatric Dentistry Volume 26 #3: 277-282.

Atasu, M & Biren, S (2000) Ellis -Van-Creveld Syndrome: Dental Findings Journal of Clinical Pediatric Dentistry, Volume 24:141-145.

Haneman, JA, et al Oral Manifestations in Ellis -Van-Creveld Syndrome (2010) Journal of Oral & Maxillofacial Surgery Volume 68#2: 456-460.

Database of Hereditary Ocular Disease. Kenny-Caffey Syndrome Type 2

Koob, M et al. (10/2010) NeuroImaging in Cockayne Syndrome. American Journal of NeuroRadiology Volume 31#9: 1623-1630. doi.org/10.3174/ajnr A2135

Alves, Inesp, (5/2/2015) BeyondAchondroplasia,.org/blogve/language/en/Orthodontics-and-dental-management-in-action.

Rushton, Alan R & Genel, Myron, Hereditary ED, Olivopontocerebellar Degeneration,short stature & Hypogonadism, (1981) Journal of Medical Genetics V18 #5 :335-339 DOI 10.1136/jmg18.5.335

Baraitser, M & Reardon, W, (6/1993) Cerebellar Ataxia & Ectodermal Dysplasia. Journal of Medical Genetics V 30#6:515-517.

Zannoli, Raffaela Dr & Inchingolo, G (8/7/2002) Ectodermal Dysplasia Syndrome. American Journal of Medical Genetics, V113#1 DOI.ORG.10.1002/ajmg,10713: 111-113, zannolli@unisi.it University of Siena Italy Pediatrics.

Dovemed.com/diseases-conditions/cerebellar-ataxia-Ectodermal-Dysplasia-Syndrome. (updated 4/23/2018)

NFED.ORG/learn/symptoms/dental-symptoms/

Omo, Julie & Ennibulele, SE. Diagnosis & Prosthodontic Treatment of a Case of Ectodermal Dysplasia. ajompm.com/index.php/ajmp/article/download/105/571. Dept of Restorative Dentistry, School of Dentistry, University of Benin Benin City Nigeria. Julie.Omo@Uniben.edu see also African Journal of Oral & Maxillofacial Path. Med. Volume 4#2 (July-Dec.2018): 39-42.

Wieckiewicz, Mieszko, et al (7/13/2014) Psychosocial Aspects of Bruxism. Biomed Research International. Volume 2014 ID# 469187. dx.doi.org/10.1155/2014/469187. Dentistry Faculty, Wroclaw Medical University,Poland- Prosthetic Dentistry Dept.

Gomez, EM et al (1998) Correlation between Drug Addiction and Increased abnormal Occluso-Muscle Function. Journal of Dental Research. Volume 77#6: 1454-1464.

Manfredini, D (2004) Psychic & Occlusal Factors in Bruxism. Australian Dental Journal Volume 49#2: 84-89.

Linuma, Kevin. Staff Sergeant,59th Medical Wing Public Affairs. (12/11/2018) 59mdw.af.mil/news/article/1710234. Regarding Lieutenant Colonel Young J Honnlee, a 59th Medical Wing - a Maxillofacial Prosthodontist. San Antonio Military Medical Center Joint Base San Antonio Fort Sam Houston Texas.

Abbott, FB, (4/1984) Psychological Assessment of the Prosthodontics Patient. Dental Clinical North America Volume 28#2:361-367. ncbi.nlm.nih.gov/pubmed/637341.

Chandrasekar, S et al (9/26/2013, 10/2013-12/2013) Mental Attitude and Psychological Adaptive Response in Completely Edentulous Patients RRJDS Volume 1#3 Rajeshwari, Raja, Dental College Hospital, Bangalore Karnataka India. Researchgate.net/publication/26263987.

Jamieson, CH (1968) Geriatrics & the Denture Patient. Journal of Prosthodontic Dentistry Volume 8: 8-13.

Krocha, KM. (1991) The Difficult Dental Patient. International Journal Psychosomatic. Volume 38: 58-62.

Koper, A. (1967) Difficult Denture Birds. Prosthetic Dentistry. Volume 17: 632-639.

Central NJ Prosthodontics.com/library/7766/ToothSensitivity.html

Chirillo, Jeffrey DMD. (Dentistry By Design) EnglewoodDentist.us/dentistry101/one-bad-tooth.

Curatola, Gerry. Dr. www.rejuvdentist.com Teeth Health Directly Tied to Whole Body Health.

Quinn, Gwendolyn et al (6/2012) Cancer Patient fears related to Clinical Trial Participation: Journal Cancer Education. Volume 27#2 :257-262. www.ncbi.nlm.nih.gov/pmc/articles/PM C 7/14/2014 doi.10.1007/s13187-012-0310-y.NIHMS 594038, PMID 22271582. Moffitt Cancer Center, Tampa Fl.

Wabnegger, Albert & Schienle, Anne. (2/2019) The Role of the Cerebellum in Skin Picking Disorder, THE CEREBELLUM, Springer Publishing-ISSN 1473-4230, doi.org/10,10071 s12311-018-0957y Volume 18#1:91-98.

Meier, Michael L (2015) Neural Systems of Pain & Related Fear Investigated on The Basis of Painful Dental Stimulation. zora.uzh.ch/id/eprint/113215/1/20152375.pdf Ph.D doctoral dissertation. University of Zurich. Science Faculty. michael.meier@uzh.ch

Meier, Michael L et al (2012) Brain Activation Induced by Dentine Hypersensitivity Pain:Journal Clinical Periodontology Volume 39: 441-447. doi:10,1111/J-1600-051X.2012.01863.X

Apkarian, AV. (2005) Human Brain. Mechanisms of Pain Perception. European Journal of Pain Volume 9:463-484

Apkarian, AV (2013) Brain Signature for Acute Pain. Trends in Cognitive Science. Volume 17 #7: 309-310

Peyron, R. (2000) Functional Imaging of Brain Responses to Pain. Clinical Neurophysiology Volume 30#5: 263-288

Dababneh, RH et al (1999) Dentine Hypersensitivity, British Dental Journal Volume 187#11: 603-611

Moulton, EA et al The Cerebellum & Pain. Brain Research Review: Volume 65#1:14-27

Orchardson, R (2006) Managing Dentin Hypersensitivity. Journal American Dental Association Volume 137#7: 990-998

Robson, David. (4/21/2019) The Utter Horror of Waking Up During Anesthesia Is more Common than you think. ScienceAlert.com

Anesthesia Awareness Registry-University of Washington at Seattle.

NY Times (1/30/2019) Awake on the Table, nytimes.com/surgery-anesthesia-awake-consciousness-trauma-depression.

Patient Safety Institute.ca/en/toolsresources/member-videos-and-stories/pages/anesthesia-awareness-incident-makes-surgery-a-nightmare-experience-2016-10.aspx Anesthesia Awareness Incident Makes Surgery a Nightmare Experience. (10/25/2016)

Shigli, Kawal & Purushottam, Giri, (3/13/2017) Oral Manifestations of Menopause. jbcrs.org/articles drpgiri1y@gmail.com

Ikeda, Etsuko et al (3/6/2019) Functional Ectodermal Organ Regeneration of Functional Organs: The Next Generation of 3D Organ Replacement Therapy. doi.org/10.1098/rsob.190010. Royal Society Publishing.org

Zanolli, R et al (2002) Cerebellar Ataxia. American Journal of Medical Genetics. Volume 113#: 111-113.

Munoz, RMV & Santos, AC. et al (10/3/1997) Cerebello-Trigeminal-Dermal-Dysplasia, American Journal Medical Genetics Volume 72#1: 34-39

Chan, JK. (10/19/2018) Case of Alemtuzumab Related Alopecia Areata jn MS. M, neurology.org/content/6/1/e516

Al-Semari, AbdulAziz, & Bohlega,S (12/13/2006) Autosomal Recessive Syndrome With Alopecia, American Journal Medical Genetics Part A Volume 143A Issue 2 onlinelibrary.wiley.com/doi/abs/10.1002/ajmg.a.31497: pg 149-160.

MunozRojas, MV et al in Roach,ES & Miller VS (eds) NeuroCutaneous Disorders , Cambridge University Press.: 306-312.

Pascual-Castroviejo Ignacio & Ruggieri, Martino. Cerebello-Trigeminal-Dermal-Dysplasia (CTD) Gomez Lopez Hernandez Syndrome. Chapter 62.

Choudhary, Anita et al (2017) Gomez Lopez Hernandez Syndrome-Intractable & Rare Disease Research Volume6#1:58-60.

Sukhudyan, Biayna et al (7/23/2010) Gomez Lopez Hernandez Syndrome European Journal of Pediatrics Volume 169: 1523-1528.

Chiruvolu, A (2006) A Term Newborn with Congenital Dwarfism Neoreviews.aappulications.org/content/7/5/e280

Kebapci, Nur et al (2009) Dwarfism Due to Congenital Partial Hypopituitarism Endocrine Abstracts Volume 20: pg319.

Kitty CH Informational Tri-Fold, chcat.org/about-ch-cats/

Kornreich, I & Horev, G et al (2002) Craniofacial & Brain Abnormalities in Laron Syndrome, European Journal of

Endocrinology Volume 146: 499-503. Imaging Dept Endocrinology Schneider Children's Medical Center of Israel Petah Tiqva 49202 + Tel Aviv University-Sackler Faculty

Halder, Ashutosh, et al (1998) Dwarfism, American Journal of Medical Genetics volume 80:12-15.

AJNR ORG/AJNR-CASE-COLLECTIONS-DIAGNOSIS (3/9/2015) American Journal of Neuroradiology.

Priesmeyer, Nicole LCSW MSW www. fulsheartransition.com/trauma-and-brain,

Holmes, Sophia E, et al (7/6/2018) Cerebellar & Prefrontal Cortical Alterations in PTSD.ncbi.nlm.nhi.gov/pmc/articles/PM Chronic Stress (Thousand Oaks) Jan-Feb 2018 doi.10.1177/2470547018786390. published online 7/6/2018.

Rabellino, Damela et al (4/17/2018) Human Brain Mapping Volume 39#8. The Cerebellum After Trauma. doi.org/10.1002/hbm.24081 onlinelibrarywiley.com

Dengler, Roni (3/20/2019) Scientists Find that Anesthetics can weaken traumatic memories. Discover Magazine.com/d-brief/2019/03/20/ scientists-weaken-traumatic-memories-with-anesthetics /#.xr17 cmr6a.

McDonald, B (2/21/2018) Prevalence of Pain Flashbacks in PTSD www.tandfonline.com/doi/full/10.1080/247.40527.2018.1435994 Canadian Journal of Pain Volume 2 #1

Shin, Myung Seop. et al (8/21/2018) Rehab. of lost teeth relative to the Maintenance of Cognitive Function Oral Diseases Volume 25#1:290-299. doi.org/10.1111/odi.12960

Ricketts, David (2011) Advanced Operative Dentistry, ScienceDirect.com/topics/pharmacology-toxicology-and-pharmaceutical-science/occlusion.

Yamazaki, Kaoruko et al (4/29/2008) Effect of Tooth Loss on Spatial Memory. Hippocampus Volume 18#6 doi.org/10.1002/hipo.20440. onlinelibrary.wiley.com/doi/abs/   10-1002/hipo.20440.

Okubo, Mai DDS & Fujinami, Yukiko DDS & Minakuchi, Shunsuke DDS (1/2010) The Effect of complete dentures on body balance during standing and walking, Journal of Prosthodontic Research Tokyo Dental University Japan. doi.org/10/1016-/.jpor.2009.09.002.

Lin,Chia-Sun (1/5/2010 Revisiting Link between cognitive decline and masticatory dysfunction, bmcgeriatric.biomedcentral.com/articles/doi.org/10.1186/s/12877-17.0693.z

Lida, Takasha & Kawara,Misao,(2009) Cerebellar Activity before teeth clenching using magnetoencephalography. Journal of Prosthodontic Research Doi,10.1016/j.jpor,2009.09.003

Suresh, S & Asopa, Vipul. (1/2011) Prosthodontic Management of Complete Edentulous Patients with NeuroMuscular Disorders. Journal Advanced Dental Research, Volume 3#1,ispcd.org Darshan Dental College Dept Prosthodontics Udaipur Rajasthan India drsuresh72@gmail.com

Glasner, Shifra, Rosenblatt, Kate, Snyder, Rose & Unger, Helen (2011-2012) Familial Dysautonomia & its Dental Manifestations, Journal of Torah & Science Volume 16: Yeshiva University Stern College for Women-Derech HaTeva: pg 23+

Preuss, Julius, (1978) Biblical & Talmudic Medicine. Sanhedrin Press NYC NY.

Moskowitz, Nicole C, The Davidic Harp: An Aeolian Awakening, :46-48.

Pasik, Dahlia (2011-2012) Short & Sweet? Not Necessarily, , Journal of Torah & Science Volume 16: Yeshiva University Stern College for Women-Derech HaTeva: 49+

Watanabe, Yutaka, DDS PHD (2/2015) sciencedirect.com/science/article/pii/s1882761614000271, doi,org/10.1016/j.jdsr.2014.09.002

Kondo, K et al (1994) Case Control study of Alzheimer's disease in Japan. Dementia Volume 5: 314-326.

Kusaga, M (2002) Mastication As Indicator of brain function in elderly people. Journal Kyushu University Nursing Social Welfare Volume 4 :179-183.

Lexomboom, D, (10/4/2012)

Chewing ability and tooth loss: association with cognitive impairment in an elderly opulation study. Journal American Geriatric Society, Volume 10:1951-1956.doi,org/10,1111/j,1532-5415 2012.04154.x.epub.2012 Oct 4

Eckerd, Marcia Dr. (5/17/2017) Surviving the dentist for Adults with Aspergers. blogs.psychcentral.com/Aspergers.

Blomqvist, M Y Dahlof,Goran & Bejerot, Suzanne (10/28/2014) Experiences of Dental Care & Dental Anxiety in Adults with Autism. Autism Research & Treatment. Volume 2014, Article id 238764. dx.doi.org/10.1155/2014/238764. Division of Pediatric Dentistry Dept of Dental Medicine. Karolinska Institute, Huddinge Sweden, copyright 2014 by Blomqvist. Dept Clinical Neuroscience Northern Stockholm Psychiatry St Goran's Hospital Stockholm Sweden, Academic Editor Manuel F Casanova. Open Access Creative Commons Unrestricted use/reproduction. Blomqvist, MY Holmberg, Kristen et al (2/2007) Salivary CortisoL Levels & Dental Anxiety in Children with ADHD.

European Journal Oral Science. Volume 115;1-6. Doi.10.1111/j.1600-0722.2007. 00423.x

Hansen, Brant. (2017) Blessed are the Misfits. DenverSeminary.edu/resources/news-and-articles/ Denver Journal Book Review, Nashville TN West Publishing Group,ISBN 978-0-7180-9631-1. + religion.blogs.cnn.com/2013/10/19 Mr Spock goes to Church: How 1 Christian copes with Asperger's Syndrome.

jamesbradfordpate.blogspot.com/2007/12 Aspergers-and-Religion.html. Jamesbradfordpate@yahoo.com (12/21/2007) James Thoughts & Musings.

Kankurette.wordpress.com/2011/03/06 (3/6/2011) The Hidden Village of Aspergers.

Autismforums.com/threads/aspergers-and-religion .7509 AspieCentral Aspergers & Autism Forum.

AutisticSymphony.com/jca.html Did Jesus have Autism? Dr Jonathon ES Talkington MD & Dr Gina A Scherzo PHD.

Stein, Leah J & Polido, Jose C et al (5/18/2011) Oral Care & Sensory Sensitivities in Children with Autism. SPECIAL CARE IN DENTISTRY. doi,10.1111fj.1754.4505.2011.00187.x pg. 102-110, Volume 31#3.

Green, Shulamite A & Ben-Sasson, Ayelet, (12/2010) Anxiety Disorders and Sensory Over-Responsivity in Children with Autism. Journal Autism & Developmental Disorders. Volume 40#12: 1495-1504. doi 10.1007/s10803-010-1007-x PMCID PMC 2980623 PMID 20383658

Milgrom, P Weinstein, P Getz T (1995) Treating Fearful Dental Patients: A Patient Management Handbook Continuing Dental Education. University of WA-Seattle. 2nd edition.

Rodd, Helen & Noble, Fiona. Psychosocial Impacts Relating to Dental Injuries in Childhood (3/4/2019) Journal Dentistry Volume 7#1:23 doi.org/10.3390/dj7020023.

Murthy, J Varsha & Vaz, Rucha. Prosthetic Management of Ectodermal Dysplasia.

Rostamzadeh, Masoumeh. (2017) Case Report of Prosthetic Treatment of a Young Patient suffering Papillon-Lefevre Syndrome. scirp.org/journal/paperinformation.asp?paperid=77256.

Jokstad, Asbjorn, (10/26/2018) Saving patients by pulling their teeth out-but killing them softly afterwards with dental implants onlinelibrary.wiley.com/doi.10.1002/cre2/2.142

Wolf, Thomas Gerhard et al (2016) Effectiveness of Self-Hypnosis on the relief of experimental dental pain- A randomized trial, www.tandfonline.com/doi/abs/10.1080/00207144.2016.1131587

Hickey, Alan Joseph DMD & Salter,Margery PhD (2006) Prosthodontic & Psychological Factors in treating patients with congenital & craniofacial defects. Journal of Prosthetics Dentistry, Volume 95:392-396 ajhfam@maine.rr.com citeseerx.1st.psu.edu/viewdoc/download?doi=10.1.1.514.7784&rep=rep1@type=pdf

Wiens et al Taylor, TD, editor. (2000) Clinical Maxillofacial Prosthetics, Chicago IL: Quintessence:pg 1-13 Psychological Management of the Maxillofacial prosthetics patient

Giddon, Donald DMD PHD (4/1980) Psychological Aspects of Prosthodontic Treatment for geriatric patients, Journal of Prosthetic Dentistry Volume 43 Issue 4: 374-379 doi.org/10.1016/0022-3913(80)90204-8

BDJ British Dental Journal (10/21/2011) Evaluation of psychological effects of prosthetic treatment. www.nature.com 211,373 nature.com/articles/sj.bdj.2011.865.ris.

Daxon, Kim DDS (12/13/2017) Treating Young Patients with Ectodermal Dysplasia: A Prosthetic Dilemma. www.perioimplantadvisory.com

Haggard, Patrick & DeBoer,Lieke (11/2014) Oral Somatosensory Awareness doi.org/10.1016/j. neubiorev 2014.09.015 Neuroscience & Biobehavioral Review, Volume 47: 469-484 sciencedirect.com/science/article/pii SO149763414002425

Yang, Z & LI J (5/2018) Influence of Temperature on Cerebellar Metabolite levels. ncbi.nlm.nih.gov/pubmed/28540835 International Journal of Hyperthermia Volume 34#3: 273-275

Moulton, ErIc Dr PHD. Principal Investigator. brainimaging@childrens.harvard.edu ChildrensHospital.org Research Centers Departmental Programs Center for Pain and thr Brain. pain research group current studies/cerebellar resection,

Trulsson, 2006. Sensory Motor Function of human periodontal mechanoreceptors ,Journal Oral Rehab. Volume 33#4 :262-273

Williams, WN (1985) Bite force discrimination by individuals with complete dentures, Journal Prosthetic Dentistry Volume 54#1:146-150

Agrawal, KK et al (2011) A study to evaluate the effect of oral stereognosis in acceptance of fixed prosthetics. Indian Journal Dental Research Volume22#4 :611 10.4103/;0970-9290.90321

Accogli, Andrea (8/9/2017 10/2017) Europepmc.org/articles/pmc5550382 Novel mutation in Pontocellular hyperplasia (PCH) Dysmorphisms & Teeth Abnormalities. PMID 28815207 PMCID PMC 5550382 American Academy of Neurology-Genetics Neurol.Genetics Volume 3#5:179 10.1212/nxg-179

Rudnik-Schoneborn, S et al (6/12/2014) Pontocerebellar Hypoplasia American Journal Medical Genetics C Seminars in Medical Genetics doi 10.1002/ajmg c.31403 166c#2 pg 173-183 PMID 24924738

Ali Aghaei, Abbas et al (5/2019) Cell & Tissue Research. Volume 376#2 :179-187. link.springer.com/article/10.1007/S00441 doi.org/10.1007/s004410180280-x Dental Pulp Stem cell transplantation,

Meyers, Arlen Dr & Burgess, Jeff Dr (11/9/2015) Management of the dental patient with neurological disease. emedicine.medscape.com/article/2091727-overview

Willoughby, K Dr & Kelly, DE Hereditary cerebellar degeneration n 3 kittens, veterinary record.bmj,com/content/151/10 .295 dx.doi.org/10.1136/vr.15/.10.295

Shanmugapriya, S & Murali, GV Murali Gopika. & Nisha, Aarthi. A unique oral manifestation in Dandy-Walker Syndrome. TamilNadu Govt Dental College/Hospital, iosrjournals.org/iosr/jdms-papers/Volume 15/ iSSUE 6 VERSION 2 W150602142-.WI 50602142.145 ,PDF

Ten Donkelaar, HJ et al (2003) Development & Developmental Disorders of the Human Cerebellum Journal of Neurology Volume 250;1025. DOI,10,9790/0853-150602142145 WWW. IOSRJOURNALS ,ORG

Warotayanont, Rungnapa. et al (5/17/2016) Case Report: Open Access Dental Considerations in Dandy-Walker Malformation, Neonatal & Pediatric Medicine, ISSN 2572-4983. O micsonline.ord /open-access/dental-considerations-in-Dandy Walker -Malformation-pdc-1000108.php?aid=73210 Division of Pediatric Dentistry Dept Orofacial Sciences University of California@ San Francisco Rungnapa.Warotayanont@ucsf,edu

Xiao, Rui et al (11/22/2017) frontiersin.org/articles/10.3389/fncel.2017,00373/full Front Cell Neuroscience doi.org/10.3389/fncel.2017.00373

Maron, Dina Fine (6/30/2015) The Anesthesia Dilemma Scientificamerican.com/article/the-anesthesia-dilemma/

Pediatrics (2011) Children w/ multiple anesthesia exposures before age 2. Pediatrics (2012) Children under 3 with 1 Anesthetic Event. Pediatrics (2012) Children under 4 for a surgical anesthetic event.

Klages, Ulrich. et al (3/3/2006) Anxiety Sensitivity as a predictor of pain in patients undergoing restorative dental procedures, doi.10.1111/j.1600-0528.2006.00265 x Community Dental Oral Epidemiology Volume 34;139-145.

www.dentistry.com (2007) /articles/Confessions_of_a_Dental_Coward.aspx dentalcare universe.com/mobile/item-confessions

Zakin, Susan, Dental Anxiety. (3/21/2003) (updated 7/30/2006) Consumer Health Interactive. Dentalcare universe.com/mobile/item-dental.ahealthyme.com/topic/dentalanxiety.

Lee, Mac, Dr Nothing Personal Doc, but I hate dentists, IHD Publishing, Edna TX

Phelps, Autumn. (11/9/2007) Spa Like Distractions. dentalcareuniverse.com/mobile/item-dentist-new-drill-spa-like-distractions.20263.html

Thompson, Allison, (2/6/2008) Fear Factor: Dentists Sink their teeth into efforts to end the dread. Sheboygan Press WI Dentalcareuniverse.com

Call Kurtis Investigates: Dentist used controversial restraint (5/4/2016) Kurtis Ming, Sacramento.cbslocal.com/2016/05/04.

McBride, Mike (9/09/2016) Childabusesurvivor.net/wordpress/2016/09/09 /sometimes it takes a root canal.

Heath, Terrance. (3/30/2014) Why American Dental Insurance is so unspeakably awful, www.salon.com/2014/03/30.

Cbsnews.com (5/18/2016) Controversial Dental Restraint used on kids sparks debate.cbsnews.com/news/dentists/controversial-restraint-kids-debate-dental-industry.

Borreli, Lizette. (11/3/2015) General Anesthesia & Human Brain: How going under may impact cognitive impact. see Journal Pediatrics Lborreli@medicaldaily,com

Elder, Jeff, (10/24/2007) Fear not costs keeps many from seeking dental care. Star-telegram.com dentalcareuniverse.com Citing Dental Fears Research Clinic University of WA Seattle.   Dr Philip Weinstein PhD Clinical psychologist. newsobserver,com/105/story/74059. Star Telegram,com /health/story/278386.html c@2007 news and observer publishing. '

Bracha, H Stefan Dr (11/7/2006) Post Traumatic Dental Care Anxiety, ncbi.nlm.nih. gov/pubmed/17152624. dentalcareuniverse.com/mobile/item-cogprints.org/5248 & Hawaii Dental Journal (9/2006-10/2006) volume 37#5: 17-19

Dejong,A & Fransen, Jet (1/13/2007) Psychological Trauma Exposure & Trauma Symptoms among individuals with dental anxiety. European Journal Oral Science British Dental Journal Volume 114: 286-292. copyright 2007 Nature Publishing group www.nature.com/bdj/journal/volume 202: n1/full/bdj.,2006,118.html. a.de.jongh@acta.nl Dejong, A & Hartman, IH.(2/2003) Trauma Related Phenomena in Anxious Dental Patients . Community Dental Oral Epidemiology Volume 31#1:52-58

Bernson, Jenny M et al (11/19/2007) Self-Reported Dental Coping Strategies among fearful adult patients. Preliminary Enquiry Explorations. dentalcareuniverse.com/mobile/item. European Journal of Oral Sciences. Volume 115#6: 484-490. doi 10.1111/j.1600-0722.2007.00496.x

Corah, Norman (1969) Corah Dental Anxiety Scale. SUNY NY School of Dentistry

Kotilainen, J et al (1995) Craniofacial & Dental Characteristics of Silver-Russell Syndrome. American Journal of Medical Genetics, Volume 56: 229-236

Saltzmann, JA & Wein, SL (1952) Dental Correlation in Pituitary Dwarfism. American Journal of Orthodontics Volume 38: 674-686.

Tsuchiya, H et al (1981) Analysis of the Dentition & Orofacial Skeleton in Seckel Dwarfism. Journal of Maxillofacial Surgery Volume 19: 170-175.

Gardner, DG & Girgis, SS (1977) Taurodontism, Short Roots & External Resorption Associated with Short Stature & Small Head. ORAL SURGERY, Volume 44:271-273

Chilvarquer, LW et al (1987) Oral Manifestations of Seckel Syndrome. Journal Dent Child Volume 54: 129-131

- Nihill, Patricia DMD & Salzmann, Larry DDS et al (1996) Esthetic Overdentures for a patient with possible Seckel Dwarfism Syndrome. SCD Special Care in Dentistry: Volume 16#5: 210-213. Dr Nihill is Assistant Professor of Restorative Dentistry at Southern ILLiNOIS University School of Dental Medicine & Adjunct Faculty at Northwestern University in Evanston IL where this case treatment was performed.
- Dr Nihill=2800 College Ave Alton IL 62002 Southern iL University School Dental Medicine.
- Dr Luh-Xuan Lin DMD=Assistant Clinical Professor in Graduate Prosthodontics
- Dr Larry Salzmann DDS= Associate Clinical Professor in Pediatric Dentistry,
- Steven Stevens CDT=Certified Dental Lab Technician Northwestern University Evanston IL,

Jeffery, Nathan & Berkovitz, BKB (4/8/2002) Morphometric Appraisal of the Skull of Caroline Crachami, Sicilian Dwarf 1815-

1824. American Journal of Medical Genetics, Volume 111: 260-270. n.jeffery@ucl.ac.uk

Berkovitz, BKB, (1998) Caroline Crachami: The Sicilian Dwarf, American Journal Medical Genetics Volume 76: 343-348.

Locastro, Adriana et al (2008) Neurologic Aspects of MOPD Type2 Dwarfism; Pediatric Neurology Volume 38#6: 435-438.

Pitts, WC (1985) Difficult Denture Patients. Volume 53: 532-534.

Alexandra, Jill (5/2017) How my dentist became my Anxiety Ally. Mighty.com/2017/05/dentist-help-anxiety/

Taneja, P (1/2015) Iatrosedation: A Holistic Tool in the Armamentarium of Anxiety Control. SAAD Digest Volume 31: 23-25. ncbi.nlm.nih.gov/pubmed/25895235. PMID 25895235

Friedman, Nathan Dr (1967) USC School of Dentistry -Journal Dental Education 02/1983, Volume 47#2: 91-95 =Iatrosedation Treatment of Fear in the Dental patient.
IATROSEDATION.dentalfearcentral.org/tips/Iatrosedation. Fear Reduction with Iatrosedation Process Journal California Dental Assn (1993) Volume 21#3:41-44 +(1998) An evaluation of the Iatrosedative process for treating dental fear.+ The Influence of Fear,Anxiety & Depression on a patient's adaptive response to complete dentures Journal Prosthetic Dentistry (1987) Volume 58:687-689 + (1988) Volume 59: 169-173.+ see Sedation 6th edition(2018) + Friedman, Nathan in Psychosedation/Iatrosedation in McCarthy, FM (ed) & in Emergencies in Dental Practice Philadelphia PA WB Saunders (1979) and see A Dentist Oriented Fear Reduction Technique ;
Iatrosedation and see pocketdentistry.com/ Compendium Continuing Education in Dentistry Volume 10#2:113. and

(4/98) Volume 19#4: 434-442 (1998) Volume 19#4 =An Evaluation of the iatrosedative process for treating dental fear: 1998 Compendium of Continuing Education in Dentistry.

McCarthy, Frank DDS MD (ed) (1967) Emergencies in Dental Practice

Poorsattar, Susan Parveen (4/1/2010) Recognizing & Managing Dental Fears: Journal of Dental Education. jdentaled.org/content/74/4/397-401 Volume 74#4@ 2010 American Dental Education Assn. poorsatt@usc.edu

Maggirias, J et al (2002) Psychological Factors & Perceptions of Pain Associated with Dental Treatment. Community Dental Oral Epidemiology, Volume 30#2:151-159.

Champong, B et al (2007) Need & Demand for Sedation or General Anesthesia in Dentistry National Survey Canadian Population Volume 52#1: 3-11. 2007 Community Dentistry & Oral Epidemiology Anesthesia Progress (2005) Published Study.

Armfield, JM et al (2007) The Vicious Cycle of Dental Fear, BMC Oral Health Volume 7#1

Mehrstedt, M et al (2007) Oral Health Related Quality of Life in Patients with Dental Anxiety. Community Dental Oral Epidemiology Volume 35:357-363.

Donaldson M et al (2007) Oral Sedation Primer on Anxiolysis for Adult patients Anesthesia Progress Volume 54#3: 118-128

Goodchild,JH et al (2004) Anxiolysis in Dental Practice. General Dentistry Volume 52#3: 264-268.

Fiedler, Randy (4/25/2013) Humor: Tales of Dental Terror. wacotrib.com/waco_today magazine/humor-tales-of-dental-terror/article_56700bc5-2cfc-572a-aeef-b9cdp4573ff.html

Foley, Katherine Ellen (3/8/2017) So many people are afraid of going to the dentist. qz.com/926892/

Woolard, Holly. (10/10/2005) Patients fear of Dentist Drill,needle, put to ease with sedation. www.marinij.com

Blende, David Dr San Francisco CA ALSO SEE WOOLARD, HOLLY, Chief of Dentistry, California Pacific Medical Center + Private office Pacific Heights CA

Kindism.org (11/20/2014) Wisdom & Teeth

Kindism.org (06/29/2014) Praying Away the Cavities

Breus, Dr Michael (10/30/2018) The SleepDoctor.com Five scary things to know about dreams and nightmares-Blog.

Coolidge, Frederick L'& Bracken, Duane D (1984) The Loss of Teeth in Dreams: An Empirical Investigation Psychological Reports Volume 54#3: 931-935.dx doi.org/10.2466/pr 0.1984.54.3.931

Yubiliana, Gilang et al (2016) Hypnodontics: The Art of suggestion to control dental anxiety. media.unpad.ac.id/files/publikasi/2016/rpm_20160807114215_9833.pdf

International Society of Hypnosis: 1st World Congress on Hypnodontics (9/28/2016) Iranian Scientific Society of Clinical Hypnosis (ISSCH) Mashhad University of Medical Sciences.

OralHealth Group.com/blogs/dental (4/11/2011) Dental Hypnotherapy

Berman, Dave. CHT (7/29/2014) Increasing Case Acceptance-Hypnodontics dentistryiq.com/dental-hygiene/clinical/hygiene/article/16360427 and Hypnodontist Because Words Matter (2014) 16360409 Dentistryiq.com/articles/2014/07/because-words-matter.html. also see hypnodontist.com and manifestpositivity.com

Acosta, Juan, (2014) Hypnodontics -Ethical Influence San Bernardino CA Hypnodontist.com

Malamed, Stanley DDS, (2010) in Sedation 5TH ed. The Spectrum of Pain & Anxiety Control

Skinner, Helen (2/19/2019) Hypnotherapy in Dentistry
nextec.com/nexlec_life/articles

Moss, Aaron DDS Clinical & Experimental Hypnosis in Medicine,
Dentistry & Psychology 2nd ed. 46 Hypnodontics; Hypnosis in
Dentistry.

Foskett, Jackie (2011) Hypnosis or Hypnotherapy for reducing
Anxiety in the Dental Office, dentistryiq.com/articles/2011/04
/hypnotherapy.html

Samuelson, Allen (2007) Iatrosedation: Treatment Planning in
Dentistry 2nd edition and (2017) 3rd edition.

Lile, Samantha (6/28/2018) Your dentist is psyching you out.
thriveglobal.com

McNeil, Daniel & Randall, Cameron (2014) Behavioral Dentistry.

Chao,John DDS MAGD "Cowards Welcome" Ostrow School of
Dentistry @USC - Behavioral Sciences. Adjunct Assistant Professor.
& Dentist in Alhambra CA.

Appukuttan, Deva Priya (2016) Strategies to manage patients with
anxiety/dental phobia. Clinical Cosmet. Investig. Dental Volume 8:35-
50.

Weissenberg, M (12/1984) Volume 20#4: 371-383. Relevant &
Irrelevant Anxiety in PAIN

Brodsgaard, Moore R (2/2001) Dentists Perceived Stress. Community
Dental Oral Epidemiology Volume 29#1: 73-80

Brahm, et al (2012) Dentists views on fearful patients, Swedish Dental
Journal Volume 36#2: 79-89.

Eli, I. (7/1993) Dental Anxiety. Int'l Endodontics Journal Volume
26#4: 251-253.

Botto, RW IN Mostofsky, DI et al (2006) Behavioral Dentistry
Oxford-Blackwell :115-125

Cohen, SM et al (10/14/2000) The impact of Dental Anxiety, British Dental Journal Volume 189#7: 385-390

Levinson, Harold. (2019) Feeling Smarter & Smarter. Springer Publishing.NYC.

Levinson, Harold (1986) Phobia Free,

Levinson. Harold (1994) A Scientific Watergate, Stonebridge Publishing.

Levinson, Harold. (1990) Total Concentration
Levinson, Harold. (1984) Smart But Feeling Dumb

Levinson, Harold (1982) A Solution to the Riddle,Springer-Verlag.

Jordao, Lidia et al (1/29/2014) Relationship between rates of attending religious services and oral health in Brazilian adolescents. Onlinelibrary.wiley.com/ doi.org/10.1111/cdoe.12098

Gatlin, Leroy. (9/23/2016) Christian Science & Dentistry: How dentists can work with their Christian Science patients to respect their faith while providing treatment www.dentistryiq.com/dental-assisting-staff-relations/article/16352519/christian-science-and-dentistry.

Easton, Kristen L MS RN CRRN-ACS & Andrews, Jonathan Ph.D ThMba (7/10/2012) The role of the Pastor in the Interdisciplinary Rehab.Team onlinelibrary.wiley.com/doi.org/10.1002/j.2048-7940.2000. tb01850.x

Connecticut Hospice Inc. Interdisciplinary Care. hospice.com/services/interdisciplinary-care/

Weiner, Stacy Staff Writer (11/21/2017) Is there a chaplain in the house? Hospitals integrate Spiritual Care. AAMC News. news.aamc.org/patient-care/article/hospitals-integrate-spiritual-care-chaplains/

Lichter, David (July-August 2017) Chaplains interdisciplinary role has made progress. www.nacc.org/vision/

Cedars-Sinai Hospital. Cedars-Sinai-edu-about-us/spiritual-care-department.

HCCN Healthcare Chaplaincy Network (2017-2018) Creating the New World of Spiritual Care.www.healthcarechaplaincy.org/docs/about /

Bunn, Steven Dr (2019) DrBunn.com /faq/st-apollonia-patron-saint-of-dentistry.

Olympia Union Gospel Mission. A trip to the dentist might lead to someone' s salvation. www.ougm.org/dental-clinic.

Huch, Pastor Larry. Unveiling ancient biblical secrets: Receiving the Miracles You have been waiting for.

Congregation Ruach Israel, Needham MA. Refuah Shlema Healing Prayer Conference Unite Boston 3/29/2019-3/30/2019. Rabbi Nathan Joiner. Healing Prayer from the Messianic Jewish Tradition- A life transforming journey. office@ruachisrael.org

Schulz, Daniel. & Peterson, Scott. & Romanik,Donald. (7/10/2013) Forced Clergy Transitions. Alban@Duke Divinity School. alban.org/archive/forced-clergy-transitions/ Congregations Magazine Volume 2#2 -Scott Peterson=Episcopal Priest. Donald Romanik=President, Episcopal Church Foundation.

Henderson, Carolyn. God the Dentist. beliefnet.com/columnists/commonsensechristianity/God-the-dentist.htm

Brachear-Pashman, Manya (1/1/2017) West Suburban dentist treats clergy for free. Chicago Tribune.com/news/ct-clergy. mbrachear@chicagotribune.com

Magro, Kerry. & Wuethrich, Louisa Ann. KerryMagro.com Diagnosed with autism as an adult my next journey will be going to college KerryMagro@gmail.com

Eby, Aaron. FFOZ.ORG (5/15/2019) Discover-messianic-jewish-calendar-i-am-the-lord-your-healer-rosh-chodesh-iyar-html The journey from Egypt to Sinai involves a physical and spiritual transformation.

Gifts of his glory.com/miriamsblog/tag/messianic-judaism (11/29/2016) My book becoming Miriam-A life transformed by God.

Moskowitz, Nicole C. (2011-2012) The Davidic Harp: An Aeolian Awakening: Derech Hateva Volume 16: pg 46-48.

Pasik, Dahlia. (2011-2012) Short & Sweet? Not Necessarily. Derech Hateva Volume 16: pg 49- see also download.yutorah.org/2012/1053/774731.pdf

Whitworth, Garrett C, The Man Nobody knew: Jesus & the Dwarf (Zacchaeus) isbn 13 soft 9781512739930 isbn 13 hard 9781512739947 and e-book 9781512739923.

Bathfire,Ezekiel (10/13/2017) God's approach to Toothache-Prayers Required , in Christ's Rottweiler-www.landoverbaptist.net/showthread.php?t=113579

Yonke, David (2/14/2009) Praying until Jesus returns. Adat Adonai Messianic Synagogue-Blade Religion Editor. also see TV program Discovering Jewish Jesus Channel 40(Michigan) & discoveringthejewishjesus.com & Rabbi Kirt Schneider at Adat Adonai Ottawa Lake Michigan

Moll, Lucy & Allchin, Sherry. (12/4/2014) Biblical Counseling Center.org /Overcoming Phobia.

Gaultiere, Bill Soul Shepherding.org/Fear of the Dentist.

Kumar, N Ashok, Pastor (10/2010) Pastoral Benefits of Visiting Church Members. www.ministry magazine.org/archive.

Hiltner, Seward. (1958) Preface to Pastoral Theology NY: Abingdon Press: p28.

Hansen, Brant (2017) Blessed are the Misfits: Denver Seminary.edu/resources/news-and-articles/ Denver Journal Book Review,Nashville W. Publishing Group. ISBN 9780718096311. + " Mr Spock goes to church. How 1 Christian copes with Asperger's Syndrome. Religion.blogs.cnn.com/(10/19/2013) follow@branthansen

Bradford Pate, James (12/21/2007) Aspergers and Religion html. James thoughts & musings Jamesbradfordpate@yahoo.com

Kankurette.wordpress.com (3/6/2011) The hidden village of Aspergers.

Autismforums.com/threads/aspergers & religion.7509. Aspergers & Autism Forum + Aspie Central

Talkington, Jonathan MD & Scherzo, Gina PhD et al. AutisticSymphony.com/jca.html DID JESUS CHRIST Have Autism? An Interdisciplinary Evidentiary Analysis

Bible Knowing Jesus.com 38 Bible verses about Robes. bible.knowing-jesus.com/topics/Robes.

www.JewishVoice.org/read blog/you can make miracles happen (12/5/2018)

Kehilanews.allisrael.com/secret behind the Messiah's miracles- (10/23/2017) 1ST Fruits of Zion Staff.

Dupre, Carol (8/25/2013) Broken: A Pastor's wife shares her story" Olive Press Publishers.com

Stump, Todd (2/15/2017) In Germany, Refugees face challenges beyond Relocation. www.usnews.com/news/world/articles.

Ichinose, Akiko MSW & Kihara, Katsunobu PhD Integration of Christian Spiritual Care into assisting the relocation of older adults with dementia. NACSW North American Association of Christians in Social Work Botsford CT NACSW.ORG /Publication/proceedings20

Jackson, Kate & Mintz, Tracy Greene & Branch-Dogans, Tach & Warchol, Kim
 (Jan-Feb 2015) Prevent Elder Transfer Trauma. Social Work Today V15#1:10.

Kozma, Chahira MD. gumc.georgetown.edu/gumc/stories/in-egypt-small-people-with-big-status. Professor of Pediatrics Georgetown University Medical Center Chief of Genetics @Medstar GUMC Hospital. and see her articles in the American Journal of Medical Genetics 2006-2011. Twombly, Renee (4/25/2012) GUMC Communications, also see www.hand-free-co.uk/disability-ancient - Egypt-disabled-pharoah also see Dwarfs in Ancient Egypt/Greece Oxford UK Clarendon Press (1993) Veronique Dasen.

Friedman, Stan (3/2/2017) Chaplain offers advice for helping in times of trauma. CovenantCompanion.com

Levi, Deborah, (June 2017) Finding Level Ground: My journey with Cerebellar Ataxia.

www.operationwearehere.com/Resources_for_ America Ministering to families affected by military deployment. Resources for America's clergy US Army Office of Chief of Chaplains Directorate of Ministry Initiatives Version 4 (9/2008) Arlington VA CHAPNET.ARMY.MIL

National Center for PTSD www.ncptsd.va.gov

www.catholic.org/saints/saints.php?/saint St John the Dwarf, lower Egypt

Young, Amos. Zacchaeus: Short and Unseen
baylor.edu/content/services/document

Preuss, Julius (1993). Biblical & Talmudic Medicine. books.google.com/books?id=occ4aqaaqb Jason Aronson Inc Northvale NJ

Eerdman, William B Publishing (2011) The Bible, Disability & The Church A new vision of the people of God. Grand Rapids MI: 10-12

BiblicalTraining.org/library/disease/Dwarfism

Hirsch, Emil. et al Jewish Encyclopedia.com/articles/5381-dwarf

Adelson, Betty M. (2005) The Lives of Dwarfs Rutgers University Press Piscataway NJ google.com/books?id-ymsxemq2p7e

Ferber, Dan (11/9/1998) Sound of Music in the Cerebellum. Sciencemag.org/news/1998/11/sounds-music-cerebellum

Hamilton, Jon (10/25/2018) The Underestimated Cerebellum gains new respect from brain scientists. www.npr.org/sections/health-shots/2018/10/25/660504533/

Marek, Scott Dr postdoctoral researcher/author Washington University St Louis MO see cell.com/neuron/full text/S0896-6273(18)30898-5.

Schmahmann, Jeremy Dr Neural Professor Harvard University

Dosenbach, Nico Dr Neural Professor Washington University St Louis Mo

Marek, Scott & Dosenbach, Nico et al (2018) Spatial & Temporal Organization of the Individual Human Cerebellum doi.org/10.1016/j.neuron.2018.10.010

Hutchinson, Siobhan et al (9/2003) Cerebellar Volume of Musicians. Volume 13#9:943-949. doi.org/10.1093/cercor/13.9.943 academic.oup.com/cercor/article/13/9/943/342632

Yourstory.com/2016/05/27 apoorva-sharma Despite being dyslexic & a dwarf. see also timesofindia.indiatimes.com/city/lucknow/even disorders cannot dwarf her achievements/articleshow/52425414.cml (5/25/2016)

Schlaug, Gottfried. Neurology Dept Palmer 1 Beth Israel Deaconess Medical Center & Harvard Medical School Boston Ma. gschlaug@caregroup.harvard.edu

Callan, Daniel, Parsons Lawrence, Kawato, Mitsuo, Turner, Robert (3/2007) Speech & Song: The role of the cerebellum. The Cerebellum V6#4:321-327. DOI.10.1080/14734220601187733

Lega, Carlotta & Vecchi, Tomaso, et al (3/2/2016) A TMS investigation on the role of the cerebellum in pitch discrimination. and timbre discrimination. Cerebellum Ataxia doi.10.1186/s40673-016-0044-4 pmcid pmc 4774184 and pmid 26937285. Volume 3#6.

Maguire, Linda. Instrumental Music Memory & The Cerebellum. George Mason University Fairfax VA Biopsychology Masters Student. lindamaguireproductions.com/website/new/music memory and the cerebellum.pdf

Tillman, Barbara, Justus Timothy & Bigand, Emmanuel (3/2008) Cerebellar patients demonstrate preserved implicit knowledge of association strengths in musical sequence. Brain Cognition Volume66#2: 161-167. pub online 9/18/2007, doi 10.1016/j.bandc.2007.07.005 pmcid pmc2271057 nih ms41288

Levitin, Daniel This is your Brain on Music.

Psychology Today. Cerebellum Damage may be at the root of PTSD, (1/15/2016) US/BLOG/THE ATHLETES WAY/201601/CEREBELLUM DAMAGE MAY BE THE ROOT PTSD IN COMBAT BEHAVIOR

Sorensen, Maria (5/2015) The Neurology of Music for PTSD Treatment St Catherine University University of Saint Thomas MSW Clinical Research Paper School of Social Work sophia.stkate.edu/cgi/viewcontent.cgi?article=1526@content=msw_paper

Jewish Voice.org/read/article/healings/miracles/muslims/accepting/yeshua

Jewish Voice.org/read/blog 5/17/2018 They hoped for a miracle & Jesus did not disappoint.

Marsden, Skip (11/25/2013) Blind Rabbi sees better than most. www.hickoryrecord.com/news/article_471f90ce-52f3 Hickory Daily Record. also see rockofisraelcongregation.org attn. Rabbi Cliff Maynard & Rabbi Jeff Grillo, Clover SC.

Ellis, Mark (01/15/2016) godreports.com/orthodox-jew-found-yeshua-jesus-in-Israel-miracles-unfolded-in-his-life.

Osbourne, Abbie & Dodd, Amber Lee (8/9/2016) Books by Dyslexics/We are Giants-The Codpast.org.

Strick, Alex. & Dodd, Amber Lee. Dwarfism, Dyslexia & Discovery. The World Thru Books. (4/7/2016) booktrust.org.uk/news-and-features

Burns, Robert (1786) Address to the Toothache.

Brown, Paul. Time Engineering, The Cerebellum & Volition. Thesis. pdfs.semanticscholar.org/Scb7/4b9fdfb078ft

Newberg, Andrew Dr MD. How God Changes Your Brain: An Introduction to Jewish NeuroTheology. NY: Ballantine (2009) static1squarespaces.com/static/52402ca4e4bf Journal, The Reform Jewish Quarterly: pg. 18-25.

Newberg, Andrew Dr MD. Principles of Neurotheology. Ashgate, Burlington VT (2010)

Newberg, Andrew Dr MD. The Neurotheology Link.

Newberg, Andrew Dr MD. Director of Research at Jefferson-Myrna Brind Center of Integrative Medicine Philadelphia PA Thomas Jefferson University Hospital email Andrew.Newberg@Jefferson.edu www.andrewnewberg.com He is Board Certified Internal/Nuclear Medicine and NeuroScience

Newberg, Andrew Dr MD Why God won't go away: Brain Science & the Biology of Belief NYC NY Random House (2001)

Shortland, Michael. (1987) Courting the Cerebellum: Early Organological & Phrenological Views of Sexuality:BJHS Volume 20: 173-199.

New Church Essays on Science, Philosophy & Religion. (1854) books.google.com/books?id=ktwraaaaiaaj

Swedenborg, Emanuel (17th Century Scientist/Philosopher/Mystic)

Hobson, J Allan MD (4/1/2004) The Dualism of John Carew Eccles. dans.org/cerebrum/2004/Neuroscience and the soul

Eccles, John Carew (1951) Nature:168: 53 and see Hypotheses relating to the brain-mind problem, Nature 1951: 168:53 and see Cerebellum as a Neuronal Machine (1966) Nobel Laureate Lecture Harvard Medical School. And see Nobel lectures: Physiology or Medicine 1963-1970 Amsterdam: Elsevier Publishing 1972

Savain, Louis (9/14/2017) Medium.com/@rebelScience/ancient-occult-facts-about-the-brain-unknown-to-neuroscientists-the-cerebellum-does-not-generate-29567efqb7a1

Arumugam, Karthika (Spring 2015) Neural Correlates of Religion & Spiritual Experiences.duo.vio.no/bitstream/handle/10852/45982/Prosjekt-karthika-pdf.1

JewsforJesus.org The Messiah would perform Signs of Healing (1/29/2019)

Extraordinary Miracles of the Messiah: free.messianicbible.com/feature

learnreligions.com Holy spirit gift of healing

FFOZ.ORG I am the Lord, your healer. Discover/Messianic-Jewish-Calendar-Rosh Chodesh iyyar.html (5/5/2019)

Roth, Sid. & Carlson, Rabbi Eric (7/20/2007) Miracles of Yeshua SIDROTH.ORG/articles/

rmcucc.org/wp-content/uploads/2016/02/A2A Guide.pdf. Any Body Every Body Christ's Body A Guide for Congregations Associations & Conferences for becoming accessible to all A2A Written/Compiled by UCC Disabilities Ministries www.uccdm.org (Spring 2016) + uccdm board of directors. also see UCC Mental Health Network+ mhn-ucc-blogspot.com and UCC Disabilities Ministries Board and chair@uccdm.org and secretary@uccdm.org

Eisland, Nancy. Encountering the Disabled God www.dsfnetwork.org/assets/uploads/disability/sunday/21206. Eisland-disabled-God.pdf and The Disabled God: Toward a Liberating Theology of Disability Nashville TN Abingdon Press (1994)

Eisland, Nancy and Sailers, Don E, eds (1998) Human Disability & The Service of God, Nashville TN Abingdon Press

Wilke, Harold (3/23/1977) Mainstreaming The Alienated: The Church Responds To A New Minority (Ministry) Christian Century www.disabilitymuseum.org/dhm/lib/catcard.html?id.1721

Wilke, Harold (1980) Creating the Caring Congregation Abingdon Press

Gaventa, William C ed. Dimensions of Faith & Congregational Ministries with Developmental Disabilities see rwjms.umdnj.edu

American Association of People With Disabilities - That All May worship: An Interfaith Welcome to People with Disabilities. Washington DC

WWW.AAPD.COM/what-we-do/interfaith/that-all-may-worship .html.

Congregational Accessibility Network (CAN) CanAccess.org

Ecumenical Disability Advocacy Network, World Council of Churches-www.edan.wcc.org/

National Organization on Disability nod.org Religion & Disability Org Washington DC

Pathways to Promise.Org St Louis MO Pathways@mimh.edu

Block, Jennie Weiss (2002) Copious Hosting: A Theology of Access for People with Disabilities NY: Continuum.

Fritzon Arne & Kabue Samuel. (2004) Interpreting Disability: A Church of All & For All. Geneva: WCC Publications.

Swinton, John (2005) Critical Reflections on Hauerwas' Theology of Disability Disabling Society Enabling Theology Haworth Press (2005)

Pailin, David A. (1992) A Gentle Touch: From a Theology of Handicap to a Theology of Human Being, London: SPCK

Reynolds, Thomas. (2008) Vulnerable Communion A Theory of Disability & Hospitality Grand Rapids MI Brazos Press.

Olyan, Saul M (2008) Disability in the Hebrew Bible Interpreting Mental & Physical Disabilities Cambridge University Press

Carter, Erik W (2007) Including People with Disabilities in Faith Communities Baltimore MD Paul H Brookes Publishing Co

Webb-Mitchell, Brett (2008) Beyond Accessibility Towards Full Inclusion of People with Disabilities in Faith Communities NY: Church Publishing Inc

Winters-Johnson, Diane. (2008) The View From Under the Pew Nashville TN Abingdon Press

Black, Kathy (1996) A Healing Homiletic: Preaching & Disability Nashville TN Abingdon Press

Foley, Edward ed (1994) Developmental Disabilities & Sacramental Access Collegeville MN Liturgical Press.

Thornburgh, Ginny ed, (2000) That All may worship: An Interfaith Welcome to People with Disabilities. NY: Natl Org on Disability.

Thornburgh, Ginny & Miller, Janet Rife (1996) From Barriers to Bridges A Community Action Guide for Congregations People with Disabilities NY Natl Org on Disability

Hartbauer, Roy E (1983) Pastoral Care of the Handicapped. Berrien Springs MI Andrews University Press.

UCC Resolution- Appendix 5 Resolution To Become Accessible to All 05-GS-32 voted 25TH General Synod Called to Wholeness in Christ: Becoming a Church Accessible to All

Mackinlay, Elizabeth ed (2008) Disability & Spirituality: Addressing the Challenge of Disability Later in Life. Phila.Pa Jessica Kingsley Publishers

Nouwen Henri, JM (1979) The Wounded Healer: Understanding the Power of Ministry in the Broken Places of our lives. NY: Image Doubleday

Roche, David (2008) The Church of 80% Sincerity NY: Perigee

Swinton, John (1999) Building a Church for Strangers Edinburgh: Contact Pastoral Trust

Sullivan, Jackie. (2007) Pastoral Care with Adults. NY: Haworth Press

Thompson, Carolyn. (2009) Ableism The Face of Oppression as Experienced by People with Disabilities in Injustice & Care of Souls Taking Oppression Seriously in Pastoral Care ed Sherly Kujawa-Holbrook, Minn MN Fortress Press: 211-226

Pidoux, Ludivine & LeBlanc, Pascale et al (7/25/2018) A subcortical circuit linking the cerebellum to the basal ganglia involved in Vocal Learning. ElifeSciences.org/articles/32167. Physiology & Pathology UMR CNRS 8119.Centre National de la Recherche Scientifique CNRS Institute for Neuro-Science & Cognition Paris Descartes University France doi 10.7554/elife.32167.
Gregory, AH, (1997) The Roles of Music in Society: The Ethnomusicological Perspective in Hargreaves, David J North (Adrian

C) The Social Psychology of Music NYC NY Oxford University Press (1997); 123-140.

Christianity.com/church/church-history /timeline/1601-1700/slave-songs-transcend-sorrow-11630165.html

harriet-tubman-org/songs-of-the-underground-railroad

 Christensen, Lauren (12/22/2017) NY TIMES .COM/Books Review.Harriet Tubman personal hymn book 1876, at Smithsonian National Museum of African American History & Culture.

Harriet Tubman Secret Messages Shared Thru Song artsedge.kennedy-center.org/education

Singing in Slavery: Songs of Survival, Songs of Freedom. Mercy-Street-blogs-mercy-street-revealed/songs -of-survival and songs of freedom during slavery.last updated by Kenyatta D'Berry Esq (1/25/2017) Mercy St Revealed Blog.

Davis, Fannette Owlcation.com The UR-A Code of Secrecy Part 2

Gray, Helen T (3/5/2012) Negro Spirituals Still Resonate.Deseret News.com /76555599

Crosby, Pamela. (Jan-Feb 2014) Interpreter. umc.org/resources/part-of-history-african-american-spirituals-still-heal

ArtsEdge.Kennedy.Center.org/education. Harriet Tubman-Secret Messages shared thru song.

Passage to Freedom-Secrets of the Underground Railroad - CivilRightsMuseum.org National Civil Rights Museum (May 2016)

Granade, Andrew, Professor Musicology Univ. Of Mo. Kansas City Mo Conservatory. Songs of Perseverance & Hope.

Jones, Randye. Gospel Truth about Negro Spirituals

Bible,org/seriespage/13-exodus-12-1521-passover-and-escape-Egypt

Colburn, David M (8/2012) Bible Seven Study, edited for bible.org

Biblehub.com/psalms/118-223.htm study bible

Biblegateway.com/passage/?search New International Version NIV

Holy Bible,NIV. 1973-2011, Biblica Inc worldwide.

Piper. John. Christian Theologian. The Rising in Faith.

Cohn-Sherbok, (2000) Messianic Judaism:pg160

King David Psalms dedicated to Musicians

Wise, Jean (12/30/2014) The Spiritual Practice of Taking Your Tambourine. healthyspirituality.org/the-spiritual-practice-of-taking-your-tambourine.

www.Timbrelpraise.org/background/tambourine-in-the-bible.

Goren, Dana PhD (06/2014) Therapy in a second language. www.psychologytoday.com/us/blog/contemporary/psychoanalysis-in-action/home-away-home-therapy in second language.

Pogosyan, Marianna PhD www.psychologytoday.com/us/blog/between-cultures/(08/2017) /when-learning -foreign-language.

Nisbet & Shucksmith, 1986, Metacognitive Abilities.

Limacher-Riebold, Dr Ute 4 Tips to learn a new language for adults.

Banach, Edo JD President/CEO NHPCO. www.musictherapy.org/about/personal_stories

Graham, Sharon MM MT-BC. Music therapy.org

Norris. Tamera. www.musictherapy.org/about/personal_stories

Franks, Jefri. amtapro.musictherapy.org

Fratianne, Richard MD, Music Therapy.

Cohen, Florence. Music Therapy.

Dicamillo, Mary Dr Music Therapy

Lipe, Anne Dr Music Therapy

Yanke, Roy (4/24/2017) Uncovering the Trauma of Forced Ministry Exits. PIR Industries -Partners in Pastor Renewal. pirministries.org (blog)

Harrison, Deanna. Moving On -Surviving the Grief of Forced Termination.

Ferentz, Lisa LCSW DAPA (8/1/2017) Navigating Abuse by the Clergy Part 2. Psychology Today.com/us/blog/healing-trauma-s-wounds-2017/07 and 2017/08 and Navigating Abuse by the Clergy Part 1 (7/13/2017)

Miller, Susan, Just Moved Ministry, Arizona. Justmoved.org

After the Boxes Are Unpacked: Moving On After Moving In by Susan Miller (Author), John Trent (Foreword, Contributor)

UMCOM.ORG/learn/tips to help pastors and families on the move. Communication: United Methodist Communications

UMCOM.ORG/Learn/Caring for Church Leaders-Burnout. Communication: United Methodist Communications

Frame, Marsha Wiggins, (1998) Relocation & Wellbeing in United Methodist Clergy & their spouses: What Pastoral Counselors Need to Know. link.springer.com/article/10.1023/a:1023098/20436 & Pastoral Psychology Volume 46#6 (1998) +Fla Annual Conference UM Clergy/Spouses. mframe@ceo.cudenver.edu University of Colorado at Denver UM Minister & Professor of Counseling Psychology

Anderson & Stark, 1985. Emerging Issues from Job Relocation in the HighTech Field. Implications for EAP'S. Employee Assistance Quarterly. Volume 1#2:37-53.

Hazler & Nass,1988. Over 20% of Americans move each year.

Lantz, Cheryl M Dr RN MS PHD (12/2009) Influence of Spirituality within older adults during relocation University of North Dakota. pdfs.semanticscholar.org 8547/ff6360594bd.6ac898ad 181f096c4fb8943d.pdf Theses & Dissertations 883 commons.und.edu/theses/883 BSN MS. Ph.D Doctoral Dissertation UMI#3406189 COPYRIGHT 2010 by Proquest LLC Ann Arbor MI 12/8/2009 -scholarly use which may be made of any material in this dissertation . Dickinson State University Dept Chair of Nursing Cheryl.Lantz@ dickinsonstate.edu Dickinson North Dakota and see July 2006 Conducting a Spiritual Assessment Sigma Theta Tau Nursing Knowledge Intl Nursing Knowledge.org/portal/main.aspx?pageid=36&sku=58860 and see Teaching Spiritual Care Journal of Nursing Education Volume 46#1: 33-38

NANDA & NANDA Relocation Stress Syndrome North American Nursing Diagnostic Assoc. 2007-2008 pg 178 Phila PA

Mallick MJ & Whipple TW 2000 Validity of the Nursing Diagnosis of Relocation Stress Syndrome. Nursing Research. Volume 49#2: 97-100.

Saunders, J (1998) Spirituality & Nursing. Collegian Volume5#1:16-19.

Stoll, RL (1979) Guidelines for Spiritual Assessment American Journal of Nursing Volume 79: 1572-1577.

Amenta, MO (1986) Spiritual Concerns Chapter 9 :115-161 in Amenta, MO & Bohnet Eds, Nursing Care of the Terminally Ill. Little Brown Boston MA.

Amenta, MO & Weiner, A (1984) Successful Relocation of elderly residents Geriatric Nursing Volume5#8: 356-360

Walton, J (1996) Spiritual Relationships -Journal of Holistic Nursing Volume 14#3: 237-250.

Narayanasamy A. (1999) A Review of Spirituality as Applied to Nursing. International Journal of Nursing Studies Volume 36#2: 117-125. AND (2002) Spiritual Coping Mechanisms in Chronically Ill Patients. British Journal of Nursing Volume 11#22: 1461-1470.

Mackinlay, Elizabeth, (2004) The Spiritual Dimension of Aging: in A Jewell ed Aging Spirituality & Wellbeing pg 42-57, London NJ Jessica Kingsley Publishing.

Young C & Koopsen C, 2005 Spirituality Health & Healing, Sudbury MA Jones & Bartlett Publishing.

Tornstam, L 2005 Great Transcendence NYC NY: Springer Publishing.

Leetun, MC 1996. Wellness Spirituality in Older Adults. Nurse Practitioner Volume 21#8:60-70

AHCA 2007 American Health Care Assn Paper A Guide for Families making the transition to Nursing Facility Life. Retrieved from longtermcareliving.com/familyguide/transition/trans3.htm

AHNA 2005 2007 2008 American Holistic Nursing Association ALTNA Standards of Holistic Nursing Practice ahna.org/about/standards.html and ahna.org/home/tabid/1231/default.aspx and 2007 Vision Mission & Philosophy Statement ahna.org/about/about.html

Kociszewski, Cynthia 06/2003. Journal of Holistic Nursing. A phenomenological pilot study of Nurses Experience providing spiritual care. Volume 21:131-148.

Berube, MS & Devinne, PB eds, (1985) American Heritage Dictionary 2nd college edition. Boston MA: Houghton Mifflin: page 1044.

Scocco, Rapattoni & Giovanna, (2006) Nursing Home Institutionalization A source of Eustress or Distress. International Journal of Geriatric Psychiatry. Volume 21:281-287.

Ackley, Betty & Ludwig, Gail (2006) Nursing Diagnosis Handbook Mosby St Louis MO 7th ed.

Fehring, RJ et al (05/1997) Spiritual Well Being, Religiosity Hope Depression & other mood states in elderly people coping with cancer. Oncology Nursing Forum Volume 24#4: 663-671

Linz, R 1990. Meaning in Old Age. Doctoral Dissertation. California School of Professional Psychology at Berkeley Alameda CA UMI 9030508

Castle, NG (2001) Relocation of the Elderly. Medical Care Research & Review Volume 58#3:291-333 doi 10.1177/107755870105800302

Brugler, C Titus, M & NYPaver (1993) Relocation Stress Syndrome: Journal of Nursing Admin. Volume 23#1: 45-50

Cress, CJ 2007 Handbook of Geriatric Care Management 2nd ed. Sudbury MA Jones & Bartlett

Coyle, J 2001 Spirituality & Health. Journal of Advanced Nursing, Volume 37#6:589-597

Kirkland K & McIlwain H 2001, 1999 Full Circle Spiritual Therapy for the elderly NYC NY Haworth Press

Koenig, HG (2004) Faith in the Future. Phila Pa Templeton Foundation Press

Koenig, HG (1998) Use of Religion & Other Emotion Regulated Coping Strategies among older adults. Gerontologist Volume 38:303-310

Koenig, HG (1994) Aging & God-Spiritual Pathways to Mental Health in Midlife & later years. Haworth Pastoral Press

Bergland A & Kirkevold M, 2006 Thriving in Nursing Homes in Norway. International Journal of Nursing Studies Volume 43#16: 681-692

Oswald F & Rowles, GD 2006 Beyond Relocation Stress in Old Age. in HW Wahl et al New Dynamics In Old Age Baywood Publishers Amityville NY:127-152

Chow, RK (2005) Life's Quest for Spiritual Well Being Geriatric Nursing (Sept-Oct 2005)

Field, L (2007) Religiosity & Spirituality at End of Life in Pruchno RA & Smyer MA eds Challenges of an Aging Society. Baltimore MD John Hopkins Press :74-113

Fischbacher Mcrae E (1988) The Aging Process for Women: Focus on the influence of Spirituality on Adaptation Doctoral Dissertation Union for Experimenting Colleges/Universities AAT 8908196

AI, AL & Mackenzie, ER (2006) The Concept of Spiritual Wellbeing & Care of Older Adults. in ER Mackenzie & Rakel eds. Complementary Alternative Medicine for Older Adults. pg 271-288. NYC Springer Publishing

Byrd, R (1997) Positive Therapeutic Effects of Intercessory prayer in a coronary care unit population: Alternative Therapeutic Health in Medicine V3:87-90

Capezuti, EM & Boltz, M et al (2006) Nursing Home Involuntary Relocation Journal of American Medical Director Assn Volume 7#8: 486-492

Barnum, BS (1996) Spirituality in Nursing NYC NY Springer Publishing.

Barry, DC (2000) Preferences of Frail elders regarding ideal living environments. Doctoral Dissertation. University of Missouri at Columbia UM1 Microfilm 9988647.

Fowler, JW (1981) Stages of Faith. San Francisco CA: Harper & Rowe Publishers

Fry, A (1998) Spirituality Communication & MH Nursing Australian & New Zealand Journal of MH Nursing Volume 7:25-32.

Golberg, B (1998) Connection: An Exploration in Spirituality in Nursing Care Journal of Advanced Nursing Volume 27: 836-842

Greenstreet, William (1999) Teaching Spirituality in Nursing. Nurse Education Today Volume 19: 649-658

Haight, N Michel Y & Hendrix S (1998) Life Review: Preventing Despair in Newly Relocated Nursing Home Residents International Journal of Aging & Human Development Volume 47#2: 119-142.

Harris, W Gouda,M & Kolb J (1999) A Randomized trial of the effects of Remote Intercessory Prayer on outcomes of patients admitted to CCU. Archives of Internal Medicine: Volume 159:2273-2278

Hasselkus BR (1981) Relocation Stress & the Elderly, Concord 29-31

Hodge, DR (2000) Spirituality Social Thought Journal of Religion in Social Services Volume 19#4: 1-20

Hungleman, J Kenke-Rossi et al (1996) Focus on Spiritual wellbeing Geriatric Nursing Volume 17#6: 262-266.

Kao, HS ET AL (2004) Relocation to a long-term care facility Journal of Psychosocial Nursing Volume 42#3: 10-16

Lapierre (2003) JCAHO Safeguards: Spiritual Care. Holistic Nursing Practice Volume 17#4: 219

Maher,P (2006) Reclaiming Spirituality in Nursing. in a History of Nursing Ideas. LC Andrist et al

Maclaren, J (2003) Spiritual Nursing. Journal of Advanced Nursing. Volume45#5:457-464.

Maier, M & Lorenzo (2004) The Importance of Prayer for the Mind.

McEwan, W (2004) Spirituality in Nursing, Orthopedic Nursing Volume 23#5

McManus, J (2006) Spirituality & Health. Nursing Management Volume36#4:24-27

McSherry, W (2004) Language of Spirituality. International Journal of Nursing Studies Volume 41#2: 151-161.

McSherry, W (2002) Dilemmas of Spiritual Assessment Journal of Advanced Nursing Volume38#5:479-488.

Mitchell, MG. Effects of Relocation on the Elderly. Perspectives Volume23#1:2-7

Morse, Donna L BSN RN (8/2000) Relocation Stress Syndrome is Real American Journal of Nursing Volume 100#8: 24a-24d DOI 10.2307/3522152 JSTOR.ORG/STABLE/3522152?SEQ=1#PAGES_S

Mowat, H (2004) Successful Aging & Spiritual Journey. in A Jewell ed. Aging Spirituality & Wellbeing. London NJ Jessica Kingsley Publishing: 42-57

Obrien, ME (2008) Spirituality in Nursing Boston MA Jones & Bartlett Publish. and (2003) Spiritual Wellbeing & Quality of Life

Pargement, KI (1997) Psychology of Religion & Coping. NYC Guilford Press.

Park CI (2007) Religion & Spiritual Issues in Health & Aging. in CM Aldwin et al Handbook of Health Psychology & Aging: NYC Guilford Press: 313-337

Ross, LA (1997) Elderly Patients Perceptions of their spiritual needs/care. Journal of Advanced Nursing Volume 26 5075

Rosswum, M (1983) Relocation & the Elderly, Journal of Gerontology & Nursing Volume 9#12: 632-637

Tredar LL (2001) Spiritual Care. Journal of Christian Nursing, Volume 18#2: 16-20

Keville, Terri D (1993) Studies of Transfer Trauma Health Matrix: The Journal of Law & Medicine, Volume 3#2:

Quigley, Lillian (1959) The Blind Men & the Elephant.

Killian, Eldon C (1970) Effects of Geriatric Transfer on Mortality Rates. SOCIAL WORK Volume 15#19 :427-436.

Borup, Jerry (1981) Relocation Attitudes Info. Network & Problems Encountered. 21 Gerontologist 501: 508-509

Borup, Jerry & Gallego, Daniel T (1981) Mortality As Affected by Institutional Relocation: 21 Gerontologist :8-12

Schulz, Richard & Brenner, Gail (1977) Relocation of the Aged. A review & theoretical analysis. Volume 32 Journal of Gerontology: 323-331

Levitan, Anson (1980) Transfer Trauma & the Non-Institutional Option: A Review of the Literature: Volume 13 Clearinghouse Review: 653

Coffman, Thomas L (1981) Relocation & Survival of Institutionalized Aged: A Re-Exam. of the Evidence. Gerontologist Volume 21: 483-493

Kowalski, N Claire (1981) Institutional Relocation: Current Programs & Applied Approaches. Gerontologist Volume 21: 512 -517

Reed vs Hurley Medical Center 395 NW 2D 12-14 Michigan Court of Appeals 1986. (See Keville, pg. 445- 449) and see 447 US 784 N16 US Supreme Court and at 793,

Shane, Cari (4/24/2013) A Moving Concern: Transitional Trauma, updated 6/24/2013 HuffPost.com/entry/downsizing-rightsizing-transitional-trauma-b3113259.

Danick, Susie. TAD Relocation Washington DC Founder/Owner

Derrick, Jolyne (4/5/2018) A place for mom. Blog Aplaceformom.org

Greene-Muniz, Tracy Social Worker -Expert Relocation Stress Syndrome

North American Nursing Diagnostic Assn (1992) Official Diagnosis: RSS Relocation Stress Syndrome.

Williams, Amber Lois (3/15/2013) On the Environmental Factors that alleviate relocation stress syndrome. commons_1827&context=theses Eastern Michigan University Digital Commons @ EMU

McKinney & Melby, 2002. Coping Resources/Constraints.

Golant, SM 2003. Conceptualizing Time & Behavior in Environmental Gerontology. The Gerontologist Volume 43#5: 638-648.

Thomas, Dr William "Eden Alternative"

Weinstein, LB 1997. The Eden Alternative: Activities Adaptation & Aging. Volume 22#4:1-8 doi 10.1300/jo16v22n0401.

Looker PA & Stichler, JF (2003) Healing Environments: Marketing Health Services: Volume 23#2

McKinney AA & Melby, V (2002) Relocation Stress in Critical Care Journal of Clinical Nursing Volume 11: 149-157.

Melrose, S (2004) Reducing Relocation Stress Syndrome in long term facilities. Journal of Practical Nursing. Volume 54#4: 15-27

Ambulgekar, Jayant Dr, Doshi, Mahan Dr, Sanadi, Rizwan Dr, Gaikwad, Subodh Dr, Full mouth rehab. of Mutilated Dentition: Case Report. (August 2013) International Journal of Research in Science, Engineering & Technology Volume2#8: 60-70 Dept Periodontics YMT Dental College/Hospital Navi Mumbai Maharashtra India. ISSN 2319-8753

Daing, Anika Dr, Singh, Aparna Dr ^& Dixit, Jaya Dr (Nov. 2011) Full Mouth Crown Lengthening: Case Report. International Journal CDS, Volume2#4:60+

NYCDentist.com Restorative/Prosthodontics.

Agrawal, S., Jose, N. P. H., Bandi, R. S., Jain, N., & Rodrigues, S. J. (2015). An Interdisciplinary Approach in Rehabilitation of an Adult Mutilated Dentition with Multiple Missing Permanent Teeth--A Case Report. *International journal of orthodontics (Milwaukee, Wis.)*, *26*(4), 45-48.

Warraich, R., Dali, M., & Naulakha, D. (2017). A Combination Prosthesis Using Thimble Copings for Reconstruction of Mutilated Dentition: A Case Report at Nobel Medical College, Biratnagar. *Birat Journal of Health Sciences*, *2*(2), 222-226. https://doi.org/10.3126/bjhs.v2i2.18532

Drug Invention Today |
Vol 10 • Issue 5 • 2018
Full mouth rehabilitation of a patient using multiple metal ceramic restorations:
A case report jprsolutions.info/files/final-file
Ashish R. Jain Research Scholar, Saveetha University, Chennai, Tamil Nadu, India
*Corresponding author: Dr. Ashish R. Jain, Maruthi Dental Clinic, No 436, Mint Street, Sowcarpet, Chennai-600079.Phone: 9884233423, E-mail: dr.ashishjain_r@yahoo.com,
Received on: 12-02-2017; Revised on: 17-04-2018; Accepted on: 09-05-2018

Jain AR, Ariga P. Full mouth rehabilitation of a patient having limited inter arch space with mandibular implant retained xed adoro fused to metal Fp-1 prosthesis and maxillary acrylic removable conventional complete denture. Int J Oral Implantol Clin Res 2013;4:112-7.

Jain AR, Nallaswamy D, Ariga P, Philip JM. Full mouth rehabilitation of a patient with reduced vertical dimension using multiple metal ceramic restorations. Contemp Clin Dent 2013;4:531-5.

Jain AR, Nallaswamy D, Ariga P, Philip JM. Full mouth rehabilitation of a patient with mandibular implant screw retained Fp-3 prosthesis opposing maxillary acrylic removable overdenture. Contemp Clin Dent 2013;4:231-5.

Jain AR, Janani T. Full mouth rehabilitation of an ectodermal dysplasia patient with hypodontia and reduced vertical dimension using metal ceramic restorations:A case report. Biol Med (Aligarh) 2016;8:335.

Jain AR. Fp1 Prosthesis in maxillary ridge defect and xed partial denture in mandibular ridge defect
A case report. Int J Dent Sci Res 2014;2:184-9.

Miles R. Cone, DMD, MS, CDT, FACP Rethinking the traditional full-mouth rehabilitation by applying minimal prosthetic dentistry for maximum patient benefit 46 GENERAL DENTISTRY November/December 2016

IOSR Journal of Dental and Medical Sciences (IOSR-JDMS) e-ISSN: 2279-0853, p-ISSN: 2279-0861.Volume 18, Issue 9 Ser.12 (September. 2019), PP 59-61 www.iosrjournals.org DOI: 10.9790/0853-180912 5961 www.iosrjournals.org 59 |
 Prosthodontic Management of True Generalized Microdontia in Pituitary Dwarfism –
A Case Report

Dr. Mohammed Ibrahim Mathar
Dr. Shaik Mohamed Shamsudeen
Dr.Mohammed Ziauddeen Mustafa
Dr.Pramod Punchiri Sadan
Dr.Syed Shujaulla

Assistant professor Dept. of Prosthetic Dental Science, Al -Rass College of Dentistry, Qassim University, Kingdom of Saudi Arabia. Assistant professor, Department of Dental Diagnostic Science, College of Dentistry, King Khalid

University,Abha, Kingdom of Saudi Arabia.
Assistant Professor, Dept. of Prosthetic Dental Science, College of
Dentistry, AlZulfi, Majmaah
University,Kingdom of Saudi Arabia.
Associate Professor, Dept. of Prosthetic Dental Science, College of
Dentistry,Qassim University, Buraidah,
Kingdom of Saudi Arabia
Assistant Professor, Dept. of Prosthetic Dental Science,College of
Dentistry,Qassim University,
Buraidah,Kingdom of Saudi Arabia.
Corresponding Author: Dr.Mohammed Ibrahim Mathar M.D.S.,
Dr. Shaik Mohamed ShamsudeenM.D.S.,

BANDODKAR, KRANTI ASHOKNATH and ARAS, MEENA
(2007) Psychological Considerations for Complete Denture Patients,
Journal Indian Prosthodontics Society, Volume 7#2: 71-76,
Prosthodontics Dept Goa Dental College Bambolim Goa India,doi 10-
,4103,0972/4052,33999 j-ips,org/article

Asulu, Sreeniv et al Dwarfism in Complete Denture.

Jain, Sumeet Dr Prosthodontic Rehab of Achon, Dwarf, Clinical
Dentistry (6/2013) V7#6,

Zemes, K & EA Holtgrave, Berlin Johanson-Blizzard Syndrome,
Clinical Genetics (May 1986) V30;177-183

Cone, Dr Miles DMD (Nov-Dec 2016) Rethinking the traditional Full
Mouth Rehab, General Dentistry: 46.

Miettunen, Katie DDS MS (8/.2011) Multi-Disciplinary Assessment
for Adults with Mutilated dentition, Thesis Temple University MS
Orthodontics Program,

Berdmore, Thomas (1768) Treatise on Disorders & Deformities of
Teeth,

Guilford, Simeon, (1889) Malposition of Human Teeth.

Abduo, Jaafar (3/2011) Innovative Prostheses Design for Rehab of severely mutilated dentition, Journal of Advanced Prosthodontics Volume 31#1: 37-42.

Dua, Parag Singh JP & Aghi Anu, (July-Sept 2011) Aesthetic Functional Rehab of a case of mutilated dentition Volume 11#3: 189-194,'doi 10,1007.s13191011100883 Journal Indian Prosthodontic Society

Bell, AM et al (1985) Multiple fixed prosthetics also enhance chances of failure. Dental Clinical North America Volume 29#4: 763-778

Preiskel, Harold Dr (9/1985) Restoration of Mutilated Dentition Volume 13#3: 173-183., Journal of Dentistry doi,org 10,1016/03005712(85) 90001-6

Paranhos, Klenise & Kanda, Harprit & Ghalili Michael & Kotick, Philip, (7/18/2017) International Comprehensive Program, NYU College of Dentistry. Reconstruction of a worn mutilated dentition, KP21@NYU.EDU

Gurav, Sandeep Vivek, Ram,Sabita, Khanna, Tulika. (2015) Occlusal Rehab of severely worn dentition, doi 10.5005 jp-journals-10031-1106 Case Report Journal of Contemporary Dental V5#1`: 48-52

Turner, KA & Missirlian DM (10/1984) Restoration of extremely worn dentition, Journal of Prosthetic Dentistry v52#4: 467-474.

Hanlin, SM (/2012) The Mutilated Dentition - Management of Debilitated Dentition. Annals R Australas College Dental Surgery Volume 21:49-50.

Bilodeau, JE (4/2009) Multidisciplinary Treatment of Mutilated Dentition. American Journal Orthodontic Dentofacial Orthopedic Volume 135 Supplement 4 pg 96-102, doi 10.1016/j.ajoda.2008,08,020 email is jeb6116@erols.com

Patel, Jayanti R (11/30/2018) Prosthodontic Management of Mutilated Dentition: A Novel Approach. www.j-ips.org Volume 18#6:109. Sankalchand Patel University Visnagar.

Wankhade, Sattyam + Lokade, Jyoti + Rajguru, Vilas, (2011) Prosthodontic Rehab. of Mutilated Dentition, International Journal of Dental Clinics, Volume 5#2:103-104. Accepted 11/13/2010, pdfs.semanticscholar.org/4826/c234169c9d5 dravw@yahoo.co.in Dr Wankhade=Asst. Lecturer Prosthodontics Dept Govt Dental College Hospital, Hanuman Nagar Medical Campus Nagpur India Ambulgekar, Jayant Dr Sanadi Rizwan Dr Doshi Manan Dr Gaikwad Subodh Dr (August 2013) Full Mouth Rehab. of Mutilated Dentition, Volume 2#8 Dept Prosthodontics YMT Dental College/Hospital Navi Mumbai Maharashtra India ISSN 2319-8753.

Daing, Anika Dr Singh Aparna Dr Dixit Jaya Dr (November 2011) Full Mouth Crown Lengthening Case Report IJCDS Volume2#4: 60+ Periodontics Dept Faculty Dental Sciences Lucknow Uttar Pradesh India,

Alsayed, Arwa, (4/17/2018) Implant supported fixed partial denture in a patient with Seckel syndrome. ISSN 2637-7764. Modern Research Dentistry Volume2#2 doi 10,31031/MRD 2018.02,000534 Email arwa.s.dau.edu.sa

Kim, Kanghyun, et al (10/28/2015) Prosthetic Management of a patient with Russell-Silver Syndrome,Clinical Report. Journal of Advanced Prosthodontics Volume 7#5:406-410. doi 10.4047/jop.2015,7.5.406 PMCID PMC 4644783 PMID 26576258.

London, Robert Dr. The Tennis Racket & The Mind. (5/4/2010) Psychology Today.

www.themartineffect.co.uk. The Tennis Psychologist/Win the Mental Battle.

Heller, Robert Dr Sports Psychology Boca Raton FL. cognitive therapy,cc/services/boca-raton-sports-psychology.

Pugliese, Lisa (3/5/2019 4/25/2018 7/4/2017) Love Serving Autism-Tennis with a therapeutic stroke. Palm Beach Post (3/5/2019) WPTV - Love Serving Autism-Therapeutic Tennis Instruction-+ Tennis as a therapeutic tool for children with Autism www.differenttbrains.org/tennis-therapeutic -tool-children-autism-spectrum-disorder (7/4/2017) Email Lisa@loveservingautism.org. 10 Reasons to play tennis for individuals with Autism. loveservingautism.org/ Lisa Pugliese, Founder Love Serving Autism

Olson, Harry Ferdinand (1967). Music, Physics, and Engineering. 2nd Edition 2. Dover Publications, New York, N.Y. 110-113.

 Chow, Lisa (2003). The Harp: Engineering the Perfect Sound. Illumin, Viterbi School of Engineering. http://illumin.usc.edu/106/the-harp-engineeringthe-perfect-sound/ (retrieved January 13, 2012).

 Swift, Dan. The Aeolian Harp, Alaska Science Forum. http://www2.gi.alaska.edu/ScienceForum/ASF10/1070.html (retrieved January 13, 2012).

 Govardhan, R.N. and Ramesh, O.N. (2005). A Stroll Down Kármán Street. Resonance, Journal of Science Education. 10:8: 25.

 Bearman, P. (2009). Understanding and Predicting Vortex-Induced Vibrations. Journal of Fluid Mechanics. 634: 1-4.

 Ferreira, R.L. et al (2004). Flow Around Modified Circular Cylinder. RETERM, Thermal Engineering Journal. 5:62-67.

 Rayleigh, John William Strutt (1896). The Theory of Sound, Volume 2. Macmillan, London, England. 412-413.

 Govardhan, R.N. and Ramesh, O.N. (2005). A Stroll Down Kármán Street. Resonance, Journal of Science Education. 10:8: 32.

 Gurr, Henry. Aeolian Harp, The University of South Carolina Aiken. http://www.usca.edu/math/~mathdept/hsg/aeolian.html (retrieved November

[House of Harrari, Biblical Harp Makers,

Spencer, Jon. (8/6/2018) Not about wins & losses: Tennis is therapeutic for a grieving father, Mansfield News Journal .com/story/923356002.

Yazici, Ahmet (5/18/2016) Tennis Enhances WellBeing in University Students. MENTAL ILLNESS Volume8#1:650.

Merglen, A (2014) Weekly Sports Practice & Adolescent Wellbeing Archives Disabled Child, Volume 99:208-210.

Jeste, Shafali (3/7/2017) Tennis Program serves up benefits for children with autism www.spectrum news .org/opinion/viewpoint.

Li, Jian Jose PHD USPTA Ambassador (January 2010) Tennis the right sport for ADHD kids, www.addvantageuspta.com/default.aspx act=newsletter.aspx& newsletter id, email Jose@adhd-tennis.org

Gardiner,Cerith (7/10/2018) 4 Tennis Players whose faith made them champions, aleteia.org/2018/07/10/4

Henley, Blair (5/11/2015) On a swing & a prayer: Faith's place in Tennis, Tennisnow.com /news/2015/may/

Wilson, Ralph F Dr (2019) Tennis mirrors Christian Life. joyfulheart.com/encourage/tennis_life.htm email pastor@joyfulheart.com

Oppenheimer, Mark (9/2/2011) Doing unto others off & on the Tennis Court. NY TIMES.COM/2011/09/03/US/03

Owen, Sam. Tennis enthusiast & Episcopal Seminarian student Berkeley Divinity School at Yale University)

Yazdgerdi, Comron, Tennis Coach @Hastings College, Nebraska & Member Fellowship of Christian Athletes.

Serve & Rally, The Art & Psychology of Tennis. serveandrally.com/2016/10/religion-in-tennis (10/16/2016)
Serve & Rally, Juan Martin Del Potro's faith is tested. (10/13/2017) serveandrally.com/2017/10/juan-martindel-potros-faith-tested.

Ashcraft Michael & Ellis Mark (2/2/2016) Serbian Christian survived bombings & became best tennis player. GodReports.com/2016/02/bombings-made-the-best-tennis-player-of-this-serbian-christian.

Djokovic, Novak aka Super Novak Memoir " Serve to Win".
Gatto, Luigi: Djokovic Novak, Faith plays an important role in my life & tennis. www. tennisworldusa.org (10/16/2018)

Lundell, Peter. What's Your Tennis Ball? cbn.com/devotions/whats-your-tennis-ball @2016

Letter to the Philippian Church Chapter 3: 12-14 NIV Bible

Eccles, John C Facing Reality (1970) NYC Springer Verlag

Levinson, Harold (1982) A Solution to the Riddle. NYC Springer Verlag

Levinson, Harold. (1986) Phobia Free. Warner Books NY

Levinson, Harold (1994) A Scientific Watergate. Stonebridge Publishing NY

Levinson, Harold (1984) Smart But Feeling Dumb. Warner Books NY

Levinson, Harold. (2019) Feeling Smarter & Smarter. Springer-Verlag NY

Thorpe, WH (1961) Biology, Psychology & Belief. London UK Cambridge University Press.

Stieglitz, Brian. A Dental Miracle in North Bellmore. (7/13/2017)
herald.com/bellmore/stories/a-dental-miracle93684 Herald Life NY

A mouth full of miracles - Herald Community Newspapers

www.liherald.com › a-mouth-full-of-miracles,120574

Dec 5, 2019 · A mouth full of miracles Book shares local dentist's life-changing procedure Posted Thursday, Dec 5, 2019, 4:29 pm Dr. Michael Schamis gave Marsha Lampert a new set of teeth.

Appendix 1:

Abnormal Cerebellar/**Ocular/Ophthalmic/Visual** traits found in Dwarfism Dental Pathology/Ectodermal Dysplasia
(Dalkiz & Dalkiz,) have observed the following **ocular** manifestations in Dwarfism Dental Pathology patients: **Nystagmus/ Nystagmoid eye movements, optic atrophy, and abnormal visual evoked responses, and ocular inflammation**. Abdel-Salam, et al, observed the following **ocular** manifestations: **Horizontal Nystagmus from Ophthalmic Exam.** (Wikipedia,,Gomez Lopez Hernandez Syndrome) shows the presence of :**Strabismus** (cerebellar**), with Short Stature Dwarfism**. (Pesic) **CCAS Cerebellar Cognitive Affective Syndrome** includes **Convergent Strabismus,** Alopecia, Learning Disabilities. ADHD, Cerebellar Dyspraxia.

 (Hou)) Mentions **ocular abnormalities** together with mandibular jaw hypoplasia, dwarfism, and small cerebellum. in Hallermann-Streiff Syndrome. (Mendelian) cites a Short Stature Dwarfism that includes cerebellar hypoplasia, hypotonia, ataxia, tooth eruption abnormality, **strabismus and nystagmus.** (Jauhari) describes Marinesco-Sjogren Syndrome that includes cerebellar ataxia, learning disabilities, short stature dwarfism,**nystagmus, esotropia, and** hypotonia. (Malacards Human Disease Database) describes a case that includes short stature dwarfism. learning disabilities cerebellar hypoplasia cerebellar ataxia, **strabismus, and** dysdiadochokinesia. (DeFraia,) mentions does **NOT** mention the cerebellum in his research on Hallermann Streiff Syndrome however he does include **Nystagmus + Hypermetropia**, concurrent with mandibular hypoplasia, dental abnormalities, severe malocclusion, receded chin, open anterior bite, excess vertical dimension of lower face, narrow upper arch, bilateral posterior crossbite, impacted teeth, double crown bicuspids, misshapen teeth, teeth aplasia, deficient psychomotor development and proportionate dwarfism-Please note that the Cerebellum is directly related to psychomotor skills, so I have included this disorder in this chapter.

Bhatia & Shukla had a patient with hypopituitary dwarfism, + spino-cerebellar ataxia and poor academic performance, cerebellar hypotonia, spatial/perceptual difficulties and **GAZE DEPENDENT NYSTAGMUS.** (Database of Hereditary Ocular Disease): **Hyperopia,** Dwarfism. Alopecia, Calcification in the Cerebellum, Normal iQ, (see Kenny-Caffey Syndrome Type 2)

(Koob, 10/2010) listed **photosensitivity**, dwarfism, cerebellar atrophy, neurodevelopmental delays, neurosensory hearing loss, dental caries, and calcified basal ganglia.

(Rushton, & Genel (1981) listed **Ocular Dysmetria,** + Ectodermal Dysplasia + motor/sensory deficits. hyperreflexia, ataxia, dwarfism, hypodontia, peg shaped teeth, midface hypoplasia. **abnormal saccadic pursuit,** cerebellar impairment of rapid alternating movement. bilateral intention tremor of limbs, ataxic gait, defective teeth enamel, malformed teeth, cerebellar atrophy, spinocerebellar degeneration. alopecia, hair thinning/loss, hyperreflexia, abnormal finger to nose dysmetria, gapped teeth, **horizontal nystagmus**, spinal lordosis, broad gait, damaged eyebrows, and loose joints.

(Zannoli, & Inchingolo, 8/7/2002) (11/15/2002) described Ectodermal Dysplasia Syndrome as including sparse eyebrows, **Ptosis of the eyelids**, Alopecia, **Hyperopia Astigmatism Strabismus, Horizontal Nystagmus**, Loose Joints, Cerebellar Ataxia, loss of balance when turning around, awkward gait, mildly ataxic arm/hand movement, weak dysmetria during finger to nose testing, ataxic handwriting, leg ataxia , discoordinated movement of limbs, & lumbar spine osteopenia.

(Munoz & Santos,10/3/1997) described Cerebello-Dermal-Dysplasia as follows: **Convergent Strabismus**, Short Stature Dwarfism, Cerebellar Ataxia, Cerebellar Anomaly,inter alia,

(Sukhudyan,7/23/2010) listed for **Gomez Lopez Hernandez Syndrome: Strabismus,** alopecia dwarfism, learning disabilities, hypotonia, cleft in cerebellar junction, abnormal horizontal orientation of cerebellar folia, horizontal side-to-side head nodding, along with midface hypoplasia and underdeveloped jaw bones,

Appendix 2

<u>**Burning Mouth Syndrome and effect on Wearing of Dental Prosthetics**</u>

(Shigli & Purushottam in their research study on Oral/Dental issues of Menopause, describe <u>**Burning Mouth Syndrome**</u> as follows: Cause=Hormonal Aspects of Menopause.

Symptoms include:

- xerostomia dry mouth, decreased flow of saliva mucosa/epithelium =thin and dry
- periodontitis periodontal symptoms, gingivitis, gum bleeding, increased gum sensitivity
- burning gum pain. usually bilaterally dento-facial pain
- anxiety that exacerbates stress and altered pain/sensory thresholds.

This situation can present as an added difficulty for wearing dental prosthetics.

<u>*A "Cosmic-like" oral-neural somato- sensory view of the Human Mouth*</u>

(Haggard & DeBoer wrote about Somatic Sensations arising within the mouth. Oral tissues have strong somatosensory innervation. -they are the locus of some of our most intense and vivid bodily experiences ,powerful oral somatosensory system-bodily awareness of the mouth-the somatosensation of noxious pain stimuli affects nerves-peripheral inputs give rise to the perception of oral devices in the mouth-the brain can perceive a gap left by a missing tooth-somatic perception involves the processing of sensory inputs to form a perception of a stimulus and the brain integrates force position and tactile signals to form an oral somatosensory perception of a stimulus-integration refers to a combining of info. from different receptor types + different regions of receptor surfaces, somatosensation afferent inputs=tooth, pain and proprioception, an oral somatosensory pathway-perceptual model of oral somatosensory awareness-starting with sensory innervation of oral tissues from the classes of peripheral receptors- -- oral tissues are among the most richly innervated tissues in the body-due to the number and variety of receptors they contain, receptors send afferent signals to the brain ie regarding thermal temperature (heat, cold) and noxious pain stimuli,

Cerebellum as a Neuronal Machine (1966, John Carew Eccles Nobel Laureate -Lecture at Harvard Medical School) (Also see Hobson, J Allan Dr ,4/1/2004):

(Dr Allan J Hobson) in a 2004 study regarding Cerebrum/Cerebellum/ NeuroScience & the Soul- discussed the "dualism" of Nobel Laureate John Carew Eccles:

Here is a brief 'recap" from that study:

Scientific knowledge is often at odds with religious belief, Eccles' most fundamental views of the world were rooted in faith. Eccles felt that positivism freed him as a scientist to rejoice even in the falsification of a cherished theory, because even this is scientific success. Eccles was Catholic...and did believe in both mystery and miracles, Eccles showed that great science can be done by people who have strong religious beliefs, Eccles felt that scientific evidence alone can never overcome assumptions based on faith simply because faith is a claim to a non-sensory non-rational form of knowledge...therefore insulated from scientific evidence. Also see Nobel lectures: Physiology or Medicine 1963-1970 (Amsterdam, Elsevier Publishing 1972) and John C Eccles Hypotheses relating to the brain-mind problem.

(Arumugam, Karthika) discussed Neural correlates of Religion and Spiritual Experiences including "God & Science meet": I decided to provide a brief overview of her opinions and ideas as follows: Religion & Spirituality continue to thrive in an age of prodigious scientific and technological development. Religion = Latin Religio - meaning to "re-connect", re-again & ligo-bind -connect adding that Psychiatrist Dr Harold Koenig MD defines it as an organized system of beliefs and practices, supported by rituals that acknowledge, worship, and communicate with the Sacred, the Divine God it is promoted and sustained by a human community and includes rules practices and rituals. Spirituality is a personal experiential thoughtful dynamic process searching for meaning, unity, connectedness, transcendence. for the highest of human potential. It includes individual experience of and relation with non-material aspects of the universe, i.e. God Higher Power, which, by person, finds meaning and relates to life in the universe. Geneticist Dean Hamer wrote a book " The God Gene: How Faith is hardwired into our genes"...Religion provides answers to questions that otherwise might seem unanswerable, it provides comfort and always anxiety,

Cerebellum as Master Computer/Controller

(Hamilton, Jon) posited that the cerebellum plays a critical role in everything from language to emotions to daily planning. 80% of it is involved in abstract thinking, planning, emotion, memory, and language while 20% is involved with physical motion/motor functions. Scott Marek & Nico Dosenbach, state that the cerebellum is wired to higher order thinking areas it's the brain's ultimate quality control unit,

Jeremy Schmahman wrote how the cerebellum is involved in everything we do and it plays a key role in human behavior, including in psychiatric disorders, (which corroborates the brilliant cerebellar - psychiatric findings of neurologist Dr Harold Levinson MD) ...and it makes a process smoother, faster and more accurate.,, what it does to motor control it does to cognition and emotion as well, ,it does it all automatically..,. when it isn't doing its job, the result may be a brain disorder...Psychiatric conditions including autism, depression, OCD all link to the cerebellum. Again, that too corroborates Dr Levinson's research findings.

Nico Dosenbach added that it is cooler than most people thought. These results are way more exciting and clear than I could have ever dreamt, the cerebellum monitors work areas of the brain and makes them perform better kind of like an editor reviewing and improving one's thoughts and decisions ,when a person is drunk, they lack cerebellar editing of their thoughts it has evolved over hundreds of millions of years...over time it expanded enormously and added extra capacity to take on functions beyond motion and motor skills,(Marek & Dosenbach, 2018) studied the spatial and temporal organization of the human cerebellum functional brain networks are elucidated in the cerebellum, cerebellar bold signals temporally lag the brain cortex by hundreds of milliseconds the frontoparietal control network is over-represented in the cerebellum ,variance in cerebellar function networks exceeds that of the brain cortex it plays a role in adaptive plasticity networks are related to both cerebellum and cerebral cortex the cerebellum contains organized networks cerebellar resting state signals lagged behind the cerebral cortex , the cerebellum exerts adaptive control of all cortical processes.

CEREBELLUM & TRICHOTILLOMANIA "hair pulling".

Over the course of the past 9 yrs. quite a number of "Trich" patients have contacted me, seeking my help/support, due to my being somewhat of a social media public figure, especially with my Facebook/Instagram Dwarfism Alopecia pages. (My moniker is DYSLEXIC DWARF WIG DIVA FASHIONISTA). The more "trich" patients came to me, their "heart rendering" stories tugged at my dyslexic dwarf alopecian heartstrings & an intuitive "trich/trick" question began popping into my dyslexic dwarf alopecian head.

What if the CEREBELLUM were involved in TRICH? Maybe the "trich" question wasn't "tricky" at all? Could the Cerebellum be the key to putting the brakes on the Trich? The more I pondered this, even more questions began popping up in my inquisitive/intuitive mind, & I knew that "thirst for knowledge driven" mind wouldn't rest until I researched this situation. Once again, my intuitive gut was RIGHT. YES, VIRGINIA there is a "MRS SANTA CLAUS" AT THE " POLES OF TRICH' (lots of laughter).

I didn't plan to write about Trich in my book, but the findings were so "thought provoking and mind blowing " that I relented to my "inner gut intuition " and decided to add this chapter on "Trich" Trick Questions and the Cerebellar No-Trick Trich Answers:

(Pereyra,) noted the presence of reduced cerebellar volumes in "Trich" and increased cerebral glucose metabolic rates in the Cerebellums of "Trich" patients.

Psychiatryonline indicated that: There is evidence for involvement of the cerebellum in "Trich". A resting state PET Positron Emission Tomography study conducted by (Swedo SE,1991) identified increased brain metabolism in the cerebellum bilaterally. The rates correlated positively with anxiety (See also Levinson, Harold who verifies that Anxiety is caused by cerebellar dysfunction) Evidence for cerebellar involvement has also been obtained in MRI studies. Keuthen et al reported evidence that shows reduced cerebellar volume in Trich patients. Cardona & Franklin stated that neuroimaging shows hyperactivity in the left cerebellum in Trich patients.

Wabnegger & Schienle examined the role of the Cerebellum in a related condition called Skin Picking Disorder (a pathological maladaptive emotion regulation strategy), Wabnegger & Schienle noted the following items:

The Cerebellum is involved in body focused repetitive behaviors such as skin picking and hair pulling ("Trich.") disorders. Patients with these disorders show altered cerebellar functional activity, as well as reduced gray matter volumes in left cerebellar lobules 5+6. There are also structural and functional abnormalities in specific subregions of the cerebellum related to motor and affective-cognitive function and altered cerebellar connectivity with area implicated in affect control. The cerebellum affects cognitive, affective, social, and motor skill areas. The cerebellum has interconnections with cortical areas and receives input from motor cortical regions-there are prefrontal cortex-cerebellar circuits that modulate cognitive-affective processes. Cerebellar dysfunction is a cognitive affective symptom constellation that includes trichotillomania. "Trich" patients demonstrate reduced cerebellar cortex volumes-reduced in both motor areas of cerebellum and emotional function areas of cerebellum+ reduced gray matter volumes in left cerebellar lobules 5&6. 5=sensorimotor function including tactile and 6=motor processes and higher-level spatial tasks, executive functions and affective processing, OCD Obsessive Compulsive disorder=smaller cerebellum in these patients especially at lobule 6. OCD also= enhanced vestibular region activity, diminished overall cerebellar activation, but increased activation of left cerebellar crus 1, Crus1=cognitive function in skin pickers. There are also differences in cerebellar connectivity with the prefrontal region, in skin pickers. Cerebellar Dysfunction = emotional dysregulation. Skin pickers have maladaptive mechanism of affect control and increased cerebellar VLPFC coupling. This reflects increasing efforts to exert more cognitive control to counter neuronal input from cerebellum.

Mystical/Religious Thoughts about the Cerebellum

(New Church Essays,) in the 19th century commented on the Cerebellum: all the involuntary of the cerebellum was manifested in the face angels to whom the cerebellum corresponds ,the cerebellum perceives all that the cerebrum does but does not publish it(AC4326)(

Emanuel Swedenborg) a 17th century scientist/philosopher/mystic said that the cerebellum is awake during sleep time when the cerebrum is asleep(AC1977).

Louis Savain wrote about "ancient' mystical-like aspects of the cerebellum and referred to biblical resources to support his "mystical-like" view of the cerebellum: & he referred to his views as "rebel science" and claimed that the neuroscientists don't know everything about the cerebellum and even said that his views might be seen as "occult facts about the brain unknown to neuroscientists". I felt that it might be "useful" to share here some of his "mystical like" views, as I am very open-minded & willing to consider alternate perspectives to my more " traditional scientific fact driven legal mindset" -Remember that in embarking on an EXPERIMENTAL DENTAL JOURNEY I had to "suspend" my facts driven "legal research writer mindset' and rely on religious/spiritual faith, and " gut intuition" and loads of prayers as well, coupled with trust in the experimental dental provider and GOD & my guardian angels.

Here is my recap of Savain's writings :He opined that New Testament Revelation & the Old Testament Book of Zechariah contain "revolutionary scientific knowledge about the brain and consciousness written in symbolic language intended to hide their true meaning" ,he also opined that many patients with cerebellar damage/defects learn to cope by quickly switching between tasks every fraction of a second he then took a "leap" to the Church in Laodicea (Chapter 3 of Revelation, New Testament) and opined that this was connected to the cerebellum: he explained that the message to the Church in Laodicea taught that the cerebellum receives its teachings from the conscious part of the brain and added too that the cerebellum learns sensorimotor behavior by knowing the names of the priests in the Temple".

Honestly, this baffled, horrified and yet intrigued me as I silently asked myself if any of this contains kernels of truth. I had no answer except to wonder & decided ultimately not to explore this "off the Richter scale" bizarre theory" any further.

Saint Apollonia- Patron Saint of Dentistry

(Bunn,) wrote about Saint Apollonia, the patron saint of Dentistry, was born in Egypt during the 3rd century and died in the year 249. She lived in a refuge for Christians and was persecuted, punished, and martyred for refusing to renounce her faith during the reign of Emperor Philip. An account of her life was written by St Dionysius to Fabian, Bishop of Antioch. Angry pagan persecutors of Christians hit her in the face and had all her teeth knocked out one at a time. She was threatened with fire unless she renounced her faith. She said a prayer and jumped into the flames-which St Augustine defended as an act of heroic faith. She is considered the patron of dental diseases and is often invoked by those with toothaches. Ancient art depicts her with a golden tooth situated at the end of her necklace. She is also featured in some art with pincers holding a tooth. Parts of her jaw and several of her teeth are housed in churches across Europe. Her feast day is Feb.9th. See for example the pincers picture at the workshop of Pierodella Francesca before 1470, Samuel H Kress collection, National Gallery of Art Washington DC. She was eventually granted sainthood.

Psychosocial stress aspects of Bruxism (tooth grinding)

Wieckiewicz, discusses the psychosocial stress aspects of Bruxism (tooth grinding) as follows. His comments are applicable and relevant in terms of dental prosthetic patients with rare unique conditions. Therefore, I am including it here in this book as I think it might be helpful to take it into consideration when treating special needs dental patients: Psycho-emotional issues can affect occluso-muscle conditions, especially in terms of chronic stress and bruxism (tooth grinding). Chronic stress connects to the development of occlusal dysfunction and can be a destructive factor. Chronic stress can also connect to functional disturbances that can include neuromuscular disorders. Chronic stress is connected to functional deficiencies of the neuromuscular system. Some patients are observed to be " venting accumulated tensions directly thru their dental arches" as increased muscle activity results from chronic stress. The increased muscle activity causes tension & rigidity, and increased muscle tone as well as overstimulation of neurons. An abnormal increase in muscle tone activity is triggered by psychological stimuli. See also (Gomez, EM et al) regarding a correlation between drug addiction and increased abnormal occluso-muscle activity. See also (Manfredini) regarding psychic, psychological & occlusal factors associated with Bruxism (tooth grinding). (Watanabe notes that one's sense of safety is linked to secretion of pleasure related substances in the brain and by oral cavity sensations during mastication.

PRAYERS/PRAYING

(Byrd) See Positive Therapeutic Effects of Intercessory Prayer in a coronary care unit population. Alternative Therapeutic Health in Medicine (Harris, Gouda & Kolb) See A Randomized Trial of the Effects of Remote Intercessory Prayer on outcomes of patients in CCU. Archives of Internal Med. (Maier Lorenzo) See: The Importance of Prayer

What is Periodontal Disease?

Periodontal disease, also known as gum disease, is an infection that affects the gums and eventually the bone that supports the teeth. In the early stages, it is treatable, and in later stages, it can be controlled with proper maintenance. Periodontal disease begins when plaque builds up around the teeth and the bacteria from the plaque causes inflammation of the gums. When not treated, it is a progressive condition and can advance rapidly. Plaque forms on teeth every day and removing the plaque is vital to prevent gingivitis and gum disease. Brushing and flossing every day, in addition to professional cleanings and regular dental exams, are essential for prevention.